Entrepreneur
MAGAZINE'S

LEGAL
GUIDE

The
Operations
Manual for
LLCs

Additional titles in Entrepreneur's Legal Guides
Helen Cicino, Esq.
Managing Editor

Bankruptcy for Businesses: The Benefits, Pitfalls, and Alternatives

Business Contracts: Turn Any Business Contract to Your Advantage

Business Structures: How to Form a Corporation, LLC, Partnership, or Sole Proprietorship (Available December 2007)

Estate Planning, Wills, and Trusts

Forming an LLC: In Any State

Forming a Partnership: And Making It Work

Harassment and Discrimination: And Other Workplace Landmines (Available December 2007)

Hiring and Firing

Incorporate Your Business in Any State

Intellectual Property: Patents, Trademarks, Copyrights, Trade Secrets

Principles of Negotiation: Strategies, Tactics, Techniques to Reach Agreements

The Small Business Legal Tool Kit

Small Claims Court Guidebook (Available January 2008)

Tax Planning for Business: Maximize Profit, Minimize Taxes

Entrepreneur
MAGAZINE'S

LEGAL GUIDE

Michael Spadaccini
Attorney at Law

The Operations Manual for LLCs

- Keep Your LLC in Compliance
- Avoid Personal Financial Risk
- Complete Reference Information for All 50 States

Publisher: Jere Calmes

Cover Design: Desktop Miracles, Inc.

Production: CWL Publishing Enterprises, Inc., Madison, Wisconsin, www.cwlpub.com

Advisory Editor for the Entrepreneur Press Legal Guide Series: Helen Cicino, Esq.

This publication is designed to provide accurate and authoritative information in regard to the subject matter covered. It is sold with the understanding that the publisher is not engaged in rendering legal, accounting, or other professional services. If legal advice or other expert assistance is required, the services of a competent professional person should be sought.

> —From a Declaration of Principles jointly adopted by
> a Committee of the American Bar Association
> and a Committee of Publishers and Associations

ISBN 13: 978-1-59918-160-8
      10: 1-59918-160-6

Library of Congress Cataloging-in-Publication Data

Spadaccini, Michael, 1964-
  Operations manual for LLCs / by Michael Spadaccini.
    p. cm.
  ISBN 978-1-59918-160-8 (alk. paper)
  1. Private companies—United States. I. Title.
  KF1380.Z9S664 2007
  346.73'0668—dc22

                                                     2007040738

Printed in Canada

11 10 09 08 07   10 9 8 7 6 5 4 3 2 1

Contents

Preface

*The Operations Manual f*or *LLCs* is built on this simple proposition: to devote more time and energy to running your limited liability company successfully and to avoid potential financial risk, you need to familiarize yourself with your state's limited liability company act and have efficient, well-organized procedures for dealing with the extensive amount of required paperwork. To accomplish this, you need to first learn about LLC formalities, internal governance, record-keeping, and LLC mechanics. This knowledge will help you:

- Avoid personal liability for company actions;
- Save money by preplanning company goals, avoiding common mistakes, and handling company maintenance in house;
- Have a better understanding of issues when consulting with your attorney and accountant; and
- Realize that LLCs are flexible entities that can be tailor-made to fit your needs.

This book is an operating manual: it will teach you how to run an LLC. From that standpoint, we presume that you already own or operate an LLC. Nevertheless, we'll touch lightly on some formation issues as background and to highlight issues that arise while operating an LLC.

The Operations Manual for LLCs strives to emphasize the areas of LLC formalities and mechanics you need to know to gain the benefits and avoid the risks of owning and operating an LLC. For example, among the many topics this handbook covers are good recordkeeping, compliance with state law, knowledge of your articles of organization and operating agreement, and member and manager meetings.

If you are just starting to learn about LLCs, it will be helpful to take a long view of LLCs to learn about some concepts. If you are familiar with corporations, some of the concepts here will be familiar to you. LLCs differ from corporations, however. If I had to define an LLC in a simple phrase, I would say that an LLC is *a special form of partnership that is granted liability protection through the effect of state law*. At first glance, the greatest difference will be in the terminology. LLC owners are not typically called *shareholders*; they are called *owners* or *members*. LLCs can be managed by their owners. This is the simpler form of LLC, called a *member-managed LLC*. Or, an LLC can be managed by a one or more managers appointed by the members. These appointed managers are not directors or officers; they are simply called *managers*. This is a slightly more complex form of LLC, a *manager-managed LLC*. We'll cover these concepts in depth in this book.

Quickly Find What You Need to Know

Limited liability companies are complicated, with numerous requirements and issues surrounding them. By breaking the issues into focused part, this book tries to make it as easy as possible for you to quickly locate the information you need.

Part One, Sources of Authority, explains and defines limited liability company acts, articles of organization, and operating agreements. Devoting a chapter to each topic, this part details:

- How state limited liability company acts provide the legal basis for forming and operating your LLC while allowing for flexibility;
- What information the articles of organization must or may contain and why this is important to you personally and to your LLC; and
- Why you need to know what your operating agreement requires and how you can structure your operating agreement to suit your particular needs.

The part closes with an overview of taxation requirements and general information for all businesses.

Part Two, The Limited Liability Company Players, identifies and describes the many participants that appear in the LLC universe. By clearly defining LLC roles—such as promoter, member, manager, and agent— you establish who is responsible for what in your LLC and you can increase your chance of success and reduce your potential personal liability

Part Three, Handling Ownership and Ownership Units, outlines the law surrounding the issuance of ownership to founders and investors and the law surrounding transfers of ownership. Chapter 7 goes further: it analyzes ways you can use your operating agreement to control ownership in your LLC.

Part Four, LLC Formalities: Meetings, Minutes, and Resolutions of Managers and Members, focuses squarely upon legally mandated formalities such as meetings of managers and meetings of members. We fully outline, with sample documents, the process for calling, noticing, and conducting such meetings. We also address how to conduct LLC meetings by informal written resolution—a real time saver.

Part Five, LLC Lawsuits and Personal Liability Protection, sets forth a framework for maximizing your LLC's personal liability protection. Chapter 11 discusses basic information about suing and being sued as an LLC, while Chapter 12 brings the point home by relating real-life cases in which the owners of LLCs and corporations were judged personally liable for injuries or debts because of lapses such as poor recordkeeping, inadequate capital, absence of resolutions and stock records, and personal use of entity funds.

Use the Book's Features as Handy References

Sample Documents, Checklists, and Forms. Throughout this book, you will find sample documents, checklists, and forms. These items are included to help you better understand the issues discussed and to demystify the limited liability company process. If you would like to use any of these forms in your LLC, it's a good idea to consult your lawyer or accountant for input and advice.

Insider Tips, Definitions, and Examples. As you read the text, notice the comments and tips in boldface located throughout the text. These tips and notes are provided to emphasize important aspects of a discussion or to highlight additional information. They are particularly helpful when reviewing a chapter or when studying one of the larger sample documents.

The Book includes two appendices:

Appendix B. Supplemental LLC Forms. You will find 11 example forms and documents here to help you create the legal language necessary to set up and manage the legalities of your LLC.

Appendix C. Glossary. Because of the legal and structured nature of LLC formalities and procedures, there may be a term or phrase within the book's discussions that you may not quite understand. To help you quickly find easy definitions to such terms as "piercing the corporate veil," "tort," and "indemnification," you can refer to the Glossary (Appendix C).

It also includes an accompanying CD on which you will find:

State Reference Information. Since the secretary of state's office (or its equivalent) will be an initial as well as follow-up resource for your LLC, both initially and continuing, we have included complete reference information for all 50 states and the District of Columbia. It contains office addresses, Web addresses, filing fees, periodic filing requirements, tax summaries, links to forms, and much more.

The forms in Appendix A are also included on the CD for your use.

A Final Thought

It would be impossible to cover all the LLC bases in one volume. One of my law professors once said, "This course will focus on the peaks." Likewise, this book focuses on the peaks of LLC formalities and law. If you are interested in exploring some the valleys, your local law library is a good source of information.

The Operations Manual for LLCs is not intended to be a substitute for competent legal and professional advice. Laws change; the business environment changes. Don't try to do it all. As a businessperson, you must develop good working relationships with a lawyer, an accountant, and an insurance agent. Be aware that laws vary from state to state and the issues presented in this book are general in nature. Use your professionals to help you make this book work for you.

With that in mind, note that this volume occasionally warns about certain topics that present potential pitfalls and complex issues that warrant a visit to your local attorney's office. Heed these warnings because small legal errors have a way of becoming enormous legal problems over time. In business law, some topics are simple and some are complex; if your needs are obviously complex, don't try to do everything yourself. Sometime the best advice an attorney can give is "get a qualified attorney."

Let's get started.

Acknowledgments

I'd like to thank Jere Calmes, editorial director of Entrepreneur Press, and the entire Entrepreneur Magazine and Entrepreneur Press team for giving me the opportunity to write this book.

I am also grateful to:

- Attorney, friend, and fellow golfer Dan Sweeney, who has contributed to this volume and to all my books by providing invaluable legal research.
- Attorney and friend Robert Kleinman, who has contributed to this volume and to all my books by providing invaluable legal research.
- My law professors at Quinnipiac University School of Law, who taught me the foundations of corporate and business law, which I now offer to you.
- All the clients who have sustained my law practice throughout the past 14 years and whose support helped me grow to become an expert in my field, with a special thanks to Don LeBuhn and his family's business, Evolution Furniture of Berkeley, California, my first clients, for whom I organized my first corporation back in 1993.
- My family and friends, who offered their support throughout the drafting of this volume.
- Emmett Ramey, president of Oasis Press, who gave me my first book contract, based not upon any experience I could demonstrate, but solely upon my repeated and vehement pronouncements that I would do a fine job.

Finally, and most important, my wife Mai.

About the Author

Michael Spadaccini is a business law author and attorney. He has practiced business law for small businesses and start-ups in San Francisco and Silicon Valley since 1993 and more recently in Austin, Texas. From 1991 to 1992, he was the Editor in Chief of *The Connecticut Probate Law Journal*, published by his alma mater, Quinnipiac University School of Law. He is the author of several business law books published by Entrepreneur Press and founded the legal education Web site, *LearnAboutLaw.com*.

PART ONE

Sources of Authority

CHAPTER 1

LLCs and Limited Liability Company Acts

The limited liability company (LLC) is America's newest form of business organization. There is little or no historical precedent for LLCs; they are essentially creations of the state legislatures. Some commentators trace the origin of the LLC to a 19th-century form of business organization called the *partnership association* or *limited partnership association*. The great bulk of laws authorizing LLCs in the United States were passed in the 1980s and 1990s. Wyoming passed the first law authorizing the LLC in 1977. Florida followed in 1982. The watershed event in the rise of the LLC was a 1988 Internal Revenue

Service ruling that recognized partnership tax treatment for LLCs. Within six years, 46 states authorized LLCs as a business form. By 1996, the last state to recognize LLCs, Vermont, had an LLC statute in place.

The LLC is often described as a hybrid business form. It combines the liability protection of a corporation with the tax treatment and ease of administration of a partnership. The limited liability company, as the name suggests, offers liability protection to its owners for company debts and liabilities.

Simplicity and Flexibility

While LLCs are essentially creations of state legislatures, corporations are truly ancient—and today's corporate law still carries some unwanted baggage. The modern American corporation has antecedents that date to Roman times, inherited by us through English law. The basic principles of American corporate law have not changed significantly in centuries. Probably the single greatest disadvantage of the corporate form is the burdensome range of formalities that corporate managers must observe. A modern corporation's heavy administrative burden is a remnant of the more traditional and formal legal system under which corporate law was cultivated.

Expert Tip

LLCs are the favorite choice for small local business entities with one to three owners who do not plan to grow their business significantly and do not expect to raise significant amounts of capital. As the number of owners grows, the corporation becomes a more attractive choice as a business form.

The LLC changed all that. The LLC offers the liability protection benefits of the corporation without the corporation's burdensome formalities. It is this simplicity that has made the LLC an instantly popular business form for smaller companies.

Another attractive feature of LLCs is their flexibility. An LLC can elect to be taxed either as a partnership or as a corporation. An LLC can be managed like a partnership (a member-managed LLC) or like a corporation (a manager-managed LLC). An LLC can create a board of directors and have a president and officers just like a corporation. An LLC can choose to have periodic meetings of its members or choose to ignore such formalities altogether.

Potential Disadvantages of the Limited Liability Company

The LLC has some disadvantages that will make it an undesirable business form for some purposes. The LLC is a new business form and courts have not yet developed a body of legal precedent governing it. Thus, LLC owners and professionals may face operating questions and issues for which they have little or no legal guidance. That said, this concern lessens as the states develop a reliable body of law concerning LLCs and is of no concern at all for very small companies.

Furthermore, for business owners who wish to pursue venture capital, accumulate a large number of shareholders, and/or eventually pursue an initial public offering, the LLC is not an appropriate alternative to a corporation. Venture capitalists and angel investors tend to shy away from investing in LLCs. Most large, publicly held companies are corporations, not LLCs.

What should the owners of an LLC do if their company grows so much that an LLC is no longer the appropriate business form? The answer is simple: it is possible to convert an LLC into a corporation. Thus, some small companies begin life as LLCs and then outgrow the LLC form, so the owners transfer the assets of their LLC to a corporation they form. Thereby, the LLC is converted to a corporation. Furthermore, as one might imagine, it is also possible to convert a corporation into an LLC or to convert nearly any business form into any other. It is also possible to reorganize a business in another state by transferring the assets of a business into a newly chartered entity. Converting business forms requires some sophisticated legal and tax analysis and it should not be attempted without the services of a qualified attorney and accountant.

The cost of setting up an LLC is roughly equivalent to setting up a corporation. The secretary of state's fees for filing articles of organization and for filing annual reports are often the same for both LLCs and corporations. Organizers who wish to seek help with organizing an LLC through an LLC formation service or through an attorney will find the fees to be roughly the same.

Advantages and Disadvantages of the Limited Liability Company

Advantages of the limited liability company:

- LLCs do not require annual meetings and require fewer ongoing formalities.
- LLC owners are protected from personal liability for company debts and obligations.
- LLCs enjoy partnership-style, pass-through taxation, which is favorable to many small businesses.

Disadvantages of the limited liability company:

- LLCs do not have a reliable body of legal precedent to guide owners and managers, although LLC law is becoming more reliable as time passes.
- An LLC is not an appropriate vehicle for businesses seeking to eventually become public or seeking to raise money in the capital markets.
- LLCs are more expensive to set up than partnerships.
- LLCs must usually make periodic filings with the state and pay annual fees.
- Some states do not allow the organization of LLCs for certain professional vocations.

Is an LLC a Type of Corporation?

An interesting question I often hear is the following: "Is an LLC a type of corporation?" The answer is "No," but LLCs bear some resemblance to corporations. First of all, a corporation is a state-chartered entity that is authorized by a state's corporation law. LLCs are authorized to be formed by a different set of statutes, never by the same state law that authorizes the formation of a corporation. LLCs have their own separate statutes in all 50 states. Thus, in the eyes of the law, an LLC is a separate type of business organization and should not be confused with a corporation, despite many similarities between the two.

How LLCs Are Formed

LLCs are formed much like corporations. Both LLCs and corporations are *chartered* entities. This means that, unlike some types of partnerships that can be created without state registration, LLCs and corporations can be created only by filing a charter document in the state of organization or incorporation. An LLC's charter document is called its *articles of organization*—a name obviously borrowed from the corporation's *articles of organization*.

Articles of organization for LLCs are very similar to articles of organization for corporations. For example, both of them state the entity's name, require the appointment of a "resident agent" (more on this below), and usually require a statement of purpose.

How LLCs Are Governed

LLCs can be governed in various ways; they are the most flexible types of business organizations in this respect.

Corporations, by statute, are required to be governed by representative management. In other words, corporations are governed by a board of directors who are elected by shareholders. (Close corporations are a partial exception to the rule of representative governance, but close corporation status is not available in all states and is hopelessly complicated.) A corporation's directors may in turn delegate some of their powers and responsibilities to officers that they appoint.

General partnerships, on the other hand, are governed by their owners. The power and authority to operate and govern a general partnership fall upon the owners directly, without any representative management. The owners of a general partnership vote in proportion to their ownership interests.

LLCs can be governed either by direct management or by representative management. LLCs must always make an election to be governed by their owners (member-managed LLCs) or by an elected body or group of managers (manager-managed LLCs). A member-managed LLC is governed by its owners (members) equally, just like a general partnership. A manager-managed LLC is governed by one or more appointed managers. These managers need not be members of the LLC. A manager-managed LLC is managed much like a corporation, by an appointed body of persons other than the owners. The managers who undertake the governing responsibilities of an LLC can form a board or a committee.

An LLC makes the election to be manager-managed or member-managed in either its articles of organization or its operating agreement. Some states dictate that the election to be manager-managed or member-managed be made in the articles of organization. Nevada is an example of a state where such an election is mandatory. Delaware, on the other hand, does not impose such an election.

Free Resource

learnaboutlaw.com maintains online question-and-answer forums operated by several practicing attorneys. Follow the links to "forums"; you can post questions for free and practicing lawyers will answer your questions or you can search the listed topics.

If your LLC's articles of organization do not require you to elect your form of management, you'll make that election in your operating agreement. An operating agreement is a close equivalent of a corporation's bylaws. Naturally, because a manager-managed LLC and a member-managed LLC are quite different, their operating agreements will differ greatly. LLC operating agreements cover matters such as who governs the LLC, how managers are appointed, how members can be ousted from the LLC, and such. Operating agreements, like bylaws, are not filed with the state. In fact, typically an LLC is not required to have any operating agreement in place, although it is advised. In the absence of an operating agreement, the LLC will follow the default rules of governance set forth in the laws of the state of organization. LLCs that operate without operating agreements are extremely rare. We discuss operating agreements in Chapter 3. In that chapter, we'll also discuss the advantages and disadvantages of the two types of governance structure.

Professional Limited Liability Companies

Professional limited liability companies (PLLCs) are simply LLCs in which the members are engaged in rendering professional services, such as the practice of medicine or law. Forming a professional LLC is slightly more difficult than forming a standard LLC. Much like the shareholders of a professional corporation, the members of a professional LLC may enjoy personal liability protection for the acts of other members; however, each member remains liable for his or her own professional misconduct. State laws generally require professional LLCs to maintain generous insurance policies or cash reserves to pay claims brought against them.

Professional LLCs are not recognized in all states, most notably California. Professional LLCs are more sophisticated enterprises than standard LLCs, and their organization should be left to a qualified attorney.

LLCs vs. S Corporations

While both S corporations and LLCs provide limited liability and partnership-like taxation, they differ in significant ways, as shown in this table. There are other important differences, and legislation that makes S corporations more attractive to investors was passed by Congress in 1996. You should work closely with your tax advisor in choosing any entity for your business.

	S Corporation	LLC
Owners (Number)	No more than 75. All shareholders must consent to the election at the time it is made.	No maximum and no minimum. All states allow single-member LLCs.
Owners (Eligibility)	Individuals, U.S. citizens and resident aliens, death estates, bankruptcy estates, and certain tax-exempt organizations.	All people and entities eligible to own S corporations plus corporations, partnerships, most trusts, nonresident aliens, and pension plans.

	S Corporation	LLC
Nature of Ownership	Single class of stock.	Different classes and priorities of ownership permitted.
Essential Documents	Articles of incorporation, bylaws, stock certificates, stock ledger, IRS and state election of S corporation status.	Articles of organization, operating agreement (optional).
Management	Managed by board of directors and officers.	Managed either by the owners or by managers appointed by the owners.
Tax Treatment	The entity is not taxed: profits and losses are passed through to the shareholders.	The entity is not taxed: profits and losses are passed through to the members.

Limited Liability Company Acts

Every state has a limited liability company act and there are many similarities from state to state, but there is no uniform law in effect in all states. When you organize an LLC in a particular state, you agree to comply with its limited liability company act and it is presumed that you know its requirements. If there is a conflict between the state statute and your articles or operating agreement, the statute will prevail.

Good to Know

There is no federal corporation law or federal LLC law. The federal government has chosen to stay out of the corporation law arena. Thus, it is not possible to charter an LLC in the United States: all U.S. corporations are chartered within one of the 50 states or other jurisdictions, such as the District of Columbia. The United States differs in this respect from some other nations, which charter their corporations at the national level.

The Uniform Limited Liability Company Act (ULLCA), drafted by the National Conference of Commissioners on Uniform State Laws in 1996 and revised in 2006, has been adopted by a few states. The ULLCA reflects the modern trend in business laws and it represents the subjects commonly found in all state LLC statutes.

Therefore, to help you better understand limited liability company act requirements and to guide this chapter's discussion, the ULLCA will serve as a model of a typical limited liability company act.

Before jumping into this discussion, two concepts should be explained.

The first is the concept of sources of authority. An LLC is a creature of statute and can only do what state laws permit it to do. All states have some written LLC laws and all states' LLC laws provide a general outline of what LLCs can and cannot do. The laws often defer to an LLC's articles of organization or operating agreement to fill in the gaps. As a result, the LLC laws and an LLC's articles of organization and operating agreement provide the sources of authority that control what an LLC can do and how it must act.

The second concept is the distinction between a *statute* and an *act*. Both terms refer to laws duly adopted by Congress or by a state legislature. All the laws adopted by Congress or a state legislature are statutes. Some of these statutes may empower an administrative agency like the Internal Revenue Service to pass rules to implement the statute. A specific body of statutes is an act. For example, in most states, all the statutes that pertain to LLCs are found together in the limited liability company act. Acts are sometimes referred to as codes, including the Internal Revenue Code, Uniform Commercial Code, or a criminal code.

Where to Find Your State Statutes

The list below gives the web address for the statutes of each state and the District of Columbia. You can also find a handy reference table at my web site at the following address: *www.learnaboutlaw.com/Corporations/50state_statutes.htm*.

State	Where to Find State Statutes
Alabama	www.legislature.state.al.us/CodeofAlabama/1975/coatoc.htm
Alaska	touchngo.com/lglcntr/akstats/statutes.htm
Arizona	www.azleg.state.az.us/ArizonaRevisedStatutes.asp

State	Where to Find State Statutes
Arkansas	www.arkleg.state.ar.us/data/ar_code.asp
California	www.leginfo.ca.gov/calaw.html
Colorado	www.michie.com/colorado
Connecticut	www.cga.ct.gov/asp/menu/Statutes.asp
Delaware	delcode.delaware.gov/index.shtml
District of Columbia	government.westlaw.com/linkedslice/default.asp?SP=DCC-1000
Florida	www.flsenate.gov/statutes/
Georgia	www.lexis-nexis.com/hottopics/gacode/
Hawaii	www.capitol.hawaii.gov/site1/docs/docs.asp
Idaho	www3.state.id.us/idstat/TOC/idstTOC.html
Illinois	www.ilga.gov/legislation/ilcs/ilcs.asp
Indiana	www.in.gov/legislative/ic_iac/
Iowa	www.legis.state.ia.us/IowaLaw.html
Kansas	www.kslegislature.org/legsrv-statutes/index.do
Kentucky	www.lrc.state.ky.us/Statrev/frontpg.htm
Louisiana	www.legis.state.la.us/lss/tsrssearch.htm
Maine	janus.state.me.us/legis/statutes/
Maryland	www.sailor.lib.md.us/MD_topics/law/_cod.html
Massachusetts	www.mass.gov/legis/laws/mgl/
Michigan	legislature.mi.gov/doc.aspx?ChapterIndex
Minnesota	www.leg.state.mn.us/leg/statutes.htm
Mississippi	www.mscode.com
Missouri	www.moga.mo.us/statutes/statutes.htm
Montana	data.opi.state.mt.us/bills/mca_toc/index.htm
Nebraska	www.nlc.state.ne.us/bestofweb/currentstatutes.html
Nevada	www.leg.state.nv.us/nrsindex/index.html
New Hampshire	gencourt.state.nh.us/rsa/html/indexes/default.html
New Jersey	www.njlawnet.com/njstatutes.html
New Mexico	www.fscll.org/Stat.htm
New York	caselaw.lp.findlaw.com/nycodes/index.html
North Carolina	www.ncga.state.nc.us/gascripts/Statutes/statutestoc.pl

State	Where to Find State Statutes
North Dakota	www.legis.nd.gov/information/statutes/ cent-code.html
Ohio	codes.ohio.gov
Oklahoma	oklegal.onenet.net/statutes.basic.html
Oregon	www.leg.state.or.us/ors/home.html
Pennsylvania	www.pacode.com/
Rhode Island	www.rilin.state.ri.us/Statutes/Statutes.html
South Carolina	www.scstatehouse.net/code/statmast.htm
South Dakota	legis.state.sd.us/statutes/index.aspx
Tennessee	www.michie.com
Texas	tlo2.tlc.state.tx.us/statutes/statutes.html
Utah	www.le.state.ut.us/Documents/code_const.htm
Vermont	www.michie.com
Virginia	leg1.state.va.us/000/src.htm
Washington	apps.leg.wa.gov/rcw/
West Virginia	www.legis.state.wv.us/WVCODE/masterfrm3 Banner.cfm
Wisconsin	www.legis.state.wi.us/rsb/stats.html
Wyoming	legisweb.state.wy.us/titles/statutes.htm

Filing Mechanics

For an LLC to "come to life," one or more LLC documents must be filed with the secretary of state. The process of bringing an LLC to life closely mirrors the process of bringing a corporation to life.

The ULLCA and all LLC acts set forth technical requirements for filing articles of organization. For example, the statute requires that articles be submitted on a form prescribed by the secretary of state. In most states, the secretary of state will provide a preprinted form of articles of organization. If you choose, you may fill in the blanks and submit the articles along with the required filing fee and you have created a LLC. Bear in mind, however, that filling in blanks on a form without more information could prove costly in the future.

Articles should always be typed or printed on a computer printer and signed by the authorized LLC organizer. One signed and one photocopied version of the articles must be submitted to the secretary of state. If the articles are approved by the secretary of state, your LLC's existence begins on the date of filing with the secretary of state. The secretary will file-stamp the photocopy of the articles and return it to you. In some states, this file-stamped copy must also be sent to the local recorder of deeds for filing. Check the State Reference Information on the accompanying CD for your local filing requirements, if you haven't formed your LLC already. When the secretary of state or local recorder returns your articles of organization, keep them in your LLC's minute book.

It is a crime to make a false statement in articles of organization. Read your articles carefully before filing. In addition, review the State Reference Information or contact the secretary of state's office before filing to determine the required filing fee. In some states, a flat fee is assessed for filing articles of organization. In a very small number of states, the fee is based on the number of members or on how much initial capital is invested in the LLC. Again, the State Reference Information includes each state's filing requirements and fees.

Articles of Organization and the Operating Agreement

What must you include in the articles of organization? As you will see, very little information is required. However, in some instances, you might want to include more information than is required. LLC statutes provide that any other lawful information may be included.

Here is a good point to note an important difference between corporations and LLCs. LLCs generally are simpler entities than corporations. They are easier to manage and operate; they tend to be run more like partnerships than like corporations. From this standpoint, they are ideal for small business. The great increase in the number of LLC formations in recent years is likely due to the simplicity of formation and operating. On the other hand, corporations are more suitable when the organizational and operational needs are more complex, as with large public companies, which may have multiple classes of stock or boards with staggered voting (e.g., where nine directors serve three-year terms and three of the nine director seats are filled by election every year). If you have an LLC already or if you are considering forming one, it's likely because you want something simple and easy to manage. As such, it's generally a good idea to keep your articles of organization as simple as possible. Chapter 2 discusses in more detail what you must include in your articles of organization.

Limited liability company acts also generally require that every LLC adopt an operating agreement for the purpose of managing and regulating the affairs of the corporation. If you don't adopt an operating agreement for your LLC, your LLC will be governed by the provisions of state law. Those provisions are not likely to be ideal for your needs. So, whether an operating agreement is required by law or not, you should promptly adopt an operating agreement after forming your LLC. More specific information pertaining to operating agreement and amendments is provided in Chapter 3.

Expert Tip

When you file your articles, provide your name and telephone number in your cover letter. Let the secretary of state's office staff know that they can contact you if they have any questions concerning your filing. In some states, minor errors in the articles can be corrected over the telephone without the need to resubmit the articles.

Purposes and Powers

For what purposes can an LLC be formed? A *purpose* is a statement of why the LLC was formed. Once formed, what *powers* may an LLC exercise? Powers tell us what an LLC can do to carry out its purpose. Because LLCs are creatures of statute, the answers to these questions are found in the state LLC acts.

Under the ULLCA and state statutes, an LLC is presumed to be formed to engage in any lawful purpose unless a more limited purpose is stated in the articles. You could state in your articles that the LLC is formed to operate a retail clothing store and for no other purpose; however, it would be foolish to limit your purposes. Without any limitation in the articles, the LLC may engage in any lawful act, subject, of course, to any other statutes or laws that might impact the LLC's activities or business. Nearly every model articles of organization provided by secretary of state's offices offers purpose language that is as broad as possible.

With respect to LLC powers, the ULLCA and other limited liability company acts include the powers for an LLC:

- To sue and be sued in the LLC name
- To make and amend its operating agreement
- To acquire and own real or personal property, whether by lease, purchase, or otherwise, and to use or improve that property
- To sell, mortgage, lease, or otherwise dispose of all or any part of its property
- To acquire stocks, bonds, or notes of other LLCs, partnerships, or other businesses
- To make contracts and guarantees; borrow money; issue notes, bonds, and other obligations; and secure any of its obligations by mortgage of any of its property
- To lend money, invest and reinvest its funds, and receive and hold real and personal property as security for repayment
- To be a promoter, partner, member, associate, or manager of any partnership, joint venture, trust, or other entity
- To conduct its business anywhere, subject, of course, to the foreign LLC statutes of other states
- To elect managers and appoint officers, employees, and agents, define their duties, fix their compensation, and lend them money and credit
- To establish benefit plans
- To make donations for the public welfare or for charitable, scientific, or educational purposes
- To transact any lawful business
- To do anything else that is not illegal and that furthers the business and affairs of the LLC

> ## Good to Know
>
> As a practical matter, banks, suppliers, and others with whom you may need to establish a credit or working relationship may request to see copies of your articles of organization and operating agreement and may be more apt to establish a relationship if some specific description of purposes and powers is included in the articles.

A Note on Prohibited Business Purposes

Some types of licensed professions are not legal purposes for LLCs and corporations. The practice of law and the practice of medicine are the most universal and most illustrative examples of this prohibition. Because lawyers and doctors face professional malpractice liability for errors that they make in their practices, it would be unfair to the public to allow such professionals to enjoy liability protection from such errors. The types of business purposes that a given state will allow will vary widely. For example, California prohibits use of the LLC or corporate forms for any profession that requires a "license, certification, or registration." This prohibition excludes more than 100 professions, including such diverse practitioners as lawyers, real estate brokers, and pest control operators.

As mentioned earlier, in states that allow it (not all do), licensed professionals must use a special form of LLC, the professional limited liability company (PLLC). We discuss the PLLC in some detail in Section VI: Related Concepts. Professional LLCs are complex entities and their formation and operation should be left to the pros.

Limited Liability Company Names

Every LLC must have a name; however, you may be surprised to learn how often the first or second choices for an LLC name are not available for one reason or another.

The most important consideration when choosing a name is ensuring that no other person or entity is currently using the name. This consideration is guided by two factors. First, your use of a company name may infringe on the trademark or service mark rights of others. Infringing on trademark or service mark rights may result in legal complications. Second, the secretary of state's office will not register a new LLC with the same name as an existing LLC.

Definition

A *trademark* is a word or mark that distinctly indicates ownership of a product and is legally reserved for the exclusive use of the owner.

A *service mark* is the same as a trademark but for services rather than goods.

The terms are interchangeable and their meanings are nearly identical.

Thus, you may wish to search the trademarks and LLC names in use to ensure that your desired name is available.

Searching for Existing Trademarks

Begin by performing a trademark search. You can hire a professional service to perform a trademark search for you. This fee for this service can range between $300 and $1,200. The value of such professional search services has been eclipsed by free services on the internet.

You can search registered and pending trademarks at the U.S. Patent and Trademark Office web site at *www.uspto.gov*, using the Trademark Electronic Search System (TESS). Use the New User Form Search. In the search window, enter the name that you wish to use in the "Search Term" box. Make sure the "Field" term is set to "Combined Word Mark." To ensure that your search effectively locates all potential conflicts, be sure to do the following:

- Search for phonetic variants of your proposed name, because phonetically similar marks can cause a trademark conflict. For example, if you want to use the name Cybertech, search for Cybertek, Cybertex, Sybertex, etc.
- Search for both the plural and singular versions of your proposed name.
- If your name uses more than one word, search for each word individually.
- Follow the instructions in the use of "wildcard" search terms.

Searching for trademarks is an imperfect science; no search can be expected to discover all potential users of a mark. Trademark rights are created by the use of a mark and not by registration. Thus, unregistered marks may be valid marks—and they are much more difficult to discover. The last step of your trademark conflict search should be an internet search with one of the popular search engines. Such a search will likely discover any use of your proposed name.

Searching the Secretary of State's Records for LLC and Corporation Names

Assuming that your name does not trigger a conflict with a registered or unregistered trademark, you should then search an online database of LLC and corporate names with the secretary of state in the state in which you intend to organize. You must search for both LLC and corporation names. Why? Because an "Inc." or an "LLC" designation at the end of an entity's name is not sufficient to distinguish between two companies; in most states, the secretary of state will not register an LLC with the same name as an existing corporation or a corporation with the same name as an existing LLC. For example, the secretary of state may not allow you to register "First American, LLC" if "First American Corp." is already registered. This decision will be a matter of secretary of state policy and will vary; contact the secretary of state's office if you wish to pursue the matter.

Nearly all secretary of state web sites offer free searching of existing corporate names. See the State Reference Information on the accompanying CD for information on locating the secretary of state's web site in your state of incorporation. Alternatively, some secretary of state offices offer informal searches over the telephone, but searching a database is always preferred.

Your LLC's name must not be confusingly similar to the name of any existing LLC or *fictitious name* registered to an LLC or any other business entity. A fictitious name is a *trade name*. For example, Publishing Services, Inc., an Oregon LLC, does business as PSI Research. The name "PSI Research" has been registered as a fictitious name with the Oregon Secretary of State.

States differ in their interpretations of what is "confusingly similar." For some states, the phrase is synonymous with "identical." In other states, even minor deviations are not permitted. For example, the names "AAA Body Shop" and "AAA Body Repair" would be considered confusingly similar in some states and not in others.

> ### Expert Tip
>
> As we'll learn in later chapters, the cornerstone of LLC liability protection is the degree of legal *separateness* between LLC and owner. For this reason, it may be unwise to use your personal name in the name of your LLC (e.g., John Jones Construction, LLC). Such a use implies a strong connection between owner and LLC and erodes the all-important separateness.

Your LLC's name should reflect LLC status. Most states require at least some sort of LLC identifier. Perhaps more important, you should always hold your company out to the public as an LLC to ensure maximum liability protection. Therefore, your LLC's name should include one of the following terms:

- Limited Liability Company
- LLC or L.L.C.

Some states allow "Limited Company" (Florida) or LC. I'd recommend avoiding any designation other than LLC or Limited Liability Company.

Your LLC's name should *not* include any of the following terms, which are usually restricted by state and/or federal law, unless your LLC meets the legal requirements for such terms:

- Bank
- Trust or Trustee
- Insurance
- Investment and Loan
- Thrift
- Doctor, Medical, Dental, and the like

- Mortgage
- Cooperative
- Olympic or Olympiad

Reserving an LLC Name

When you have selected an appropriate name, you may wish to reserve the name of the LLC. This step is optional. In my law practice, I almost always skip reserving a company name. The form for reserving an LLC name is typically nearly as long as the form for filing the articles of organization! To me, name reservation just creates more work. If my search reveals that a name has not been taken, I simply file the articles within a few days. If my filing is rejected, I simply work with my client to pick a new name and file again.

If name reservation is important to you, nearly all states offer a name reservation service. Typically, the service requires you to file a brief name reservation application with the secretary of state's office. See the State Reference Information on the accompanying CD for the basics on name reservation for each state, appropriate forms, and associated filing fees.

Expert Tip

Before you submit your articles of organization, make certain that the name that you have chosen is available. When selecting a name, have two or three choices ready in the event that your first choice is not available.

A foreign corporation may have established name recognition in one state, but when it seeks authority to do business in another state, it may find that the name it has been using is unavailable because it is already being used.

Name availability is also a concern for foreign LLCs. A *foreign LLC* is an LLC formed in another state. (LLCs from foreign nations can also be foreign LLCs.) LLCs formed and organized pursuant to the laws of your state are considered *domestic LLCs*. For example, a California LLC that is doing business in Nevada is a foreign LLC in Nevada and a domestic LLC in California. We discuss foreign LLCs in more detail below in this chapter.

If a foreign LLC has established name recognition in one state, but finds that name is already being used in another state, this could be a problem. For example, say you own and operate Advantis LLC in California. Later, you expand into Nevada, so you try to register in Nevada as a foreign LLC, but there is an Advantis Corporation that is a domestic corporation in Nevada. Nevada may not let your LLC qualify there.

Here are some steps you can take to secure and preserve your LLC name:

- Register your LLC name or logo as a trademark or service mark pursuant to federal laws and acquire the right to use your name anywhere in the country, subject to the right of persons using the name prior to your registration of the mark.
- Use state trademark or service mark registration laws to protect your name within the state where you register.
- Reserve the LLC name in all states where your LLC will do business. Name reservations are generally available for no more than 60 to 90 days. Some states do not permit renewal of a name reservation.

Registered Office and Registered Agent

A *registered agent* (or *registered office* or *resident agent*—the terms are synonymous) is a person or entity authorized and obligated to receive legal papers on behalf of an LLC. (Corporations have registered agents also.) The registered agent is identified in the articles of organization, but it can typically be changed by filing a notice with the secretary of state. The registered agent serves an important function: an LLC is not a physical person, so it would be impossible to serve legal papers on an LLC if there were no designated representative. The registered agent is designated by language such as "The name and address in the State of California of this LLC's initial agent for service of process are John Jones, 123 Elm Street, San Francisco, California 94107."

Your state of organization may use a term other than *registered agent*. In addition to *registered office* or *resident agent*, typical equivalents include *agent for service of process* and *local agent*.

Expert Tip

Professional Registered Agents Can Help. If you are organizing your LLC yourself, registered agents can be valuable sources of information about the state in which you are filing. Because most registered agents work so closely with the secretary of state's office on behalf of many companies, they become experts in dealing with the secretary of state's office. Remember: paid resident agents want your business, the yearly fees, so they won't mind answering a few questions free. You might confirm with them the amount of the filing fees to include with your articles of organization or you might ask for a free sample of articles of organization that they recommend.

The agent can be you, a family member, an LLC officer, an attorney, or a professional company that specializes in corporation and LLC support services. With millions of corporations and LLCs in America, professional resident agent services are big business. The registered agent's name is a public record; if you desire anonymity, then hire a professional to perform this service. The agent must have a physical address in the state of organization. Thus, if your business does not operate in the state of organization, you will need to hire a registered agent in that state. You must consider this additional expense when organizing out of state. Such services typically range from $50 to $350 per year.

Expert Tip

Don't overpay for resident agent services. The prices vary widely. If you are paying more than $75, you did not shop around enough. In Delaware, the cheapest and best is Harvard Business Services ($50 per year, *www.delawareinc.com*). In Nevada, use Resident Agents of Nevada ($90 per year, *www.nevada.org*). (These two states are popular choices for incorporation, for reasons discussed later in this chapter.) In all other states, I use Business Filings, Inc., which offers resident agent and formation services in all 50 states. Check *www.bizfilings.com.*

Using an attorney or professional firm as your agent has advantages, if you don't mind the cost. The primary role of an agent is to receive service of legal papers; an attorney or a professional firm is likely to maintain a consistent address and is likely to understand the nature of any legal papers served. The agent will also receive important state and federal mail such as tax forms, annual report forms, legal notices, and the like.

Expert Tip

Don't use a PO box as a resident agent address. First, some states don't allow it. Second, any correspondence sent to a registered agent is likely to be important; with a PO box you may not receive the correspondence as quickly.

Note that most secretary of state offices where you file your LLC organization papers will not check to see if you have properly secured the services of a registered agent. If you do not select a registered agent properly, the secretary of state will simply mail to the registered agent's address any documents that you submit with your articles of organization. If you do not select a registered agent properly, you will not receive them. Thus, you should hire your registered agent either before or when filing your articles of organization.

Here is a sample letter:

Sample Letter to Registered Agent Accompanying Articles of Organization

Michael Spadaccini
123 Elm Street
San Francisco, CA 94107
415-555-1212

March 21, 20__

Harvard Business Services, Inc.

16192 Coastal Highway

Lewes, DE 19958

To Whom It May Concern,

I have enclosed a copy of articles of organization I am filing today. As you can see, I have used you as our registered agents in the state of Delaware.

Please use the following contact information:

17 Reasons, LLC
c/o Michael Spadaccini
123 Elm Street
San Francisco, CA 94107

I have enclosed a check for $50.00 to cover the first year's services.
Yours truly,

Michael Spadaccini

Membership Interest: The LLC Equivalent of Corporate Stock

We need to begin our discussion of "LLC stock" by examining some differences in terminology between corporations and LLCs. Let's begin by discussing corporate stock. Then we'll see how the concept and the terminology adapt to the legal structure of LLCs.

A corporation issues shares of stock to its owners as part of the organization process. Shares of stock represent the ownership of the corporation; shareholders are the owners.

LLCs, on the other hand, issue *membership units*, *membership shares*, or *member's interest*. There are other, less used terms, such as *percentage interest*, *percentage share*, or *LLC share*—all proper terminology. In this sense, the ownership terminology of LLCs is more akin to the terminology of partnerships, where the ownership is expressed in terms of *percentage interest* or *percentage share*, rather than in a defined number of shares of stock. In the business world, you might hear the phrase "LLC stock." That phrase is not necessarily incorrect; it simply is not used often. It is better to discuss LLC ownership in terms of *percentage* or *share*. Throughout this book, we'll use several terms for LLC shares.

Now, you won't issue any membership shares until after your articles of organization are filed. You cannot have owners until you have a legal entity that they can own. You may wish to designate more than one class of ownership shares; this designation must be made in the articles of organization. Such a designation can be made with the filing of your articles or it can be made by an amendment any time after the original filing, with a bit of paperwork. You should have a good road map of your ownership structure early in the organization process, because you must set forth that structure in the articles of organization.

Classes and Types of Membership

All LLCs must have at least one class of ownership with voting rights. Without at least one class of voting ownership shares, an LLC's owners could not vote and therefore the LLC would be powerless to take any legal action. The overwhelming majority of LLCs, especially small LLCs, have only one class of ownership with voting rights. Typically, you won't need to overtly claim a voting class of ownership in your articles of organization; the state statute will imply that your LLCs owners enjoy voting rights.

Your LLC may have one or more additional classes of membership interest, if you designate additional classes. Secondary classes of voting interest appear in infinite varieties. But secondary classes are rare and I have never advised their use in my law practice unless it served a very good purpose.

To go forward, we'll need to borrow some terminology from corporate law. Types of corporate stock can be broadly categorized into three groups: common, preferred, and hybrid. Similarly, an LLC could create multiple classes of ownership. Nevada, for example, allows LLCs to create multiple classes of membership shares.

Common stock is simply plain voting stock, the simplest form of stock. This is equivalent to an LLC's ordinary membership units.

From here, things get very complicated. Typically, but not always, *preferred* stock is stock that entitles its holder to a monetary priority or preference over another class of shares. Often, preferred stock entitles the holder to priority in receipt of dividends and, if the corporation liquidates, asset distributions. In other words, preferred stockholders get paid first and common stockholders get what remains. Preferred stock often carries no voting rights. Sometimes preferred stock contains provisions establishing that it can be converted to common stock.

Often, investors who bring capital into the company will insist on getting preferred stock for their investment, so that they get paid first if the company is liquidated. Another common reason for investors insisting on preferred stock is that it entitles them to mandatory dividends.

While a dividend or liquidation preference is the most common feature of preferred stock, preferred stock can have other features. Though it's far less common, preferred stock can be *supervoting*. Supervoting preferred stock is a class of stock that entitles the holder to a greater voting percentage per share than a company's other class or classes of stock. Many states allow the authorization and issuance of supervoting stock and supervoting classes of LLC ownership. Such stock can have 10 votes per share, 100 votes per share, 1,000 votes per share—there is no legal limit on the number of votes per share. Supervoting stock is a powerful device if one wishes to maintain voting control of a corporation or an LLC.

Expert Tip

Don't issue multiple classes of stock unless you have a clear need. Consider this decision carefully. Multiple classes of stock create a good deal of complexity and increase operating costs; they are more appropriate for larger entities. In my practice, clients often ask me to create and issue multiple classes of shares when it really isn't necessary. Nearly as often, clients complain later that they should have taken my advice and authorized only one class of stock.

Hybrid stock refers to debt instruments that are convertible into ownership—they are not true equity instruments. For example, a promissory note—a document evidencing a loan—that is convertible into shares of an LLC's ownership is hybrid stock.

The rights and privileges of all an LLC's classes of ownership must be set forth in the articles of organization with a certain degree of particularity. Sample clauses establishing multiple classes of shares that you can include in your articles of organization appear in the articles of organization forms in this book.

Fundamental Changes

All limited liability company acts provide technical and mechanical rules for fundamental changes—changes that impact on the LLC in a significant way. For example, merger or consolidation, dissolution or liquidation, reorganization, sale of most of an LLC's assets, and amending the articles of organization are considered fundamental changes.

Some fundamental changes are beyond the scope of this book. Mergers, dissolutions, and the sale of a business are complicated transactions with diverse legal implications. Tax, securities, and antitrust are only a few of the legal issues that may be involved. Because your focus is on running your business, consider using the services of a competent business attorney in these areas.

A brief discussion of the more common fundamental changes follows.

Merger or Consolidation

A *merger* is the combination of one or more corporations, LLCs, or other business entities into a single business entity. Mergers are complex and flexible events. Mergers can involve two or more companies, even dozens of companies. Mergers can also consolidate entities of different types: an LLC can merge with a corporation or with a partnership. When two LLCs enter into a merger, one entity (the *disappearing* LLC) is absorbed into the other (the *surviving* LLC). The disappearing LLC ceases to exist for all purposes, with only the surviving LLC continuing. In general, the surviving LLC takes over all rights, liabilities, debts, and obligations of the disappearing LLC.

A *consolidation* is quite similar, involving an agreement of two or more corporations of LLCs to unite as a single entity. Often, a consolidation involves the formation of a third entity into which the assets and liabilities of the constituent entities are transferred.

For most limited liability company acts, the concepts of merger and consolidation are treated in the same fashion. If you're considering either, consult with your business attorney.

The mechanics of a merger work as follows. To effect a merger of two entities, the board of directors or managers of both entities cause a plan of merger to be prepared. If a corporation, the board votes to approve the plan and recommends that the plan be submitted to the shareholders for approval. If an LLC, either the members vote or the managers vote and then present their vote to the members for a separate vote. Specifics regarding member and manager meetings and voting are found in later chapters.

A plan of merger includes:

- The names of the entities participating in the merger
- A clear statement of which entity will survive and which entity will disappear
- The date when the merger will take effect; if this is not stated, then the merger is effective upon filing with the secretary of state
- A calculation outlining how much ownership in the surviving entity the owners of the disappearing entity will receive
- Any other information that the entities wish to include (for example, whether the name of the surviving entity will change when the merger becomes effective, whether a new registered agent or office will be appointed, whether there are any contingencies that must occur before the merger is effective)

A sample plan of merger for two fictitious LLCs, providing for a one-for-one ownership exchange, is located at the end of this chapter.

Once the plan of merger has been approved by the managers and owners of both entities, articles of merger must be prepared and submitted to the secretary of state. This is a document separate from the plan of merger. Generally, articles of merger are very brief. Like articles of organization, many secretary of state offices will provide form articles of merger for your use. In some states, you must attach a plan of merger to the articles of merger; in other states, you simply indicate in the articles of merger that the plan of merger is on file. If the merger involves a foreign entity, articles of merger must be sent to the secretary of state in both states.

Articles of merger should include:

- A copy of the plan of merger (if required by the state; if not, an indication that the plan is on file at company headquarters)
- The percentage interest or number of shares voted for and against the plan of merger
- An undertaking on the part of the surviving entity to assume the debts and liabilities of the disappearing entity or entities, if not already included in the plan of merger
- The signature of authorized officers of each entity

Expert Tip

When you contact the secretary of state's office to obtain articles of merger, specify whether or not a parent/subsidiary merger is involved. Different forms of articles of merger are used depending on the type of merger. Some states have short, fill-in-the-blank merger forms. The secretary of state will also tell you the fee for filing articles of merger. Don't forget to consult with your business attorney as well.

The following is a sample plan of merger. The first two paragraphs identify the merging LLCs. The merger is intended to qualify as a tax-free reorganization. Aluminum and Bituminous Coal, LLC (ABC) will be the survivor, assuming all the rights, properties, and liabilities of Dutch Everlight Foundry, LLC (DEF). Ownership shares will be exchanged on a one-for-one basis.

ABC's articles will govern, as amended, to change the name of the entity to ABC/DEF, LLC. ABC's managers will continue as the managers of the surviving LLC. Both ABC and DEF will continue to operate in their ordinary course of business until the merger. The members of both LLCs must approve the plan.

Sample Plan of Merger

Agreement and Plan of Merger

This Agreement and Plan of Merger is made this February 14, 20__ between Aluminum and Bituminous Coal, LLC, a Washington LLC (ABC), and Dutch Everlight Foundry, LLC, an Oregon LLC (DEF).

Recitals

ABC is a Washington LLC with its principal place of business located in Spokane, Washington.

DEF is an Oregon LLC with its principal place of business located in Portland, Oregon. Both ABC and DEF are manager-managed LLCs. The elected managers of ABC and DEF agree that it is in the best business interests of the LLCs and their owners that DEF be merged into ABC, in accordance with the terms and conditions of this Agreement and Plan of Merger, in such manner that this transaction qualify as a reorganization within the meaning of Section 368(a)(1)(A) of the Internal Revenue Code of 1954, as amended.

Therefore, in consideration of the mutual covenants set forth in this Agreement and subject to the terms and conditions of this Agreement, the parties agree as follows:

1. DEF shall merge with and into ABC, which shall be the surviving LLC.
2. On the effective date of the merger, the separate existence of DEF shall cease and ABC shall succeed to all the rights, privileges, immunities, and franchises, and all the property, real, personal, or mixed of DEF, without the necessity for any separate transfer. ABC shall thereafter be responsible and liable for all liabilities and obligations of DEF, and neither the rights of creditors nor any liens on the property of the absorbed LLC shall be impaired by the merger.
3. The resulting ownership of the surviving LLC shall be computed as follows.
   a. Concurrently with and immediately following the merger, the owners of DEF shall relinquish their ownership interest in DEF in exchange for an ownership in the surviving LLC (ABC) in accordance with and in the amount dictated by this Plan of Merger.
   b. The ownership of the surviving LLC following the merger shall be apportioned such that the existing owners of ABC shall hold fifty percent (50%) of the ownership interest in the surviving LLC; such owners of ABC shall bear this reduction in overall ownership interest pro rata.

c. The ownership of the surviving LLC following the merger shall be apportioned such that the existing owners of DEF, in exchange for their relinquishment of ownership in DEF, shall hold fifty percent (50%) of the ownership interest in the surviving LLC; such owners of DEF shall be granted this ownership interest pro rata.

4. The articles of organization of ABC shall continue to be its articles of organization following the effective date of the merger, subject to the following amendment:

Article I of the articles of organization shall be amended to read as follows:

The name of the LLC is ABC/DEF, LLC.

5. The operating agreement of ABC shall continue to be its operating agreement following the effective date of merger.

6. The managers of ABC on the effective date of the merger shall continue as the managers of ABC for the full unexpired terms of their offices and until their successors have been elected or appointed and qualified.

7. Neither ABC nor DEF shall, prior to the effective date of the merger, engage in any activity or transaction other than in the ordinary course of business, except that each LLC may take all action necessary or appropriate under federal or state law to consummate this merger.

8. This Agreement and Plan of Merger shall be submitted for the approval of the owners of ABC and DEF, such approval to be obtained on or before December 31, 20__.

9. The effective date of this merger shall be the date when a certificate of merger is issued by the Secretary of State of the State of Washington.

In witness whereof, the parties have executed this Agreement and Plan of Merger as of the date set forth above.

Aluminum and   **Dutch Everlight**
Bituminous Coal, LLC   **Foundry, LLC**

by _____   by_____
   President   President

Sale of Assets

An LLC has the power to buy, sell, and dispose of its property by virtue of powers granted in the limited liability company act. Without this power, the

LLC would be hard-pressed to conduct business. No member or manager approval is required to approve purchases or sales of LLC property in the ordinary conduct of the LLC's business. If the LLC proposes to sell all or most of its assets or make an unusual sale outside of its ordinary course of business, manager approval is required. Member approval may be required as well, depending on the state. If approval is required, the managers adopt a resolution authorizing the sale and requesting that the sale be submitted to the members for approval. Of course, in a member-managed LLC, the members are the managers, so the approval would be one step rather than two.

Below, we'll cover how to conduct member meetings and votes and manager meetings and votes.

Unless the articles or operating agreement require a higher percentage approval or super majority, the sale would require only majority member approval. Unlike merger or dissolution, no articles respecting the sale of business assets need to be filed with the secretary of state.

Good to Know

What becomes of an LLC following the sale of all its assets? Does the LLC survive? Yes. An LLC that is separated from its assets becomes a *shell LLC*; it remains a legal entity that is free to begin a new business enterprise, much in the same manner as a newly formed LLC. Shell LLCs often lie dormant for years before beginning a new business enterprise.

Dissolution and Liquidation

Dissolution is the decision to stop the active conduct of a business and formally dissolve the LLC's charter. There are three types of dissolution:

1. A voluntary dissolution is the intentional dissolution of an LLC by its own owners.
2. An administrative dissolution is a dissolution ordered either by the secretary of state, an equivalent department, or any other authorized state official.

3. A judicial dissolution is a dissolution ordered by a court of law. Judicial dissolutions are very rare.

During the dissolution process, all activities of the LLC are geared to an orderly winding up of the LLC's business and liquidating of its assets.

Like merger and consolidation, voluntary dissolution usually requires approval by the managers (if the LLC is manager-managed) and by the members. Dissolution also requires the filing of articles of dissolution with the secretary of state. In some states the secretary of state will not approve the voluntary dissolution of an LLC that is not in good standing or that has an outstanding tax liability. This is an interesting paradox, because the eventual penalty for delinquency in LLC filings and franchise taxes is administrative dissolution.

The secretary of state enjoys the power to order the administrative dissolution of an LLC. The secretary of state may exercise this power if an LLC becomes seriously delinquent in meeting its statutory requirements, such as periodic filing and tax reporting requirements. What constitutes a delinquency serious enough to warrant an administrative dissolution will differ widely from state to state. Some states allow a *reinstatement* of good standing following an administrative dissolution, if the LLC properly files and pays all back taxes. In Nevada, this process is called *reinstatement*; in Delaware, it's called *revival*.

A court of law may order the judicial dissolution of an LLC upon the request of a state attorney general, a member, or a creditor. A member, for example, may bring an action to dissolve an LLC if the LLC is wasting its assets, if the member's rights are being abused by other members, or if there's a voting deadlock among members or managers.

You should always endeavor to avoid dissolution. Dissolution can lead to a failure of an LLC's liability protection. See the State Reference Information on the accompanying CD for periodic reporting requirements and tax requirements in your state of organization. You should exercise great care if voluntarily dissolving an LLC. Do not allow it if the LLC has substantial debt. If you are a member of a dissolved LLC with outstanding liabilities, those liabilities may be attributed to you personally.

Articles of dissolution typically provide:

- The name of the LLC to be dissolved
- The date the dissolution was authorized by the board of managers and members
- The percentage of ownership interest voting for and against the dissolution
- The signature of an authorized manager of the LLC

The dissolution is effective on the date the articles of dissolution are filed with the secretary of state unless a different date is set forth in the articles. There is usually a fee charged for filing articles of dissolution.

Activities During Dissolution

What can an LLC do after it has filed articles of dissolution? The LLC may

- Continue to exist as an LLC to wind up and liquidate its business and affairs.
- Collect its assets.
- Dispose of properties that will not be distributed to its members.
- Discharge or make provision for discharging its liabilities.
- Distribute its remaining properties among its members according to their interests.

What can't the LLC do after articles of dissolution have been filed? It can't do anything not reasonably calculated to conclude its business. For example, signing a long-term contract to supply goods to another business or obligating the dissolving LLC to purchase goods over a long term would not be consistent with an intent to dissolve the LLC.

Good to Know

Because of the serious consequences of dissolution, the managers should notify each member of the proposed dissolution plan and the time, place, and date of the members' meeting to vote on the plan. In some states, even the holders of nonvoting shares may be eligible to vote on a plan to dissolve.

How Does a Dissolving LLC Manage Claims Made Against It?

The procedure for managing claims made against a dissolving LLC will vary widely. There are, however, a few common principles, which are expressed in the Uniform Limited Liability Company Act (ULLCA). The ULLCA divides claims made against a dissolving LLC into two kinds: those that the LLC knows about and those that it does not.

For claims that the LLC knows about (contract, government obligations, etc.), it must notify each creditor in writing of the dissolution and the need for the creditor to submit its claim. The notice should specify a deadline for submitting claims, but in no event can the deadline be sooner than 120 days following the written notice. Creditors that fail to file their claims before the deadline will find their claims are barred.

Unknown claims are commonly in areas of product liability, negligence, and environmental disputes. For example, a product that the LLC manufactures contains a defect that the managers and members do not know about. Sooner or later, the defect will be discovered, resulting in the possibility that claims will be filed against the LLC.

For unknown claims, the dissolving LLC should publish a notice of dissolution in a newspaper that is circulated generally in the county where the LLC is located. The notice should describe the LLC and its business and provide that claims against the LLC must be filed within five years. The notice will specify when and how claims are to be filed. Claims not filed within five years of publication will be barred. If the claim is not barred, the claim can be

---

Expert Tip

Managing the claims of a dissolving LLC can involve a significant amount of work and hassle. Avoid it by keeping your LLC alive and forgoing dissolution. If your LLC has debts, you can keep it legally alive as a *liability basket*. It may cost you some annual fees, but it's safer than dissolving it and then trying to protect your personal assets from aggressive creditors. As long as your LLC is in good standing and properly maintained, creditors and other claimants will be forced to hopelessly pursue claims against the LLC, but you won't have to manage a group of angry claimants.

---

enforced "against a member of the dissolved company to the extent of the member's proportionate share of the claim or the company's assets distributed to the member in liquidation." As a member of an LLC, you would obviously endeavor to conduct your dissolution so as not to leave lingering liabilities.

Enforcing Claims Against Dissolved LLCs

Under the ULLCA and in many states, claims of those who respond within the claim period may be enforced against the LLC. Recovery is limited to those assets that the LLC has not already distributed to its members or other creditors. If the assets have been distributed, claims may be enforced against the members, but recovery is limited to the value of assets distributed to the members. In the absence of fraud or other unusual circumstance, no member shall be personally liable for claims amounting to more than the value of assets distributed to him or her. Courts will not permit an LLC or its members to transfer LLC assets if the purpose of the transfer is to defraud claimants. In certain circumstances, entity transfers to one claimant may be attacked by another claimant if the LLC unfairly preferred the first claimant over the second.

Because dissolution involves the potential that a creditor could come knocking on your door to recover the value of assets distributed to you, it is important to follow any statutory claims procedure. Also, because of tax and other aspects of a dissolution, you would be wise to work closely with a good business attorney.

The following form is a sample certificate of dissolution for use in Delaware, which is fairly representative. (In Delaware, they call it *cancellation*.) You'll need to check with your specific state, because the forms will differ widely and your state may have additional requirements. All secretary of state offices offer sample certificates of dissolution. These documents are rarely longer than one page.

Sample Certificate of Dissolution

STATE OF DELAWARE

CERTIFICATE OF CANCELLATION OF LLC

1. The name of the limited liability company is <u>DEF LLC</u>.

2. The certificate of formation of the limited liability company was filed on

_____.

IN WITNESS WHEREOF, the undersigned has executed this Certificate of Cancellation this

_____ day of _____, 20__.

By: _____
    Signature of Authorized Officer

Name: _____
      Print or Type

Title: _____

Dissenters' Rights/Members' Appraisal Rights

Members don't always agree with each other. One may believe that a merger is the best thing for an LLC and another may feel just the opposite. In addition, not all members are equal. Some own voting shares; others may own nonvoting shares. One member may own more than 50 percent of the outstanding voting interest of an LLC and thus be considered a *controlling* member, at least for matters requiring majority approval. Members who don't own a controlling interest in stock are considered *minority* members. Minority members are obviously subject to getting outvoted on issues.

Statutory Protection for Minority Members

Because members don't always agree and because minority members can be directly impacted by decisions of the controlling members, most state statutes provide for *dissenters' rights* or *members' appraisal rights* when the LLC's majority seeks to undertake a serious event, such as to sell the business. These rights are intended to protect any minority member who does not believe that a proposed fundamental change is in the best interests of the LLC or in his or her best interests. A member exercising his or her dissenters' or appraisal rights can compel the LLC to purchase his or her shares. The degree of protection that minority members enjoy depends on the state. For example, California is very protective of minority members, whereas Nevada minority members receive comparatively little protection.

Under California law, dissenters' rights arise whenever:

- A plan of merger is submitted.
- Any exchange of shares between two companies is proposed (if the member has voting rights).
- The LLC proposes to sell all or most of its assets outside of the ordinary conduct of its business.
- The LLC proposes to take any other action to which the articles or operating agreement attach dissenters' or appraisal rights.

If an LLC proposes any action to which dissenters' or appraisal rights apply, the notice to members noting the meeting's time, date, and place must also indicate that dissenters' rights are available. Upon receipt of this notice, a member must notify the LLC of his or her election to exercise dissenters' rights.

If the proposed action is later approved, an LLC must notify all members who indicated their intent to exercise dissenters' rights. This notice must include a form of demand for payment and a timetable by which the members must submit their demands. In addition, the LLC must include financial information and a statement indicating its estimate of the value of the LLC's ownership interests and how it arrived at its estimate.

Good to Know

Members who wish to take advantage of dissenters' rights can't vote their shares in favor of the proposed LLC action. If they do, the dissenters' rights are no longer available to them. In addition, both members and the LLC would be wise to come to an agreement concerning the value of shares without resorting to the courts. Legal action in the courts is uncertain and expensive.

The member can accept the LLC's estimate and submit a demand for payment. If the member does not agree with the estimate, he or she should submit a demand for payment that indicates his or her estimate of value. If the LLC does not agree with the estimate, the parties can petition the local court to determine its value.

LLC Records

There is a common misconception that LLCs can operate with nearly no formalities. Certainly, the formalities required of LLCs are less than those required of corporations. When LLCs first began appearing as an alternative to corporations, many professionals and academics loudly touted the lack of formalities as a key selling point. But as time has passed, there have been some court decisions that are tending to indicate that LLCs will be held to a fairly high standard in order to preserve the their liability shield. We discuss LLC liability protection in detail in Section V: LLC Lawsuits and Personal Liability Protection, with some actual personal liability cases.

Remember: state statutes will only dictate the minimum standard of formalities and record-keeping that an LLC must follow. One should always endeavor to follow a higher standard of formalities and record-keeping than the statutory minimum. There are several important benefits to following higher standards.

The single greatest reason is for liability protection. The central concept in LLC liability protection is separateness. Formalities and record-keeping support this concept. A lack of formalities and record-keeping can be interpreted by a court to indicate a lack of separateness of individual and entity. The judge in *Labadie Coal Co. v. Black* said it better than I ever could: "Faithfulness to the formalities is the price paid to the corporation fiction, a relatively small price to pay for limited liability."

If you ever sell your business, a potential buyer and his or her professional team will examine your records. If those records are in a poor state, it will tend to lower the price you'll get or delay the sale.

Good records can ward off action by the IRS. The IRS imposes its own standards for record-keeping; generally those standards are higher than the statutory minimum.

So, you should venture to maintain formalities and keep appropriate records. Key concepts in maintaining LLC liability protection are separateness, as mentioned above, and *control and domination*. (One of the elements considered in disallowing liability protection is whether LLC members exercise such complete control that the entity is merely the "alter ego" of its members.) So, if you are an owner of a single-member LLC, you must strive even harder to observe formalities and keep appropriate records.

LLCs are required to keep the following records, and we discuss some of these specific topics later in the book:

- Minutes of all member and manager meetings, as well as copies of all notices to members and managers, and any proxy voting materials
- A record of all material and substantive actions taken by the managers or owners without a meeting (We'll discuss later the sorts of actions that are material and substantive and should be submitted to a proper vote and recorded.)
- A record of all actions taken by any committee of the managers
- A list of the names and addresses of current managers and owners
- All written communication by the LLC to its owners within the last five years
- All periodic reports of the LLC submitted to the secretary of state

With respect to financial statements, there is generally no requirement that an LLC provide formal financial statements to its members. Such a practice would tend to develop by the practices that an LLC chooses to follow. Providing such information, however, is good company governance and can be very good for owner relations.

The financial statements should contain the report of the public accountant who prepared the statements or, if prepared by the LLC without the use of a public accountant, a statement of the person preparing the report indicating whether or not the report was prepared in accordance with *generally accepted accounting principles* (GAAP). Finally, the LLC must provide a written summary to owners of any indemnification or loans or advances to managers and of any decision by the managers to issue ownership shares in exchange for promissory notes or future services. This notice must be provided with or before any notice of owners' meetings.

LLC records are a major topic in this book that we'll cover at length throughout.

Foreign LLCs

As mentioned earlier, an LLC conducting business in a state other than its state of organization is deemed a foreign LLC in the state in which it is a "guest." States require foreign LLCs conducting business within their borders to register. This process of registering as a foreign LLC is known as *qualification*. What constitutes "conducting business" for the purposes of determining the qualification threshold differs from state to state, but universally states will define "conducting business" broadly.

But why do states require foreign LLCs to suffer the expensive and burdensome task of filing for qualification? There are several reasons.

First, foreign LLCs must pay for the privilege of doing business in a particular state. After all, an Oregon LLC competing for sales in California competes with California corporations and Californian LLCs—all of which have paid organizational fees in California. If out-of-state businesses were not required to qualify, they would enjoy a competitive advantage over domestic businesses. Thus, requiring all to register or qualify evens the playing field.

The second reason is for consumer protection. Once an LLC qualifies as a foreign LLC, it admits to jurisdiction in the foreign state, it appoints an agent for service of legal process, and it can be sued there. It is much easier to serve a company with legal process in one's home state than in the state in which it was organized. Thus, consumers in the state where the LLC is qualified are more protected from any misdeeds committed by the LLC. Consequently, foreign LLCs are more accountable to consumers.

Qualifying as a foreign LLC closely mirrors the process of organization. LLCs must typically file their articles of organization in the foreign state, along with an additional filing that includes information specific to the foreign state, such as the resident agent in the foreign state. Every state's procedure for foreign qualification will differ slightly. The filing fees for qualification are always at least as high as for filing articles of organization and often higher.

The decision whether to qualify in a foreign state must be made cautiously. Once qualified, an LLC must file periodic reports in the foreign state, will likely need to file tax returns and pay taxes there, and must appoint a local agent. Also, qualification in a foreign state makes it much easier for creditors to serve process and bring lawsuits against the LLC in the foreign state.

While the requirements of foreign qualification are clear and obvious, in practice such requirements are routinely ignored by smaller companies. Smaller companies simply lack the resources to register in each state in which they do business. Even though every state requires foreign LLCs to qualify, no state makes a meaningful effort to enforce its requirement. However, this is not to say that it is wise to ignore the obligation to qualify as a foreign LLC. The law is the law and you should always endeavor to obey it.

The Concept of "Doing Business"

This raises an important question: what constitutes "operations" or "business activity" in a particular state? As mentioned above, all states define it somewhat differently—but universally they define "doing business" broadly. For example, California defines it as "actively engaging in any transaction for the purpose of financial or pecuniary gain or profit." It does not take a lawyer to get the crux of the meaning of that phrase. Quite simply, California interprets a single transaction taking place within its borders as "doing business."

Why do states define business activity so broadly (thereby requiring local registration of foreign LLCs)? There are two reasons. First, registered LLCs pay lucrative filing fees and franchise fees. Second, as mentioned above, each state has an interest in protecting its consumers from unscrupulous out-of-state companies, LLC or otherwise. A state can better protect its consumers from misconduct by out-of-state businesses if the state has registration and contact information on file for each company operating within its borders. Furthermore, by registering, a company automatically submits to the jurisdiction in which it is registered, so it can be sued more easily.

The ULLCA provides a partial list of individual acts that do *not* constitute doing business. You will note that the ULLCA is far more lenient than California. It includes:

- Maintaining, defending, or settling any proceeding
- Holding meetings of the board of managers or members within the state or carrying on other activities involving internal governance matters, such as committee meetings
- Maintaining bank accounts
- Maintaining stock transfer offices
- Selling through independent contractors
- Soliciting or obtaining orders, whether by mail or through employees or agents or otherwise, if the orders require acceptance outside their state before they become contracts
- Creating or acquiring indebtedness, mortgages, and security interests in property securing the debt
- Owning, without more, real or personal property
- Conducting an isolated transaction that is completed within 30 days and is not one in the course of repeated transactions of a like nature
- Transacting business in interstate commerce

States are seeking to expand the types of activities and level of business which constitute doing business. For example, businesses that rely heavily on mail order sales are under attack by several states that want to impose sales tax on mail order sales despite a U.S. Supreme Court case to the contrary. In addition, the Commonwealth of Massachusetts now seeks to impose its sales tax laws on vendors who come into the state to appear at trade shows. Previously, such an action would have been considered to be an isolated transaction.

Any significant physical presence or large volume of income or expense attributable to a particular state is a good indication that the LLC is doing business in that state. If in doubt, consult your business attorney.

What If You Fail to Get Permission?

So, is every LLC in the United States properly registered and qualified in every state in which it does business? No. Right or wrong, many thousands of

LLCs regularly ignore the foreign registration requirements imposed by states in which they conduct business. Foreign LLC registration in California, for example, runs $800 per year in taxes, plus resident agent fees.

Good to Know

We have researched and compiled the fees and filing information for foreign qualification for all 50 states and the District of Columbia in the State Reference Information on the accompanying CD.

LLCs that engage in business without obtaining the necessary certificate of authority from the secretary of state are subject to the following potential sanctions:

- The LLC cannot sue in the foreign state and it may not be able to defend claims against it until it qualifies.
- The state can assess a penalty for each day the LLC is not qualified to do business, up to a stated maximum. (These penalties are sometimes waived where excusable neglect can be shown.)

If an LLC that has qualified to do business in a state no longer engages in the business, it can formally apply to withdraw by filing an application for *certificate of withdrawal* with the secretary of state. In the application, the LLC will designate the secretary of state for the foreign state as its agent for service of process.

Where Do You Organize?

Your LLC's life begins when you file articles of organization with the secretary of state or its equivalent. Several factors will guide you in deciding which state is the best for your organization. Those factors include:

- The state or states in which your business operates
- State taxation
- Initial LLC filing fees

- Annual filing fees and annual reporting requirements
- State-specific advantages, such as privacy rights and members' rights

As a general rule, if your business is small and operates and sells only in one state, then you should organize in your state of operation. This advice will apply to most LLCs and your inquiry should go no further. As discussed above, states generally require a foreign LLC to register and pay fees if it operates within their borders. These registration rules limit the benefits of organizing out of state, because you'll likely need to register in your home state anyway.

If, however, your business operates in several states or if you expect to expand nationally, then you should consider organizing in the state that is most favorable for you.

You've likely seen advertisements touting the benefits of Delaware and Nevada corporations and LLCs. These states certainly aim to be business-friendly, and there are some benefits to larger entities.

There are many benefits to organizing in Delaware, including the following:

- Delaware law permits LLCs to liberally shield their managers from personal liability resulting from their actions as managers.
- Delaware has a separate court system, the Court of Chancery, that specifically litigates corporate and business entity matters. The Court of Chancery is widely respected and has developed a sophisticated body of corporate law.
- Delaware permits LLCs to operate with a great degree of anonymity.
- No minimum capital investment is required to form a Delaware LLC.
- The Delaware Division of Corporations is easy to reach on the telephone, although its web site needs improvement.
- Delaware organization offers some degree of prestige.
- Delaware offers incorporation on a few hours' notice (for a fee, of course).

Delaware organization carries a few drawbacks:

- Delaware, surprisingly, has fairly poor customer services support.

- Delaware's secretary of state's department has developed, over the decades, dozens of unwritten, idiosyncratic rules and procedures that stifle even the most experienced business attorneys.

Nevada has emerged recently as America's most popular corporate and LLC haven, and its features deserve mention. However, Nevada is not perfect.

The initial organization expenses in Nevada (about $280 for a bare-bones organization) far exceed Colorado's $50 organization filing fee or Florida's $70 filing fee. Nevada has recently nudged its fees upwards and, judging from that increase, one can reasonably expect that it will continue to do so. Also, Nevada requires organizers to name at least one member or manager in the articles of organization. This appointment then becomes part of the entity's public record, ultimately searchable by anyone over the internet or through the secretary of state's office. Despite this, Nevada is otherwise generally a "privacy state," one that offers its owners (but not necessarily its managers) a great degree of anonymity. We'll discuss Nevada's privacy rules at length below.

But why has Nevada become America's hottest corporate and LLC haven? Advertisements touting Nevada's advantages appear everywhere, from airline magazines to e-mail spam. The answer is that over the last few decades, the Nevada legislature has undertaken a conscious, deliberate, and effective program to make the state business-friendly.

Organizing in Nevada offers many benefits, among which are the following, and all of which are described in detail below:

- Nevada does not tax corporate or LLC profits. Nevada has no personal income tax. So naturally, Nevada has no income tax division or department. As a result, Nevada does not have any information-sharing agreement with the Internal Revenue Service.
- Nevada does not tax corporate shares or LLC ownership. Some states (not many, mind you) tax individual shares in a company.
- Nevada has no franchise tax, although it requires an annual filing fee, along with an annual statement of LLC managers or members.
- Owners of a Nevadan LLC are not a matter of public record: members can remain completely anonymous.

- Officers and managers of a Nevada LLC can be protected from personal liability for lawful acts of the LLC.
- Nevada LLCs may purchase, hold, sell, or transfer shares of their own stock.
- Nevada LLCs may issue stock for capital, services, personal property, or real estate, including leases and options. The managers determine the value of any of these transactions—and their decision is final.
- The Nevada secretary of state provides excellent customer service and excellent web support.

Nevada enjoys a windfall of tax revenues from its most notable industry: gaming. As a result, Nevada's residents and businesses enjoy some of the lowest state taxes anywhere. Unlike many other states, such as New York and California, Nevada does not impose a tax on corporate profits. California even imposes a 1.5 percent income tax on LLCs (with a minimum of $800 per year). It should be noted that California's LLC income tax is presently the subject of several legal challenges. Ultimately, the LLC income tax may be abolished.

Nevada imposes no franchise tax. A franchise tax is a tax levied in consideration for the privilege of either incorporating, organizing, or qualifying to do business in a state. A franchise tax may be based upon income, assets, outstanding shares, or a combination. Put another way, a franchise tax is a tax for "just being there." Many states impose franchise taxes on businesses.

While Nevada's secretary of state touts the absence of a personal income tax as a benefit to businesses, this is more of a reason to reside in Nevada than a reason to organize there. Personal income tax is paid in an individual's state of residency and not in the state where his or her entities are chartered. For example, a California resident who operates a Nevada LLC will be subject to California's personal income tax on LLC income paid to him or her— the same as if he or she had chosen to organize in Delaware or Wyoming or any other state.

Nevada offers a tremendous degree of privacy to owners of businesses chartered there. However, this degree of privacy is not extended to managers, directors, and officers of Nevada entities. As mentioned above, Nevada has no information-sharing agreement (ISA) with the Internal Revenue Service—and

Nevada is not afraid to boast about it.

The IRS has an ISA with 34 states. The purpose of the ISA is to combat abusive tax avoidance.

The IRS and the states that have signed the ISA will share information on abusive tax avoidance transactions and those taxpayers who participate in them. As reported by the IRS, the states participating in the ISA are Alabama, Arizona, Arkansas, Connecticut, Georgia, Florida, Hawaii, Idaho, Illinois, Indiana, Iowa, Kansas, Kentucky, Minnesota, Mississippi, Missouri, Montana, New Hampshire, New Mexico, New York, North Carolina, North Dakota, Ohio, Oklahoma, Oregon, Pennsylvania, Rhode Island, South Carolina, South Dakota, Utah, Vermont, Washington, West Virginia, and Wisconsin.

Even if Nevada participated in the agreement, it would have no information to share. Because Nevada has no corporate or LLC income tax and no personal income tax, it has no corresponding tax forms and no corresponding tax department.

Along the same lines, owners of Nevada LLCs need not identify themselves in any public records. This makes it very difficult for the government, police, or third parties to determine who owns a Nevada entity.

Unfortunately, Nevada's privacy protections are widely misused. By way of example, and not by way of recommendation, many individuals and businesses have improperly and illegally used Nevada business entities to hide assets from creditors and even their own spouses. The other obvious misuse is tax avoidance.

Despite occasional abuse, Nevada's privacy protections do offer value to the legitimate and law-abiding businessperson. Probably the single greatest benefit of Nevada's privacy protections is that they serve to protect business owners from unscrupulous creditors, aggressive attorneys, and frivolous litigation.

In my law practice, I have served as counsel to several companies that have been the victims of lawsuits that could only be fairly described as totally baseless. Often, the owners of businesses are dragged into suits as defendants simply as an intimidation tool. Frivolous lawsuits are an unfortunate reality in today's business climate. Also, lawsuits are never win-win: they are always win-lose. The successful defense of a lawsuit following the time and expense of a trial is not a pure victory: it is a victory that comes at great cost.

The real victory is not to ever be sued. Experienced businesspersons and lawyers know this. Nevada's privacy protections can go a long way toward achieving this goal by effectively hiding business owners from public view and thereby protecting them from litigation. Of course, Nevada's privacy protections are not absolute. A good plaintiff's lawyer with enough money and time (it would take a lot of both) could ultimately identify the owners of a Nevada entity. Overall, though, Nevada's privacy protections are quite valuable.

The other obvious benefit of Nevada's privacy protections for the businessperson is shelter from government prying. This benefit is obvious, even to a completely law-abiding company or company owner. Our government, police, and courts, while the finest anywhere, are capable of occasionally pursuing the innocent. Again, the successful defense of a criminal matter following the time and expense of a trial is a victory that comes at great cost.

Privacy, for lack of a better term, is good. I am quite comfortable advising my business clients to maintain their privacy as much as possible in their business affairs, regardless of the type of business they conduct. As a general rule, that which need not be disclosed should not be disclosed.

Nevada's privacy rules have an important exception, however. They protect owners, but not company officers and managers. Nevada is one of a few states that require an organizer to appoint by name at least one initial member or manager in an LLC's articles. The articles are a public record and anyone can request copies by paying a small fee.

Even worse, however, is the requirement that every Nevada LLC or foreign LLC qualified there file an "Annual List of Managers." The oft-dreaded Annual List requires companies to disclose the full names of their managers or members. The information is then posted on the Nevada secretary of state's web site and anyone can search it. This public database makes it remarkably easy for any member of the public to identify a Nevada entity's management team. Nevada offers a great degree of privacy to owners: as long as they do not participate as managers, owners can easily remain anonymous. By comparison, Delaware and many other states do not so publicly reveal the identities of managers.

> ## Expert Tip
>
> Nevada's dual approach to privacy (complete anonymity for members, but complete disclosure of managers and officers) has produced an interesting new profession: the *nominee director/manager*. This is an appointed manager/officer who serves as the appointed public representative of an LLC or corporation. The nominee director/manager is often charged with a solemn duty: to serve as the guardian of an entity's owners' privacy. The entity's owners "hide" behind the publicly disclosed nominee manager. A common use of a nominee manager is to protect assets: a Nevada entity owner that wishes to hide assets can assign them to the Nevada entity and can then appoint a nominee manager and direct that person to serve the owner's interest. The use of nominee managers has little value to an ordinary small business, but it's effective for asset protection.

You should also consider the initial cost of organization, as well as periodic filing fees and periodic reporting requirements. The State Reference Information on the accompanying CD includes filing fees and periodic reporting requirements.

Why Are You Required to File Documents?

When an LLC is formed, it files articles of organization. An LLC will also file periodic reports and a host of other public documents. These public filings serve the purpose of providing public notice. For example, articles of organization notify the public that an LLC has been formed and identify the person to contact in the event of a claim against the LLC, articles of merger inform the public that two companies are becoming one, and articles of dissolution inform the public that an LLC is discontinuing its business.

Notice is important. It identifies an entity, which in turn makes it easier for government agencies to assess the entity for its share of taxes and other fees. Notice also protects consumers and creditors: it lets them know whom to serve with lawsuits and where in the event of a dispute.

Final Thoughts on Limited Liability Company Acts

To help you remember what's in a limited liability company act, the statutory checklist at the end of this chapter lists the items that are usually found in these acts. The second list describes the most common documents that are filed with the secretary of state. Most of these documents are required or permitted to be filed by a limited liability company act.

More important, remember that most sections of limited liability company acts are prefaced with this language: "Unless otherwise provided in the articles of organization or operating agreement...." You have the flexibility to customize your LLC to fit your needs. The statutes are important, but your articles and operating agreement will more often than not establish requirements for your corporation.

Use this checklist to identify areas where you may need to refer to your state's statute to determine the proper course of action. Many of these concepts are described in later chapters.

Checklist: Statutory Matters

- ❏ Filing requirements
- ❏ Organizers
- ❏ Articles of organization
- ❏ Liability for preorganization transactions
- ❏ Operating agreement
- ❏ Emergency operating agreement
- ❏ LLC purposes and powers
- ❏ LLC name
- ❏ Name reservation
- ❏ Registered office and registered agent
- ❏ Changing registered office or agent
- ❏ Resignation of registered agent
- ❏ Service of process on LLCs
- ❏ Terms of classes or series of ownership interests
- ❏ Issuance of ownership interests
- ❏ Liability of owners

❑ Restriction on transfer of ownership interests

❑ Distributions to owners

❑ Owner annual and special meetings

❑ Court-ordered owners' meetings

❑ Consent resolutions by owners without meeting

❑ Notice of owners' meetings

❑ Waiver of notice of owners' meetings

❑ Record date

❑ Owners list for meeting

❑ Voting entitlement for membership interests

❑ Proxies

❑ LLC acceptance of member votes

❑ Quorum and voting requirements for voting groups

❑ Modification of quorum or voting requirements

❑ Voting for managers/cumulative voting

❑ Voting trusts

❑ Voting agreements

❑ Derivative lawsuits

❑ Requirements and duties of appointed managers

❑ Qualifications of managers

❑ Number and election of managers

❑ Election of managers by certain classes of owners

❑ Terms of managers

❑ Staggered terms for managers

❑ Resignation of managers

❑ Removal of managers by owners

❑ Removal of managers by judicial proceeding

❑ Compensation of managers

❑ Managers' meetings

❑ Action by managers without meeting/consent resolutions

❑ Notice of managers' meetings

❑ Waiver of notice of managers' meetings

❑ Quorum and voting at managers' meetings

❑ Committees of the managers
❑ General standards of conduct for managers
❑ Conflicts of interest
❑ Loans to managers
❑ Required officers for LLC
❑ Duties of officers
❑ Standard of conduct for officers
❑ Resignation and removal of officers from office
❑ Authority to indemnify managers
❑ Advances to managers and officers for expenses
❑ Court-ordered indemnification
❑ Determination and authorization of indemnification
❑ Indemnification of officers, employees, and agents
❑ Amending the articles of organization
❑ Merger
❑ Sale of assets
❑ Dissenting owners' rights
❑ Dissolution
❑ Authority of foreign LLC to transact business
❑ Consequences of transacting business without authority
❑ Application for authority to transact business
❑ Amendment to application for authority
❑ Name of foreign LLC
❑ Registered office and agent of foreign LLC
❑ Change of registered office or agent of foreign LLC
❑ Resignation of registered agent of foreign LLC
❑ Service of process on foreign LLC
❑ Withdrawal of a foreign LLC
❑ LLC records required
❑ Inspection rights of owners
❑ Scope of owners' inspection rights
❑ LLC annual report
❑ Penalty for signing a false document

Checklist: Frequently Filed Documents

Your secretary of state requires LLCs to file certain documents. These documents will usually include the following:

❑ Request to reserve LLC name (optional)
❑ Fictitious name reservation, aka assumed business name
❑ Articles of organization
❑ Amendment to articles of organization
❑ Annual report
❑ Change of registered office or registered agent
❑ Request for certificate of good standing
❑ Application for certificate of authority
❑ Articles of merger
❑ Articles of dissolution
❑ Application for withdrawal of certificate of authority
❑ Appointment of secretary of state for certificate of service
❑ Application to reinstate LLC charter

Articles of Organization

In terms of importance and ultimate authority, your state's limited liability company act has first priority, your articles of organization are second, and your operating agreement is considered third. In the event of a conflict between the articles of organization and your state's act, the act will control. If a conflict exists between the articles and the operating agreement, the provision in the articles will prevail.

This book is intended as an operations manual, so you may already have filed your articles of organization. If so, you may want to skip this chapter.

The life of an LLC begins with the preparation and filing of articles of organization. Typically a one-page document, the articles of organization set out the following basic information:

- The name of the LLC
- The name and address of the agent for service of process, the person or entity authorized to receive legal papers on behalf of the LLC
- A statement of the LLC's purpose
- Declaration as being member-managed or manager-managed (required by some states)
- Name of at least one member or manager (required by some states)

To form an LLC, you file articles of organization with the secretary of state or equivalent department. See the State Reference Information on the accompanying CD for contact information for the appropriate department. With the articles, you must also submit a filing fee, which differs by state.

Use the Secretary of State's Model Articles of Organization

The best place to start in preparing your articles of organization is to visit the secretary of state's web site in the state in which you want to organize. In most cases, these sample articles will be all you need.

In the past few years, many states have offered fill-in-the-blank articles. The use of such forms is now mandated in several states, most notably Nevada. Bear in mind that fill-in-the-blank forms are going to offer only the minimum. If you have additional clauses that you wish to add, such as additional classes of ownership or specific limits on the liability of officers and managers for actions on behalf of the LLC, you'll need to add those clauses on continuation pages.

Expert Tip

Don't file organization papers in the closing weeks of a fiscal year, such as in the last weeks of December—you may be required to file tax returns for the entire year. Wait until January 1 to file your organization papers.

Expert Tip

You can usually pick your date of organization. If you would like a special date, such as January 1 or a birthday, contact the secretary of state's office in the state in which you intend to organize. Almost all states will let you designate a special date of organization when you file.

Expedited Service May Be Available

If you want to form your LLC immediately or at least very quickly, some states offer expedited service available for an additional fee. Delaware and Nevada, where organization is a cottage industry, both offer expedited filing. Nevada offers a 24-hour service for an additional $100. Delaware goes further: it offers the fastest organization in the country, with 24-hour service for $50, same-day service for $100, two-hour service for $500, and one-hour service for $1,000.

Online Resource

You will find links to the web sites of the secretaries of state for all 50 states at www.learnaboutlaw.com.

What Information Should You Include in Your Articles?

Your articles of organization should include all the required items listed above, as well as any of the optional items that are required by your state. Next, determine how much information you wish to make public.

Don't Disclose the Unnecessary

As a general rule, don't appoint initial members or managers in your articles of organization—except if the state requires it, such as Nevada. And, generally, I recommend that LLCs be operated as manager-managed LLCs: that's a theme we'll talk about throughout the book. Managers can easily be appointed immediately by the organizer after filing the articles of organization. So, if it's optional, don't name managers or members in the articles. Articles of organization are a public record and available for inspection. As a result, many business owners wish to reveal as little information as possible about their LLCs in the articles, relying instead on the operating agreement and LLC minutes to store this information. You should always strive to operate your LLC as discreetly as possible.

Expert Tip

Never disclose the names of the owners of an LLC if it's not required. Although it happens only rarely, sometimes aggressive lawyers suing a company will sue the company's owners in order to harass and gain leverage—even if the owners have done nothing wrong.

It is virtually impossible to hide the identity of your LLC managers, however. Even if the articles do not name your managers, most annual reports to the secretary of state will require disclosure of this information. Annual reports are also public records.

Good to Know: What Entity Is It?

Two brothers decide to form an LLC in order to operate a pool cleaning business. One of the brothers mails the articles of organization to the secretary of state's office, but the articles are lost in the mail and never filed. They discover the problem months later, after the business is going strong. What entity did they form? It's not an LLC, because the papers were never filed. They entered into a joint enterprise for the purpose of pursuing profit. Thus, the entity they formed is a partnership.

How Do You Amend Your Articles?

Most changes to the articles of organization require filing an amendment to the articles. The amendment process satisfies the requirements in your state's statutes. Owners have no vested right resulting from any provision in the articles of organization, including provisions pertaining to the management, control, capital structure, dividend entitlement, purpose, or duration of the LLC. So long as you follow the proper procedures, you may amend your articles.

For certain minor changes to the articles of organization, the organizer or appointed manager may sometimes amend the articles of organization on his or her own. These changes include the following:

- Extending the duration of an LLC formed for a limited (not perpetual) duration
- Deleting the names and addresses of the initial managers
- Changing the address or name of the registered office or registered agent
- Changing each issued and unissued authorized share of an outstanding class to a greater number of whole shares, if the LLC has only shares of that class outstanding
- Changing the name to substitute the term "LLC," "LC," "Limited Liability Co.," or other LLC indicator

However, once an LLC has issued ownership interests to any persons, all changes to the articles of organization except the minor ones noted above require the approval of the managers (if the LLC is manager-managed) and the members. Unless a greater majority is required by the articles or operating agreement, a simple majority of any quorum is sufficient to authorize an amendment. (A quorum is the minimum number of managers or members who must be present to transact business.)

Any amendment that would affect a particular class or series of ownership interests will generally require that owners of that class, the owners affected by that change, have the right to vote on the change. This is true even if the class or series of ownership interests is otherwise nonvoting. This situation would be rare, encountered by more sophisticated LLCs. This right would arise in the following situations, for example:

- Reclassifying a class or series of ownership interest into a different class or series, as when an LLC seeks to extinguish a preferred class of ownership and convert the preferred holders into ordinary members
- Changing the rights or preferences of any class of ownership, as when

an LLC might seek to eliminate or change the dollar amount of a dividend preference enjoyed by a class of holders

To be legally effective, articles of amendment must be filed with the secretary of state in the same manner as the articles of organization were filed. Articles of amendment should include the following:

- The name of the LLC
- The full text of each amendment adopted
- The procedures to be followed to implement the change, if the amendment provides for the exchange, reclassification, or cancellation of issued shares
- The date each proposed amendment was adopted
- A statement that no owner action was required, if the managers were allowed by law to adopt the amendment without a vote by the members
- A statement that the percentage of votes in favor was sufficient for approval, if approval of the amendment by the members was required

Amendments to articles can also be made part of a reorganization plan. For example, articles of merger may indicate that the name of the surviving LLC shall be changed after the merger from "Aluminum and Bituminous Coal, LLC" to "TonoSilver, LLC." This change would take effect on the date the articles of merger are filed.

In addition, if you are qualified to do business in more than one state, you will likely be required to amend your application for certificate of authority in each state where you are qualified every time you amend your articles.

The secretary of state's office charges a fee for filing articles of amendment. Contact the office to learn the fee and any peculiar filing requirements in your state.

Should You Organize by Yourself or Hire an Attorney?

At this stage in your organization, you must decide whether you will file and organize your LLC on your own, hire a discount organization service, or hire an attorney. Each approach has its advantages and disadvantages.

Self-Organization

Obviously, the greatest benefit of self-organization is initial savings. Self-organization costs the least initially. LLCs are easier to form than corporations because they are generally simpler entities. You must analyze your own needs. How complex will your entity be? Will you require multiple classes of ownership interest? Do you expect to have more than a few members? Will you operate in an industry with a formidable degree of potential liability? If your needs are not complex, you are a good candidate for organizing your LLC yourself.

Of course, as with any legal matter, cutting costs can often cost more later. For example, if your LLC is not properly organized, ambitious creditors may later reach your personal assets by piercing the corporate (LLC) veil. See Part Five: LLC Lawsuits and Personal Liability Protection for more information on preserving your LLC's full liability protection.

For further assistance with self-organization, Entrepreneur Press offers two helpful books: *Forming an LLC: In Any State* and *Entrepreneur Magazine's Ultimate Guide to Forming an LLC in Any State*. These two books use a step-by-step approach to forming business entities.

Discount Organization Services

A slightly more expensive alternative is to hire a discount organization service. Such services, streamlined but competent, range from $200 to $300 per organization. Of course, such services are essentially filing services that do only the following:

- File articles of organization with the appropriate state office
- Select close LLC status
- Prepare boilerplate operating agreement
- Prepare boilerplate minutes of organizational meeting of managers

Such services generally do not include steps after filing the articles of organization, such as the following, which you must do on your own:

- Review and revise operating agreement, if necessary

- Review and revise minutes for organizational meeting of managers or members, if necessary
- Conduct organizational meeting of managers or members
- Ensure compliance with state securities laws
- File initial LLC reports with the secretary of state
- File periodic reports with the secretary of state

Discount organization services offer value. They can often navigate the bureaucratic complexities of state government and can provide prompt service and tested documents. However, the boilerplate operating agreement and proposed minutes of organizational meeting provided by discount incorporation services often contain fill-in-the-blank and optional provisions that can baffle an inexperienced organizer. On balance, you might find that you are better off organizing your entity on your own. You'll save money and you'll likely have an entity that more accurately suits your needs.

Hiring an Experienced Business Attorney

Finally, you may wish to hire a business attorney to organize your business for you. The general rule is that the bigger you are, the bigger your needs are. So, a simple LLC with one or two owners is fairly simple to set up on one's own. However, when the number of participants rises, the complexity of the issues increases.

A qualified business attorney can do the following:

- Suggest alternatives and solutions that would not occur to even the most diligent layperson
- Anticipate problems before they arise
- Prepare operating agreement and minutes of the organizational meeting of managers or members according to your specific needs
- Ensure that no federal or state securities laws are violated when interests in the entity are sold to raise capital for the business

How can you find a qualified business attorney?

- Recommendations from friends and associates usually yield excellent matches between attorney and businessperson.

- Local bar associations in major metropolitan areas usually operate referral services. They screen attorneys, so you can be assured of the experience of any attorney you hire.

The rate for business attorneys ranges from $175 to $350 per hour. The lower end of the scale will apply outside of major metropolitan areas and for less experienced attorneys. Business attorneys often charge a flat fee for services such as forming LLCs. You can expect to pay between $500 and $2,000 for complete organization services.

Final Thoughts on Articles of Organization

Articles of organization are of critical importance. Once filed, your LLC springs into existence, at least in the eyes of the state. Your articles are a public document, available to anyone who might request a copy from the secretary of state or view them on the internet. At a minimum, the articles tell the public who you are and how you may be contacted, who the managers are and their addresses, the business in which the LLC will engage, and any restrictions that may be imposed upon the voting rights of managers and owners.

Unlike operating agreements, which can often be amended by a vote of managers with no public declaration, most amendments to the articles of organization require approval by the owners according to procedures and

---

Expert Tip

Don't clutter your articles of organization with clauses that you can easily put in your operating agreement instead. Articles of organization require much more work to change than operating agreements because they require approval by the owners rather than only by the managers, require a filing with the state, and require a filing fee. The general rule: put clauses into your articles if you want them to be hard to change. For example, a clause dictating the number of managers of an LLC can appear either in the articles or in the operating agreement. But if you put that clause in your articles, you'll be running back to the secretary of state every time you want to raise or lower the number of managers. If the clause is in your operating agreement, a simple managers' resolution can effect the change.

---

requirements established in the statutes and the operating agreement and the filing of articles of amendment with the secretary of state.

What you don't say in your articles can have important consequences. Failure to provide for preemptive rights or cumulative voting in your articles will mean that your LLC won't have such rights in certain states or will have them in others. It's important to know your state law before you file your articles.

Expert Tip

When filing your articles of organization, take the time to verify the accuracy of the information. It is expensive and somewhat embarrassing to be required to run around and amend your articles because you omitted information or provided information that was incorrect.

For your review, two sample forms of articles of organization follow this chapter. The samples, short form and long form, demonstrate the types of provisions that are required or considered optional in the articles. It would be rare indeed to find a set of articles filed recently that contain all the sample provisions. Work with your business lawyer to develop articles that best fit your needs.

Sample Articles of Organization, Short Form

The following sample articles are as brief as articles can be. They cover only the bare minimum—the name of the LLC, the business purpose, and the resident agent. These articles are offered for illustration; you should use a state-specific form to organize your LLC.

ARTICLES OF ORGANIZATION
OF
[LLC NAME]

1. The name of this Limited Liability Company is [LLC NAME].
2. The purpose of the LLC is to engage in any lawful act or activity for which an LLC may be organized.

> 3. The name and address in the State of [STATE] of this LLC's initial agent for service of process are [NAME AND ADDRESS].
>
> Dated:
>
> _____
>
> Donald Leland
> Organizer

Sample Articles of Organization, Delaware Long Form with Optional Provisions

The following sample articles are long-form articles suitable for use in Delaware. Note that in Delaware articles of organization are called a certificate of formation, but the meaning is exactly the same. The articles contain the required provisions: the name of the LLC, the purpose, and the resident agent. The articles also contain the following optional provisions. Note that these articles favor the managers rather than the members:

- Multiple classes of membership, with a regular voting class and a preferred nonvoting class with a dividend preference and a liquidation preference (Article Four).
- A statement of perpetual existence (Article Five).
- A statement that the number of managers shall be determined by the operating agreement (Article Six).
- A statement that the managers have the power to amend the operating agreement (Article Seven).
- Strong indemnity provisions for managers and members (Article Eight).
- A provision allowing managers to appoint managers to fill vacancies; the alternative would be to require a vote by the members (Article Nine).
- A provision stating that notifications to owners shall be governed by the operating agreement. This provision is noteworthy: it gives the managers the power to notice owners in a manner different from the Delaware act. So, for example, the managers could shorten the time required for delivery of notice to owners of an upcoming vote if the operating agreement so provides (Article Ten).

- A provision specifically limiting the members' rights regarding amendment to the articles to the absolute minimum rights conferred by state law (Article Eleven).

CERTIFICATE OF FORMATION OF TONOSILVER RESOURCES, LLC

ARTICLE ONE. The name of this LLC is TONOSILVER RESOURCES, LLC (the "LLC").

ARTICLE TWO. The address of the LLC's registered office in the State of Delaware is 874 Walker Road, Suite C, City of Dover, Zip Code: 19904, County of Kent, and the name of its registered agent is United Corporate Services, Inc.

ARTICLE THREE. The nature of the business or purposes to be conducted or promoted by the LLC is to engage in any lawful act or activity for which LLCs may be organized under the Limited Liability Company Act of Delaware.

ARTICLE FOUR. This LLC is authorized to issue two classes of ownership interest: Class A Voting Membership and Class B Preferred Non-Voting Membership.

The Class A Voting Membership shall be the sole voting membership interest of the LLC.

The Class B Preferred Non-Voting Membership shall not vote upon any matter brought before the Class A Voting Membership. The Class B Preferred Non-Voting Membership has a liquidation preference. Upon the liquidation or dissolution of the LLC, holders of the Class B Preferred Non-Voting Membership are entitled to receive out of the assets available for distribution to owners, before any payment to the holders of the Class A Voting Membership, the sum of $____ for each percentage of interest of the total outstanding Class B Preferred Non-Voting Membership. If the assets of the LLC are insufficient to pay this liquidation preference to the holders of the Class B Preferred Non-Voting Membership, all of the entire remaining assets shall be paid to holders of the Class B Preferred Non-Voting Membership and holders of the Class A Voting Membership. After the liquidation preference has been paid or set apart for holders of the Class B Preferred Non-Voting Membership, the remaining assets shall be paid to holders of the Common Stock.

The Class B Preferred Non-Voting Membership has a dividend preference. Holders of the Class B Preferred Non-Voting Membership are entitled to receive dividends on a noncumulative basis at the rate of $____ for each percentage of interest of the total outstanding Class

---

B Preferred Non-Voting Membership, as and when declared by the managers of the LLC from funds legally available for dividends and distributions. The holders of the Class A Voting Membership may not receive dividends or other distributions during any fiscal year of the LLC until dividends on the Class B Preferred Non-Voting Membership in the total amount of $____ for each aggregate percentage of interest of the total outstanding Class B Preferred Non-Voting Membership during that fiscal year have been declared and paid or set apart for payment. The payment of such dividends is discretionary, and the holders of the Class B Preferred Non-Voting Membership shall not enjoy a right to dividends if such dividends are not declared, even if the LLC has sufficient funds to lawfully pay such dividends.

ARTICLE FIVE. The LLC is to have perpetual existence.

ARTICLE SIX. The LLC shall be managed by a board of managers. The number of managers that constitute the whole board of managers of the LLC and the manner of their election shall be designated in the Operating Agreement of the LLC.

ARTICLE SEVEN. In furtherance and not in limitation of the powers conferred by statute, the board of managers is expressly authorized to make, alter, amend, or repeal the Operating Agreement of the LLC.

ARTICLE EIGHT.

(a) To the fullest extent allowed by the Delaware Limited Liability Company Act, a member or manager or other person shall not be liable to the LLC or to another member or manager or to another person that is a party to or is otherwise bound by a limited liability company agreement for breach of fiduciary duty for the member's or manager's or other person's good faith reliance on the provisions of the LLC Operating Agreement.

(b) To the fullest extent allowed by the Delaware Limited Liability Company Act, the LLC Operating Agreement shall provide for the limitation or elimination of any and all liabilities for breach of contract and breach of duties (including fiduciary duties) of a member, manager, or other person to the LLC or to another member or manager or to another person that is a party to or is otherwise bound by the LLC Operating Agreement, provided that the Operating Agreement may not limit or eliminate liability for any act or omission that constitutes a bad faith violation of the implied contractual covenant of good faith and fair dealing.

ARTICLE NINE. Vacancies created by newly created manager positions, created in accordance with the Operating Agreement of this LLC, may be filled by the vote of a majority, although less than a quorum, of the managers then in office or by a sole remaining manager.

ARTICLE TEN. Advance notice of new business and member nominations for the election of managers shall be given in the manner and to the extent provided in the Operating Agreement of the LLC.

ARTICLE ELEVEN. The LLC reserves the right to amend, alter, change, or repeal any provision contained in this Certificate of Formation, in the manner now or hereafter prescribed by statute, and all rights conferred upon members herein are granted subject to this reservation.

Dated: _____

_____

Donald Leland
Organizer

CHAPTER 3

The Limited Liability Company Operating Agreement

The third part of the sources of authority trilogy is the LLC's operating agreement. An operating agreement is a written agreement containing rules and procedures that address such things as meetings of members and managers, officers, quorums, and notice requirements for meetings. While there is no magic number of pages or provisions that an operating agreement must contain, a good operating agreement should be comprehensive.

As long as members and managers are in accord, little attention is paid to the formal requirements and procedures found in the operating agreement; however, the more members, managers, and officers, the greater likelihood of disagreement and the need to resort to the operating agreement.

For example, assume that your LLC has three members and is manager-managed. Historically, each member has worked well with the others. Now, however, one of the members has rebelled. For whatever reason, the member no longer agrees with the other two and refuses to sign consent resolutions or cooperate with LLC decisions. When all members of an LLC agree on all matters, the management of an LLC is simple: most decisions would be made with unanimous consent resolutions without formal meetings. When members disagree and wish to assert their individual rights, the members and managers must turn to the operating agreement to determine the procedures for resolution. In our example, the operating agreement will dictate the rules for calling, noticing, and conducting a meeting.

We must revisit an important difference between corporations and LLCs. That difference is that corporations are always managed by representatives appointed by shareholders, who are not involved in operations. LLCs, as we noted above, can be operated by their members in the manner of a partnership or by an appointed group of managers in the manner of a corporation. This fundamental difference means that whichever election an LLC makes—to be member-managed or manager-managed—will dictate what manner of operating agreement it adopts. As these two types of LLCs will be governed differently, their operating agreements will differ. So, in this chapter, we discuss both member-managed and manager-managed LLCs, and at the end of the chapter are two sample operating agreements. Remember that an LLC can change from one form of management to the other as its needs change.

The following issues concerning members, membership, and their rights are commonly addressed in an operating agreement:

- Authority of the members or managers to fix the location of the LLC's principal executive office
- Location of members' meetings (either the LLC's principal place of business or wherever the managers or members may choose)

- Time for annual members' meetings, usually designated as the "second Monday of December" or "February 1" or in similar language
- Manner of calling special meetings of the members
- Minimum percentage ownership that can call a membership meeting (typically 10 percent to call a special membership meeting), in order to prevent calling meetings to discuss insubstantial or nuisance matters
- Manner in which members receive notice of meetings (e.g., by a written notice mailed or personally delivered to all members not more than 60 nor less than 10 days before the meeting)
- Minimum quorum required to take a membership vote, usually more than 50 percent of the outstanding percentage interest unless the operating agreement or articles set a higher percentage
- Voting at member meetings, including such issues as cumulative voting, record date, proxies, and election inspectors (all of which are discussed in later chapters)

For a manager-managed LLC, the operating agreement will cover a wider range of topics. It will typically address issues pertaining to the managers or board of managers, including the following:

- Management structure (managers organized as a committee or a board or not at all, typically each manager having one vote, regardless of management structure)
- Powers and authority of the managers
- Number of managers and the qualifications required
- Manner of electing managers and length of terms
- Procedure for filling managerial vacancies
- Procedures for calling regularly scheduled or special meetings of the managers
- Manner in which the board can act without meeting, by written consent or written resolution
- Standard of care that managers must exercise when dealing with the LLC or with each other

Operating agreements may also address optional maintenance matters, including these:

- Restrictions regarding loans to or guarantees of manager or member debts
- Persons authorized to sign LLC checks
- Required records and reports
- Maintenance and inspection of LLC records
- Procedures for amending the operating agreement

As you can see, operating agreements cover a lot of territory. Operating agreements provide technical rules of procedure. Your operating agreement should be tailored to fit your LLC. Because so many provisions of the limited liability company acts can be modified by the operating agreement, you should actively participate in creating your agreement. If you don't, you could lose flexibility and be burdened by procedural safeguards that you don't want.

For example, you own more than 50 percent of TonoSilver, LLC and Jane and Joan together own 49 percent. You wish to sell TonoSilver, LLC, but Jane and Joan don't agree. Over cocktails, you learn from a lawyer friend that under the state statute a sale requires only a majority vote of the members; that statute favors you, since you control a majority. As the lawyer drifts away, she suggests that you check the LLC operating agreement to see if the simple majority requirement has been modified. So you dust off the operating agreement that you acquired when you bought your LLC minute book and you are appalled to learn that your proposed sale of the business requires a two-thirds member approval and not a simple majority. You think, "I would never have agreed to that." No sale.

This brings us to an important point. How can founders of an LLC ensure that management or ownership will never fall into the hands of incompetent or unwelcome persons? Because LLC ownership is property, it can be passed in a will, sold, or given away, possibly to someone whom the other members would consider undesirable. It is possible for founders to exert control over the manner in which LLC interests are passed to third parties. We cover these issues in Chapter 7: Agreements to Control Ownership and Management.

How Is an Operating Agreement Made Effective?

First of all, an operating agreement can become effective only after articles of organization are filed. Until then, there would be no legal entity for the operating agreement to govern. Members can prepare and sign an operating agreement before filing their articles of organization, but the operating agreement will become effective only after the articles are filed. Alternatively, the organizers of the LLC can file the articles of organization and enter into an operating agreement soon thereafter; this is more typical. So, either concurrently with the filing of the articles of organization or soon thereafter, the members of an LLC join to either prepare or review a proposed operating agreement. Once they agree to the operating agreement, they execute it just as they would execute a contract. In the manner of a contract, the operating agreement binds the parties to certain responsibilities to the LLC and to each other.

The operating agreement goes into effect when it is executed by the members. The operating agreement also serves to "admit" members to the LLC—much in the way that partnerships require additional owners to be admitted by the current owners. The sample LLC operating agreements that we have included in this chapter contain clauses that require the current members to approve new members by majority vote. The operating agreement should also serve to document both the amount of the capital contribution of each member and the percentage interest held by each member.

When a new member is admitted into the LLC, that person should execute a copy of the operating agreement (because he or she must necessarily agree to be bound by it), and the amount of his or her capital contribution and percentage interest should be recorded.

How Do You Amend Your LLC's Operating Agreement?

Generally, under state law the board of managers retains the right to amend or repeal an LLC operating agreement. However, articles of organization or operating agreements can contain optional provisions that require approval by the members to amend all or certain portions of the operating agreement. The sample operating agreements at the end of this chapter require member approval to amend the agreement.

Whether manager or member approval is required, a majority vote is usually sufficient unless a higher percentage is required by the articles or operating agreement. The amendment process would be handled in the manner described in Chapters 8, 9, and 10 pertaining to manager and member meetings. Also, even if the articles and operating agreement don't require member approval to amend the operating agreement, members can take the initiative to amend or repeal the operating agreement.

Final Thoughts on Operating Agreements

Remember those words that preface most portions of limited liability company acts: "Unless otherwise provided in the articles of organization or operating agreements …" Those words provide the opportunity to modify your LLC to fit your needs. This is especially true for operating agreements.

Operating agreements provide rules and procedures for the internal governance of your LLC. How are managers elected? Are there to be any supermajority voting requirements for special events, such as mergers or dissolution? The operating agreement defines issues of vital importance to the health and well-being of the entity.

The two sample operating agreements below illustrate the importance of the operating agreement. There are many other forms of operating agreement that can be used. Appendix A, Supplemental LLC Forms includes two more complex sample operating agreements (one for a manager-managed LLC and one for a member-managed LLC). Following the sample operating agreement, there is a checklist to guide you in preparing your own operating agreement.

Sample Short-Form Operating Agreement for Member-Managed LLC

OPERATING AGREEMENT OF [FULL NAME OF LLC]

THIS OPERATING AGREEMENT (the "Agreement") is hereby entered into by the under-signed, who are owners and shall be referred to as Member or Members.

RECITALS

The Members desire to form [FULL NAME OF LLC], a limited liability company (the "Company"), for the purposes set forth herein, and, accordingly, desire to enter into this Agreement in order to set forth the terms and conditions of the business and affairs of the Company and to determine the rights and obligations of its Members.

NOW, THEREFORE, the Members, intending to be legally bound by this Agreement, hereby agree that the limited liability company operating agreement of the Company shall be as follows:

ARTICLE I. DEFINITIONS

When used in this Agreement, the following terms shall have the meanings set forth below.

1.1 "Act" means the Limited Liability Company Law of the State in which the Company is organized or chartered, including any amendments or the corresponding provision(s) of any succeeding law.

1.2 "Capital Contribution" means the amount of cash and the agreed value of property, services rendered, or a promissory note or other obligation to contribute cash or property or to perform services contributed by the Members for such Members' Interest in the Company, equal to the sum of the Members' initial Capital Contributions plus the Members' additional Capital Contributions, if any, made pursuant to Sections 4.1 and 4.2, respectively, less payments or distributions made pursuant to Section 5.1.

1.3 "Code" means the Internal Revenue Code of 1986 and the regulations promulgated thereunder, as amended from time to time (or any corresponding provision or provisions of succeeding law).

1.4 "Interest" means the ownership Interest, expressed as a number, percentage, or frac-tion, set forth in Table A, of a Member in the Company.

1.5 "Person" means any natural individual, partnership, firm, corporation, limited liability company, joint-stock company, trust, or other entity.

1.6 "Secretary of State" means the Office of the Secretary of State or the office charged with accepting articles of organization in the Company's state of organization.

ARTICLE II. FORMATION

2.1 Organization. The Members hereby organize the Company as a limited liability company pursuant to the provisions of the Act.

2.2 Effective Date. The Company shall come into being on, and this Agreement shall take effect from, the date the Articles of Organization of the Company were or are filed with the Secretary of State in the state of organization or charter.

2.3 Agreement: Invalid Provisions and Saving Clause. The Members, by executing this Agreement, hereby agree to the terms and conditions of this Agreement. To the extent any provision of this Agreement is prohibited or ineffective under the Act, this Agreement shall be deemed to be amended to the least extent necessary in order to make this Agreement effective under the Act. In the event the Act is subsequently amended or interpreted in such a way to validate any provision of this Agreement that was formerly invalid, such provision shall be considered to be valid from the effective date of such amendment or interpretation.

ARTICLE III. PURPOSE; NATURE OF BUSINESS

3.1 Purpose; Nature of Business. The purpose of the Company shall be to engage in any lawful business that may be engaged in by a limited liability company organized under the Act, as such business activities may be determined by the Member or Members from time to time.

3.2 Powers. The Company shall have all powers of a limited liability company under the Act and the power to do all things necessary or convenient to accomplish its purpose and operate its business as described in Section 3.1 here.

ARTICLE IV. MEMBERS AND CAPITAL CONTRIBUTIONS

4.1 Members and Initial Capital Contribution. The name, address, Interest, and value of the initial Capital Contribution of the Members shall be set forth on Table A attached hereto.

4.2 Additional Capital Contributions. The Members shall have no obligation to make any additional Capital Contributions to the Company. The Members may make additional Capital Contributions to the Company as the Members unanimously determine are necessary, appropriate, or desirable.

ARTICLE V. DISTRIBUTIONS AND ALLOCATIONS

5.1 Distributions and Allocations. All distributions of cash or other assets of the Company shall be made and paid to the Members at such time and in such amounts as the majority of the Members may determine. All items of income, gain, loss, deduction, and credit shall be allocated to the Members in proportion to their Interests.

ARTICLE VI. TAXATION

6.1 Income Tax Reporting. Each Member is aware of the income tax consequences of the allocations made by Article V here and agrees to be bound by the provisions of Article V here in reporting each Member's share of Company income and loss for federal and state income tax purposes.

6.2 Tax Treatment. Notwithstanding anything contained herein to the contrary and only for purposes of federal and, if applicable, state income tax purposes, the Company shall be classified as a partnership for such federal and state income tax purposes unless and until the Members unanimously determine to cause the Company to file an election under the Code to be classified as an association taxable as a corporation.

ARTICLE VII. MANAGEMENT BY MEMBERS

7.1 Management by Members. The Company shall be managed by its Members, who shall have full and exclusive right, power, and authority to manage the affairs of the Company and to bind the Company to contracts and obligations, to make all decisions with respect thereto, and to do or cause to be done any and all acts or things deemed by the Members to be necessary, appropriate, or desirable to carry out or further the business of the Company.

7.2 Voting Power in Proportion to Interest. The Members shall enjoy voting power and authority in proportion to their Interests. Unless expressly provided otherwise in this Agreement or the Articles of Organization, Company decisions shall be made by majority vote.

7.3 Duties of Members. The Members shall manage and administer the day-to-day operations and business of the Company and shall execute any and all reports, forms, instruments, documents, papers, writings, agreements, and contracts, including but not limited to deeds, bills of sale, assignments, leases, promissory notes, mortgages, and security agreements, and any other type or form of document by which property or property rights of the Company are transferred or encumbered, or by which debts and obligations of the Company are created, incurred, or evidenced.

7.4 Officer Positions of Members. The Members shall be empowered to appoint Members to the following officer positions: president, secretary, and chief financial officer. Further, the Members shall be empowered to delegate responsibilities among themselves in accord with such appointments. No such appointment, however, shall affect the voting power of such Members as outlined herein.

ARTICLE VIII. BOOKS AND RECORDS

8.1 Books and Records. The Members shall keep, or cause to be kept, at the principal place of business of the Company true and correct books of account, in which shall be entered fully and accurately each and every transaction of the Company. The Company's taxable and fiscal years shall end on December 31. All Members shall have the right to inspect the Company's books and records at any time, for any reason.

ARTICLE IX. LIMITATION OF LIABILITY; INDEMNIFICATION

9.1 Limited Liability. Except as otherwise required by law, the debts, obligations, and liabilities of the Company, whether arising in contract, tort, or otherwise, shall be solely the debts, obligations, and liabilities of the Company, and the Members shall not be obligated personally for any such debt, obligation, or liability of the Company solely by reason of being Members. The failure of the Company to observe any formalities or requirements relating to the exercise of its powers or the management of its business or affairs under this Agreement or by law shall not be grounds for imposing personal liability on the Members for any debts, liabilities, or obligations of the Company. Except as otherwise expressly required by law, the Members, in such Members' capacity as such, shall have no liability in excess of (a) the amount of such Members' Capital Contributions, (b) such Members' share of any assets and undistributed profits of the Company, and (c) the amount of any distributions required to be returned according to law.

9.2 Indemnification. The Company shall, to the fullest extent provided or allowed by law, indemnify, save harmless, and pay all judgments and claims against the Members, and each of the Company's or Members' agents, affiliates, heirs, legal representatives, successors, and assigns (each an "Indemnified Party") from, against, and in respect of any and all liability, loss, damage, and expense incurred or sustained by the Indemnified Party in connection with the business of the Company or by reason of any act performed or omitted to be performed in connection with the activities of the Company or in dealing with third parties on behalf of the Company, including costs and attorneys' fees before and at trial and at all appellate levels, whether or not suit is instituted (which attorneys' fees may be paid as incurred), and any amounts expended in the settlement of any claims of liability, loss, or damage, to the fullest extent allowed by law.

9.3. Insurance. The Company shall not pay for any insurance covering liability of the Members or the Company's or Members' agents, affiliates, heirs, legal representatives, successors, and assigns for actions or omissions for which indemnification is not permitted hereunder, provided, however, that nothing contained here shall preclude the Company from purchasing and paying for such types of insurance, including extended coverage liability and casualty and worker's compensation, as would be customary for any Person owning, managing, and/or operating comparable property and engaged in a similar business, or from naming the Members and any of the Company's or Members' agents, affiliates, heirs, legal representatives, successors, or assigns or any Indemnified Party as additional insured parties thereunder.

9.4 Non-Exclusive Right. The provisions of this Article IX shall be in addition to and not in limitation of any other rights of indemnification and reimbursement or limitations of liability to which an Indemnified Party may be entitled under the Act, common law, or otherwise.

ARTICLE X. AMENDMENT

10.1 Amendment. This Agreement may not be altered or modified except by the unanimous written consent or agreement of the Members as evidenced by an amendment hereto whereby this Agreement is amended or amended and restated.

ARTICLE XI. WITHDRAWAL

11.1 Withdrawal of a Member. No Member may withdraw from the Company except by written request of the Member given to each of the other Members and with the unanimous written consent of the other Members, the effective date of withdrawal being the date on which the unanimous written consent of all of the other Members is given or upon the effective date of any of the following events:

(a) the Member makes an assignment of his or her property for the benefit of creditors;

(b) the Member files a voluntary petition of bankruptcy;

(c) the Member is adjudged bankrupt or insolvent or there is entered against the Member an order for relief in any bankruptcy or insolvency proceeding;

(d) the Member seeks, consents to, or acquiesces in the appointment of a trustee or receiver for, or liquidation of the Member or of all or any substantial part of the Member's property;

(e) the Member files an answer or other pleading admitting or failing to contest the material allegations of a petition filed against the Member in any proceeding described in Subsections 11.1 (a) through (d);

(f) if the Member is a corporation, the dissolution of the corporation or the revocation of its articles of incorporation or charter;

(g) if the Member is an estate, the distribution by the fiduciary of the estate's Interest in the Company;

(h) if the Member is an employee of the Company and he or she resigns, retires, or for any reason ceases to be employed by the Company in any capacity; or

(i) if the other Members owning more than fifty percent (50%) of the Interests vote or request in writing that a Member withdraw and such request is given to the Member (the effective date of withdrawal being the date on which the vote or written request of the other Members is given to the Member).

11.2 Valuation of Interest. The value of the withdrawing Member's Interest in all events shall be equal to the greater of the following: (a) the amount of the Member's Capital Contribution or (b) the amount of the Member's share of the Members' equity in the Company, plus the amount of any unpaid and outstanding loans or advances made by the Member to the Company (plus any due and unpaid interest thereon, if interest on the loan or advance has been agreed to between the Company and the Member), calculated as of the end of the fiscal quarter immediately preceding the effective date of the Member's withdrawal.

11.3 Payment of Value. The value shall be payable as follows: (a) If the value is equal to or less than $500, at closing, and (b) If the value is greater than $500, at the option of the Company, $500 at closing with the balance of the purchase price paid by delivering a promissory note of the Company dated as of the closing date and bearing interest at the prime rate published in *The Wall Street Journal* as of the effective date of withdrawal, with the principal amount being payable in five (5) equal annual installments beginning one (1) year from closing and with the interest on the accrued and unpaid balance being payable at the time of payment of each principal installment.

11.4 Closing. Payment of the value of the departing Member's Interest shall be made at a mutually agreeable time and date on or before thirty (30) days from the effective date of withdrawal. Upon payment of the value of the Interest as calculated in Section 11.3 above: (a) the Member's right to receive any and all further payments or distributions on account of the Member's ownership of the Interest in the Company shall cease; (b) the Member's loans or advances to the Company shall be paid and satisfied in full; and (c) the Member shall no longer be a Member or creditor of the Company on account of the Capital Contribution or the loans or advances.

11.5 Limitation on Payment of Value. If payment of the value of the Interest would be prohibited by any statute or law prohibiting distributions that would
(a) render the Company insolvent; or
(b) be made at a time that the total Company liabilities (other than liabilities to Members on account of their Interests) exceed the value of the Company's total assets;
then the value of the withdrawing Member's Interest in all events shall be $1.00.

ARTICLE XII. MISCELLANEOUS PROVISIONS

12.1 Assignment of Interest and New Members. No Member may assign such person's Interest in the Company in whole or in part except by the vote or written consent of the other Members owning more than fifty percent (50%) of the Interests. No additional Person may be admitted as a Member except by the vote or written consent of the Members owning more than fifty percent (50%) of the Interests.

12.2 Determinations by Members. Except as required by the express provisions of this Agreement or of the Act:
(a) Any transaction, action, or decision which requires or permits the Members to consent to, approve, elect, appoint, adopt, or authorize or to make a determination or decision with

respect thereto under this Agreement, the Act, the Code, or otherwise shall be made by the Members owning more than fifty percent (50%) of the Interests.

(b) The Members shall act at a meeting of Members or by consent in writing of the Members. Members may vote or give their consent in person or by proxy.

(c) Meetings of the Members may be held at any time, upon call of any Member or Members owning, in the aggregate, at least ten percent (10%) of the Interests.

(d) Unless waived in writing by the Members owning more than fifty percent (50%) of the Interests (before or after a meeting), at least two (2) business days' prior notice of any meeting shall be given to each Member. Such notice shall state the purpose for which such meeting has been called. No business may be conducted or action taken at such meeting that is not provided for in such notice.

(e) Members may participate in a meeting of Members by means of conference telephone or similar communications equipment by means of which all Persons participating in the meeting can hear each other, and such participation shall constitute presence in person at such meeting.

(f) The Members shall cause to be kept a book of minutes of all meetings of the Members in which there shall be recorded the time and place of such meeting, by whom such meeting was called, the notice thereof given, the names of those present, and the proceedings thereof. Copies of any consents in writing shall also be filed in such minute book.

12.3 Binding Effect. This Agreement shall be binding upon and inure to the benefit of the undersigned Members, their legal representatives, heirs, successors, and assigns. This Agreement and the rights and duties of the Members hereunder shall be governed by, and interpreted and construed in accordance with, the laws of the Company's state of organization or charter, without regard to principles of choice of law.

12.4 Headings. The article and section headings in this Agreement are inserted as a matter of convenience and are for reference only and shall not be construed to define, limit, extend, or describe the scope of this Agreement or the intent of any provision.

12.5 Number and Gender. Whenever required by the context here, the singular shall include the plural, and vice versa and the masculine gender shall include the feminine and neuter genders, and vice versa.

12.6 Entire Agreement and Binding Effect. This Agreement constitutes the sole operating agreement among the Members and supersedes and cancels any prior agreements, representations, warranties, or communications, whether oral or written, between the Members relating to the affairs of the Company and the conduct of the Company's business. No amendment or modification of this Agreement shall be effective unless approved in writing as provided in Section 10.1. The Articles of Organization and this Agreement are binding upon and shall inure to the benefit of the Members and Agent(s) and shall be binding upon their successors, assigns, affiliates, subsidiaries, heirs, beneficiaries, personal representatives, executors, administrators, and guardians, as applicable and appropriate.

IN WITNESS WHEREOF, this Agreement has been made and executed by the Members effective as of the date first written above.

_____

(member)

_____

(member)

_____

(member)

Table A: Names, Addresses, and Initial Capital Contributions of the Members

Name and Address of Member	Value of Initial Capital Contribution	Nature of Member's Initial Capital Contribution (i.e., cash, services, property)	Percentage Interest of Member

Sample Short-Form Operating Agreement for Manager-Managed LLC

OPERATING AGREEMENT OF [FULL NAME OF LLC]

THIS OPERATING AGREEMENT (the "Agreement") is hereby entered into by the under-signed, who are owners and shall be referred to as Member or Members.

RECITALS

The Members desire to form [FULL NAME OF LLC], a limited liability company (the "Company"), for the purposes set forth herein, and, accordingly, desire to enter into this Agreement in order to set forth the terms and conditions of the business and affairs of the Company and to determine the rights and obligations of its Members.

NOW, THEREFORE, the Members, intending to be legally bound by this Agreement, hereby agree that the limited liability company operating agreement of the Company shall be as follows:

ARTICLE I. DEFINITIONS

When used in this Agreement, the following terms shall have the meanings set forth below.

1.1 "Act" means the Limited Liability Company Law of the State in which the Company is organized or chartered, including any amendments or the corresponding provision(s) of any succeeding law.

1.2 "Capital Contribution" means the amount of cash and the agreed value of property, services rendered, or a promissory note or other obligation to contribute cash or property or to perform services contributed by the Members for such Members' Interest in the Company, equal to the sum of the Members' initial Capital Contributions plus the Members' additional Capital Contributions, if any, made pursuant to Sections 4.1 and 4.2, respectively, less payments or distributions made pursuant to Section 5.1.

1.3 "Code" means the Internal Revenue Code of 1986 and the regulations promulgated thereunder, as amended from time to time (or any corresponding provision or provisions of succeeding law).

1.4 "Interest" means the ownership Interest, expressed as a number, percentage, or fraction, set forth in Table A, of a Member in the Company.

1.5 "Manager" means any natural person who has authority to govern the Company according to the terms of this Agreement.

1.6 "Person" means any natural individual, partnership, firm, corporation, limited liability company, joint-stock company, trust, or other entity.

1.7 "Secretary of State" means the Office of the Secretary of State or the office charged with accepting articles of organization in the Company's state of organization.

ARTICLE II. FORMATION

2.1 Organization. The Members hereby organize the Company as a limited liability company pursuant to the provisions of the Act.

2.2 Effective Date. The Company shall come into being on, and this Agreement shall take effect from, the date the Articles of Organization of the Company were or are filed with the Secretary of State in the state of organization or charter.

2.3 Agreement: Invalid Provisions and Saving Clause. The Members, by executing this Agreement, hereby agree to the terms and conditions of this Agreement. To the extent any provision of this Agreement is prohibited or ineffective under the Act, this Agreement shall be deemed to be amended to the least extent necessary in order to make this Agreement effective under the Act. In the event the Act is subsequently amended or interpreted in such a way to validate any provision of this Agreement that was formerly invalid, such provision shall be considered to be valid from the effective date of such amendment or interpretation.

ARTICLE III. PURPOSE; NATURE OF BUSINESS

3.1 Purpose; Nature of Business. The purpose of the Company shall be to engage in any lawful business that may be engaged in by a limited liability company organized under the Act, as such business activities may be determined by the Manager or Managers from time to time.

3.2 Powers. The Company shall have all powers of a limited liability company under the Act and the power to do all things necessary or convenient to accomplish its purpose and operate its business as described in Section 3.1 here.

ARTICLE IV. MEMBERS AND CAPITAL CONTRIBUTIONS

4.1 Members and Initial Capital Contributions. The name, address, Interest, type of property, and value of the initial Capital Contribution of the Members shall be set forth on Table A attached hereto.

4.2 Additional Capital Contributions. The Members shall have no obligation to make any additional Capital Contributions to the Company. The Members may make additional Capital Contributions to the Company as the Members unanimously determine are necessary, appropriate, or desirable.

ARTICLE V. DISTRIBUTIONS AND ALLOCATIONS

5.1 Distributions and Allocations. All distributions of cash or other assets of the Company shall be made and paid to the Members at such time and in such amounts as a majority of the Managers may determine. All items of income, gain, loss, deduction, and credit shall be allocated to the Members in proportion to their Interests.

ARTICLE VI. TAXATION

6.1 Income Tax Reporting. Each Member is aware of the income tax consequences of the allocations made by Article V here and agrees to be bound by the provisions of Article V here in reporting each Member's share of Company income and loss for federal and state income tax purposes.

6.2 Tax Treatment. Notwithstanding anything contained herein to the contrary and only for purposes of federal and, if applicable, state income tax purposes, the Company shall be classified as an association taxable as a corporation for such federal and state income tax purposes unless and until the Members determine to cause the Company to file an election under the Code to be classified as a partnership.

ARTICLE VII. MANAGERS AND AGENTS

7.1 Management by Managers. This Company shall be a manager-managed LLC. The Members shall elect and appoint the Managers who shall have the full and exclusive right, power, and authority to manage the affairs of the Company and to bind the Company, to make all decisions with respect thereto, and to do or cause to be done any and all acts or things deemed by the Members to be necessary, appropriate, or desirable to carry out or further the business of the Company. The number of Managers of the Company shall be 3. All decisions and actions of the Managers shall be made by majority vote of the Managers as provided in Section 12.3. No annual meeting shall be required to reappoint Managers.

Such Persons shall serve in such offices at the pleasure of the Members and until their successors and are duly elected and appointed by the Members. Until further action of the Members as provided herein, the Persons whose names appear on Table B below are the Managers of the Company.

7.2 Optional Appointment of Officers. The Managers are empowered to undertake the appointment of officers, including, without limitation, a chairperson or a president, or both, a secretary, a chief financial officer, and any other officers with such titles, powers, and duties as shall be determined by the Managers or Members. An officer may, but need not, be a Member or Manager of the limited liability company and any number of offices may be held by the same person. Officers, if any, shall be appointed by the Managers and shall serve at the pleasure of the Managers, subject to the rights, if any, of an officer under any contract of employment. Any officer may resign at any time upon written notice to the limited liability company without prejudice to the rights, if any, of the limited liability company under any contract to which the officer is a party.

7.3 Agents. Without limiting the rights of the Members or the Managers, or the Company, the Managers shall appoint the Person(s) who is (are) to act as the agent(s) of the Company to carry out and further the decisions and actions of the Members or the Managers, to manage and to administer the day-to-day operations and business of the Company, and to execute any and all reports, forms, instruments, documents, papers, writings, agreements, and contracts, including but not limited to deeds, bills of sale, assignments, leases, promissory notes, mortgages, and security agreements, and any other type or form of document by which property or property rights of the Company are transferred or encumbered, or by which debts and obligations of the Company are created, incurred, or evidenced, which are necessary, appropriate, or beneficial to carry out or further such decisions or actions and to manage and administer the day-to-day operations and business.

ARTICLE VIII. BOOKS AND RECORDS

8.1 Books and Records. The Managers shall keep, or cause to be kept, at the principal place of business of the Company true and correct books of account, in which shall be entered fully and accurately each and every transaction of the Company. The Company's taxable and fiscal years shall end on December 31. All Members shall have the right to inspect the Company's books and records at any time, for any reason.

ARTICLE IX. LIMITATION OF LIABILITY; INDEMNIFICATION

9.1 Limited Liability. Except as otherwise required by law, the debts, obligations, and liabilities of the Company, whether arising in contract, tort, or otherwise, shall be solely the debts, obligations, and liabilities of the Company, and the Members shall not be obligated personally for any such debt, obligation, or liability of the Company solely by reason of being Members. The failure of the Company to observe any formalities or requirements relating to the exercise of its powers or the management of its business or affairs under this Agreement or by law shall not be grounds for imposing personal liability on the Members for any debts, liabilities, or obligations of the Company. Except as otherwise expressly required by law, the Members, in such Members' capacity as such, shall have no liability in excess of (a) the amount of such Members' Capital Contributions, (b) such Members' share of any assets and undistributed profits of the Company, and (c) the amount of any distributions required to be returned according to law.

9.2 Indemnification. The Company shall, to the fullest extent provided or allowed by law, indemnify, save harmless, and pay all judgments and claims against the Members or Managers, and each of the Company's, Members', or Managers' agents, affiliates, heirs, legal representatives, successors, and assigns (each an "Indemnified Party") from, against, and in respect of any and all liability, loss, damage, and expense incurred or sustained by the Indemnified Party in connection with the business of the Company or by reason of any act performed or omitted to be performed in connection with the activities of the Company or in dealing with third parties on behalf of the Company, including costs and attorneys' fees before and at trial and at all appellate levels, whether or not suit is instituted (which attorneys' fees may be paid as incurred), and any amounts expended in the settlement of any claims of liability, loss, or damage, to the fullest extent allowed by law.

9.3. Insurance. The Company shall not pay for any insurance covering liability of the Members or the Managers or the Company's, Members', or Managers' agents, affiliates, heirs, legal representatives, successors. and assigns for actions or omissions for which indemnification is not permitted hereunder; provided, however, that nothing contained here shall preclude the Company from purchasing and paying for such types of insurance, including extended coverage liability and casualty and worker's compensation, as would be customary for any Person owning, managing. and/or operating comparable property and engaged in a similar business or from naming the Members or the Managers and any of the Company's, Members', or Managers' agents, affiliates, heirs, legal representatives, successors, or assigns or any Indemnified Party as additional insured parties thereunder.

9.4 Non-Exclusive Right. The provisions of this Article IX shall be in addition to and not in limitation of any other rights of indemnification and reimbursement or limitations of liability to which an Indemnified Party may be entitled under the Act, common law, or otherwise.

ARTICLE X. AMENDMENT

10.1 Amendment. This Agreement may not be altered or modified except by the unanimous written consent or agreement of the Members as evidenced by an amendment hereto whereby this Agreement is amended or amended and restated.

ARTICLE XI. WITHDRAWAL

11.1 Withdrawal of a Member. No Member may withdraw from the Company except by written request of the Member given to each of the other Members and with the unanimous written consent of the other Members (the effective date of withdrawal being the date on which the unanimous written consent of all of the other Members is given), or upon the effective date of any of the following events:

(a) the Member makes an assignment of his or her property for the benefit of creditors;

(b) the Member files a voluntary petition of bankruptcy;

(c) the Member is adjudged bankrupt or insolvent or there is entered against the Member an order for relief in any bankruptcy or insolvency proceeding;

(d) the Member seeks, consents to, or acquiesces in the appointment of a trustee or receiver for, or liquidation of the Member or of all or any substantial part of the Member's property;

(e) the Member files an answer or other pleading admitting or failing to contest the material allegations of a petition filed against the Member in any proceeding described in Subsections 11.1 (a) through (d);

(f) if the Member is a corporation, the dissolution of the corporation or the revocation of its articles of incorporation or charter;

(g) if the Member is an estate, the distribution by the fiduciary of the estate's Interest in the Company;

(h) if the Member is an employee of the Company and he or she resigns, retires, or for any reason ceases to be employed by the Company in any capacity; or

(i) if the other Members owning more than fifty percent (50%) of the Interests vote or request in writing that a Member withdraw and such request is given to the Member (the effective date of withdrawal being the date on which the vote or written request of the other Members is given to the Member).

11.2 Valuation of Interest. The value of the withdrawing Member's Interest in all events shall be equal to the greater of the following: (a) the amount of the Member's Capital Contribution or (b) the amount of the Member's share of the Members' equity in the Company, plus the amount of any unpaid and outstanding loans or advances made by the Member to the Company (plus any due and unpaid interest thereon, if interest on the loan or advance has been agreed to between the Company and the Member), calculated as of the end of the fiscal quarter immediately preceding the effective date of the Member's withdrawal.

11.3 Payment of Value. The value shall be payable as follows: (i) If the value is equal to or less than $500, at closing, and (ii) If the value is greater than $500, at the option of the Company, $500 at closing with the balance of the purchase price paid by delivering a promissory note of the Company dated as of the closing date and bearing interest at the prime rate published in *The Wall Street Journal* as of the effective date of withdrawal with the principal amount being payable in five (5) equal annual installments beginning one (1) year from closing and with the interest on the accrued and unpaid balance being payable at the time of payment of each principal installment.

11.4 Closing. Payment of the value of the departing Member's Interest shall be made at a mutually agreeable time and date on or before thirty (30) days from the effective date of withdrawal. Upon payment of the value of the Interest as calculated in Section 11.3 above: (a) the Member's right to receive any and all further payments or distributions on account of the Member's ownership of the Interest in the Company shall cease; (b) the Member's loans or advances to the Company shall be paid and satisfied in full; and (c) the Member shall no longer be a Member or creditor of the Company on account of the Capital Contribution or the loans or advances.

11.5 Limitation on Payment of Value. If payment of the value of the Interest would be pro-

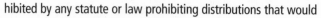

hibited by any statute or law prohibiting distributions that would

(a) render the Company insolvent; or

(b) be made at a time that the total Company liabilities (other than liabilities to Members on account of their Interests) exceed the value of the Company's total assets;

then the value of the withdrawing Member's Interest in all events shall be $1.00.

ARTICLE XII. MISCELLANEOUS PROVISIONS

12.1 Assignment of Interest and New Members. No Member may assign such person's Interest in the Company in whole or in part except by the vote or written consent of the other Members owning more than fifty percent (50%) of the Interests. No additional Person may be admitted as a Member except by the vote or written consent of the Members owning more than fifty percent (50%) of the Interests.

12.2 Determinations by Members: Except as required by the express provisions of this Agreement or of the Act:

(a) Any transaction, action, or decision which requires or permits the Members to consent to, approve, elect, appoint, adopt, or authorize or to make a determination or decision with respect thereto under this Agreement, the Act, the Code, or otherwise shall be made by the Members owning more than fifty percent (50%) of the Interests.

(b) The Members shall act at a meeting of Members or by consent in writing of the Members. Members may vote or give their consent in person or by proxy.

(c) Meetings of the Members may be held at any time, upon call of any Manager or a Member or Members owning, in the aggregate, at least ten percent (10%) of the Interests.

(d) Unless waived in writing by the Members owning more than fifty percent (50%) of the Interests (before or after a meeting), at least two (2) business days' prior notice of any meeting shall be given to each Member. Such notice shall state the purpose for which such meeting has been called. No business may be conducted or action taken at such meeting that is not provided for in such notice.

(e) Members may participate in a meeting of Members by means of conference telephone or similar communications equipment by means of which all Persons participating in the meeting can hear each other, and such participation shall constitute presence in person at such meeting.

(f) The Managers shall cause to be kept a book of minutes of all meetings of the Members in which there shall be recorded the time and place of such meeting, by whom such meeting was called, the notice thereof given, the names of those present, and the proceedings thereof. Copies of any consents in writing shall also be filed in such minute book.

12.3 Determinations by Managers. Except as required by the express provisions of this Agreement or of the Act and if there shall be more than one Manager:

(a) Any transaction, action, or decision which requires or permits the Managers to consent to, approve, elect, appoint, adopt, or authorize or to make a determination or decision with respect thereto under this Agreement, the Act, the Code, or otherwise shall be made by a majority of the Managers.

(b) The Managers shall act at a meeting of the Managers or by consent in writing of the Managers. Managers may vote or give their consent in person only and not by proxy.

(c) Meetings of the Managers may be held at any time, upon call of any agent of the Company appointed pursuant to Section 7.2 of this Agreement or any Manager.

(d) Notice of any meeting shall be given to a majority of the Managers at any time prior to the meeting, in writing or by verbal communication. Such notice need not state the purpose for which such meeting has been called.

(e) The Managers may participate in a meeting of the Managers by means of conference telephone or similar communications equipment by means of which all Persons participating in the meeting can hear each other, and such participation shall constitute presence in person at such meeting.

(f) The Managers may cause to be kept a book of minutes of all meetings of the Managers in which there shall be recorded the time and place of such meeting, by whom such meeting was called, the notice thereof given, the names of those present, and the proceedings thereof. Copies of any consents in writing shall also be filed in such minute book.

12.4 Binding Effect. This Agreement shall be binding upon and inure to the benefit of the undersigned, their legal representatives, heirs, successors, and assigns. This Agreement and the rights and duties of the Members hereunder shall be governed by, and interpreted and construed in accordance with, the laws of the Company's state of organization or charter, without regard to principles of choice of law.

12.5 Headings. The article and section headings in this Agreement are inserted as a matter of convenience and are for reference only and shall not be construed to define, limit, extend, or describe the scope of this Agreement or the intent of any provision.

12.6 Number and Gender. Whenever required by the context here, the singular shall include the plural, and vice versa, and the masculine gender shall include the feminine and neuter genders, and vice versa.

12.7 Entire Agreement and Binding Effect. This Agreement constitutes the sole operating agreement among the Members and supersedes and cancels any prior agreements, representations, warranties, or communications, whether oral or written, between the Members relating to the affairs of the Company and the conduct of the Company's business. No amendment or modification of this Agreement shall be effective unless approved in writing as provided in Section 10.1. The Articles of Organization and this Agreement are binding upon and shall inure to the benefit of the Members and Agent(s) and shall be binding upon their successors, assigns, affiliates, subsidiaries, heirs, beneficiaries, personal representatives, executors, administrators, and guardians, as applicable and appropriate.

IN WITNESS WHEREOF, this Agreement has been made and executed by the Members effective as of the date first written above.

_____ [MEMBER]

_____ [MEMBER]

_____ [MEMBER]

Table A: Names, Addresses, and Initial Capital Contributions of the Members

Name and Address of Member	Value of Initial Capital Contribution	Nature of Member's Initial Capital Contribution (i.e., cash, services, property)	Percentage Interest of Member

---

Table B. Managers

Name of Manager	Address of Manager
_____	_____
_____	_____

Checklist: Key Matters for Operating Agreement

❏ Most important, is your LLC manager-managed or member-managed?

❏ Do the managers have the power to fix the principal office location of the LLC?

❏ What are the time, date, and place of annual members' meetings?

❏ Are there procedures for calling a special members' meeting?

❏ Is notice required for members' meetings and are there provisions for waiving notice?

❏ What are quorum requirements for members' meetings?

❏ Is there a procedure for adjourning members' meetings?

❏ Are there any requirements for voting at members' meetings by proxy?

❏ How are the record date and eligibility to vote determined?

❏ Can members vote by consent resolutions or is a formal vote required in all cases?

❏ Who designates election inspectors? Are they required?

❏ What are the powers of managers?

❏ How many managers are there?

❏ Who can be a manager? Are there any limits or qualifications?

❏ How are managers elected? What are their terms of office? How do you fill managerial vacancies?

❏ Who sets the time, place, and date of annual or regularly scheduled meetings or is the date stated in the operating agreement?

❏ Who can call special meetings of the managers? Can any single manager call a special meeting? Can any single member call a special meeting?

❑ What constitutes a quorum for managers' meetings?

❑ Can managers vote by written consent resolutions in lieu of formal noticed meetings?

❑ What are the managers' standards of care?

❑ Can managers appoint committees to delegate certain responsibilities?

❑ Does the LLC have officers in addition to managers and, if so, which officers must the LLC appoint and which are optional?

❑ What are the officers' duties?

❑ How are officers removed and who fills officer vacancies?

❑ To what degree are managers, officers, employees, and agents of the LLC to be indemnified by the LLC?

❑ Are there any restrictions on the transfer of ownership interests?

❑ To what extent are there restrictions upon admitting new members to the LLC? Does the admission of a new member require a vote of the current members?

❑ What reports, if any, are required?

❑ To what extent do the members have the right to inspect the books and records of the LLC?

❑ How is the operating agreement amended?

❑ Are there any supermajority voting requirements on significant LLC actions?

❑ Are there preemptive rights or cumulative voting?

❑ Can members' or managers' meetings be held by conference call? Electronically?

CHAPTER 4

Taxes and General Information for All Businesses

Local Taxes, Local Licenses

You can reasonably expect that your state and local jurisdiction will carry licensing and filing responsibilities for your business, regardless of the business form you choose. Local licensing rules will vary from jurisdiction to jurisdiction; expect more stringent requirements in cities. These are some common requirements:

- City and/or county business license
- City and/or county local taxation
- State sales tax registration and filings for owners who sell goods subject to sales tax
- Unemployment tax

- Registration for certain industries (requirements vary wildly from state to state)
- Registration for fictitious business names

Of course, the wide variation of local regulations places this topic far beyond the scope of this book. The best way to learn about your local regulations is to either call or visit your city hall or county administration. Some municipalities even have guides to help you get started.

For further information on local regulations in your state, consider obtaining a state-specific guide to starting a business. Entrepreneur Press offers business start-up guides for each of the 50 states in its SmartStart series, available from any major bookstore.

Expert Tip

If you get stuck in the bureaucracy trying to figure out your local regulations, call the office of an elected representative, such as a county supervisor or the mayor (you'll likely reach an assistant), and ask to be directed to the right person or department. Typically, elected representatives are more responsive than non-elected bureaucrats.

Partnership Taxation

A notable feature of LLCs (and subchapter S corporations) is that they are taxed in the same manner as partnerships. Technically speaking, partnerships are not taxed: partnership income passes freely through the partnership but is ultimately taxed in the form of wages, dividends, and distributions of profits that are paid to the owners and employees. This manner of taxation is familiarly known as *partnership taxation*. In most circumstances, smaller businesses will incur a lower overall tax liability with partnership taxation. Another common term for this tax treatment is *pass-through taxation*, because the income passes through the entity to its members. Although partnerships, LLCs, and subchapter S corporations pay no federal tax, they are required to disclose their earnings and distributions to the Internal Revenue Service and state tax authorities on annual information returns.

Partnerships report their annual income or loss on Form 1065, *U.S. Return of Partnership Income*. Also, each partner submits his or her individual Schedule K-1, *Partner's Share of Income*, which is part of Form 1065.

Online Resource

To get IRS forms and explanatory publications, visit *www.irs.gov/formspubs* and use the "Search Forms and Publications" link.

LLC Taxes: What to File and How to File at Year-End

Because an LLC is a business entity, it must file a tax return each year and pay any taxes that are due. Tax returns are generally always due to the IRS and may be due to the state, depending on where your LLC is headquartered and where your LLC does business. To determine if your LLC must file a tax return in your state of headquarters or state of operation, a good place to start is the State Reference Information accompanying CD. The information provides a brief overview of each state's taxation requirements. (For example, Nevada does not tax LLC profits, so no LLC tax return is due in Nevada.) However, keep in mind that we only offer summaries here; you might need to do a little research or talk to an accountant to determine if you need to file a state return.

Single-Member LLCs vs. Multi-Member LLCs

Single-member LLCs file taxes differently from multi-member LLCs. Generally, when an LLC has only one member, the LLC is ignored or disregarded for the purpose of filing a federal tax return. This is solely for tax purposes; this filing status does not affect the LLC's status as a separate entity. If the single member is a person, he or she reports the LLC income and expenses on Form 1040, Schedule C, E, or F. If the single member is a corporation, the LLC's income and expenses are reported on Form 1120, *U.S. Corporation Income Tax Return*, or Form 1120S, *U.S. Income Tax Return for an S Corporation*.

Figure 4.1 shows a very simple Schedule C completed for a single-member LLC called "Acme LLC," with a notation "John Wilson, sole owner."

Note that the LLC files its Schedule C using an employer ID number rather than a Social Security number. Then, the owner simply attaches the Schedule C to his or her 1040 form. As you can see in our example, the LLC earned $50,000 of income in the year 2006 and had $12,000 in expenses. A single-member LLC is required to use the same tax year as its owner, which will be a calendar year.

A multi-member LLC will file a Form 1065, *U.S. Return of Partnership Income*, which is the same form that a partnership files. There is a rare but important exception to this filing rule: some LLCs elect to be taxed as corporations by making the election available on Form 8832, *Entity Classification Election*. You probably would never want to make a complex election like that without the help of a qualified accountant or tax attorney. And remember that if the LLC makes no tax election—if someone simply organizes the LLC, gets a tax ID, and does nothing more—the LLC is automatically taxed as a partnership. So, for our purposes, 99 percent of the multi-member LLCs will file a Form 1065 partnership return.

Form 1065 is more complicated than Schedule C. Form 1065 is four pages (Schedule C is only two pages) and the instructions for Form 1065 are 41 pages. As such, a complete instruction guide for Form 1065 would be a book in itself. A good low-priced accountant can usually put together a Form 1065 for a small, simple LLC for a few hundred dollars.

An LLC must also provide an additional tax form to each of its owners, a Schedule K-1, *Partner's Share of Income, Deductions, Credits, etc.*, detailing each owner's share of the LLC's income and deductions for the year.

We have included a sample K-1 for a fictitious LLC called "Acme LLC" and a fictitious owner named John Wilson. In our sample, John Wilson is a 25 percent owner, so he shares 25 percent of the LLC profits and 25 percent of the LLC losses. His distributive share of the income is $26,000: $25,000 of ordinary income, $500 of interest income, and $500 of other income. This sample K-1 is fairly representative of a K-1 you would see used in a small LLC.

SCHEDULE C **(Form 1040)** Department of the Treasury Internal Revenue Service (99)	**Profit or Loss From Business** (Sole Proprietorship) ▶ **Partnerships, joint ventures, etc., must file Form 1065 or 1065-B.** ▶ **Attach to Form 1040, 1040NR, or 1041.** ▶ **See Instructions for Schedule C (Form 1040).**	OMB No. 1545-0074 20**06** Attachment Sequence No. **09**

Name of proprietor ACME LLC, John Wilson sole owner		Social security number (SSN)	

A	Principal business or profession, including product or service (see page C-2 of the instructions) SALE OF ROADRUNNER TRAPS	B Enter code from pages C-8, 9, & 10
C	Business name. If no separate business name, leave blank.	D Employer ID number (EIN), if any

E	Business address (including suite or room no.) ▶ 123 MAIN STREET City, town or post office, state, and ZIP code OMAHA, NEBRASKA
F	Accounting method: (1) ☑ Cash (2) ☐ Accrual (3) ☐ Other (specify) ▶
G	Did you "materially participate" in the operation of this business during 2006? If "No," see page C-3 for limit on losses ☑ Yes ☐ No
H	If you started or acquired this business during 2006, check here . . . . ▶ ☐

Part I Income

1	Gross receipts or sales. **Caution.** If this income was reported to you on Form W-2 and the "Statutory employee" box on that form was checked, see page C-3 and check here . . . . . ▶ ☐	1	50000	00
2	Returns and allowances	2		
3	Subtract line 2 from line 1	3		
4	Cost of goods sold (from line 42 on page 2)	4	10000	00
5	**Gross profit.** Subtract line 4 from line 3.	5	40000	00
6	Other income, including federal and state gasoline or fuel tax credit or refund (see page C-3). . .	6		
7	**Gross income.** Add lines 5 and 6 . . . . ▶	7		

Part II Expenses. Enter expenses for business use of your home **only** on line 30.

8	Advertising	8	1000	00	18	Office expense	18	1000	00
9	Car and truck expenses (see page C-4)	9			19	Pension and profit-sharing plans	19		
					20	Rent or lease (see page C-5):			
10	Commissions and fees . .	10			a	Vehicles, machinery, and equipment .	20a		
11	Contract labor (see page C-4)	11			b	Other business property. . .	20b		
12	Depletion	12			21	Repairs and maintenance . .	21		
13	Depreciation and section 179 expense deduction (not included in Part III) (see page C-4)	13			22	Supplies (not included in Part III)	22		
					23	Taxes and licenses	23		
					24	Travel, meals, and entertainment:			
14	Employee benefit programs (other than on line 19). .	14			a	Travel	24a		
15	Insurance (other than health) .	15			b	Deductible meals and entertainment (see page C-6)	24b		
16	Interest:				25	Utilities	25		
a	Mortgage (paid to banks, etc.) .	16a			26	Wages (less employment credits) .	26		
b	Other	16b			27	Other expenses (from line 48 on page 2)	27		
17	Legal and professional services	17							

28	**Total expenses** before expenses for business use of home. Add lines 8 through 27 in columns . ▶	28	2000	00
29	Tentative profit (loss). Subtract line 28 from line 7	29	38000	00
30	Expenses for business use of your home. Attach **Form 8829**	30		
31	**Net profit or (loss).** Subtract line 30 from line 29. ? If a profit, enter on both **Form 1040, line 12,** and **Schedule SE, line 2,** or on **Form 1040NR, line 13** (statutory employees, see page C-6). Estates and trusts, enter on Form 1041, line 3. ? If a loss, you **must** go to line 32.	31	38000	00
32	If you have a loss, check the box that describes your investment in this activity (see page C-6). ? If you checked 32a, enter the loss on both **Form 1040, line 12,** and **Schedule SE, line 2,** or on **Form 1040NR, line 13** (statutory employees, see page C-6). Estates and trusts, enter on Form 1041, line 3. ? If you checked 32b, you **must** attach **Form 6198.** Your loss may be limited.	32a ☐ All investment is at risk. 32b ☐ Some investment is not at risk.		

For Paperwork Reduction Act Notice, see page C-8 of the instructions.	Cat. No. 11334P	Schedule C (Form 1040) 2006

Figure 4.1. Sample Schedule C for Single-Member LLC

Page **2**

Part III **Cost of Goods Sold** (see page C-7)

33 Method(s) used to value closing inventory: **a** ☑ Cost   **b** ☐ Lower of cost or market   **c** ☐ Other (attach explanation)

34 Was there any change in determining quantities, costs, or valuations between opening and closing inventory?
If "Yes," attach explanation . . . . ☐ Yes ☑ No

35	Inventory at beginning of year. If different from last year's closing inventory, attach explanation . .	35	10000 00
36	Purchases less cost of items withdrawn for personal use	36	
37	Cost of labor. Do not include any amounts paid to yourself	37	
38	Materials and supplies	38	10000 00
39	Other costs	39	
40	Add lines 35 through 39	40	20000 00
41	Inventory at end of year	41	10000 00
42	**Cost of goods sold.** Subtract line 41 from line 40. Enter the result here and on page 1, line 4 . .	42	10000 00

Part IV **Information on Your Vehicle.** Complete this part **only** if you are claiming car or truck expenses on line 9 and are not required to file Form 4562 for this business. See the instructions for line 13 on page C-4 to find out if you must file Form 4562.

43 When did you place your vehicle in service for business purposes? (month, day, year) ? . . . . / . . . . / . . . . . .

44 Of the total number of miles you drove your vehicle during 2006, enter the number of miles you used your vehicle for:

a Business . . . . **b** Commuting (see instructions) . . . . **c** Other . . . .

45 Do you (or your spouse) have another vehicle available for personal use?. . . . . ☐ Yes ☐ No

46 Was your vehicle available for personal use during off-duty hours? . . . . ☐ Yes ☐ No

47a Do you have evidence to support your deduction? . . . . ☐ Yes ☐ No

b If "Yes," is the evidence written? . . . . ☐ Yes ☐ No

Part V **Other Expenses.** List below business expenses not included on lines 8–26 or line 30.

. . . .		
. . . .		
. . . .		
. . . .		
. . . .		
. . . .		
. . . .		
. . . .		
48 Total other expenses. Enter here and on page 1, line 27	48	

Schedule C (Form 1040) 2006

Figure 4.1. Sample Schedule C for Single-Member LLC (continued)

		651106
☑ Final K-1	☐ Amended K-1	OMB No. 1545-0099

Schedule K-1
(Form 1065)   20**06**

Department of the Treasury
Internal Revenue Service

For calendar year 2006, or tax
year beginning _____ , 2006
ending _____ , 20___

Partner's Share of Income, Deductions, Credits, etc.

⌐ **See back of form and separate instructions.**

Part I   Information About the Partnership
A   Partnership's employer identification number
04-0000000
B   Partnership's name, address, city, state, and ZIP code

ACME LLC
   123 MAIN STREET
   AUSTIN, TX 78701

C   IRS Center where partnership filed return
FORT WORTH
D ☐ Check if this is a publicly traded partnership (PTP)
E ☐ Tax shelter registration number, if any _____
F ☐ Check if Form 8271 is attached

Part II   Information About the Partner
G   Partner's identifying number
000-55-1212
H   Partner's name, address, city, state, and ZIP code

JOHN WILSON
   123 MAIN STREET
   AUSTIN, TX 78701

I ☐ General partner or LLC member-manager   ☐ Limited partner or other LLC member

J ☐ Domestic partner   ☐ Foreign partner

K   What type of entity is this partner? _____

L   Partner's share of profit, loss, and capital:

	Beginning	Ending
Profit	25 %	25 %
Loss	25 %	25 %
Capital	25 %	25 %

M   Partner's share of liabilities at year end:

Nonrecourse . . . .$	25000
Qualified nonrecourse financing . .$	
Recourse . . . .$	

N   Partner's capital account analysis:

Beginning capital account . . . .$	25000
Capital contributed during the year .$	0
Current year increase (decrease) . .$	0
Withdrawals & distributions . . .$ (	0)
Ending capital account . . . .$	25000

☑ Tax basis   ☐ GAAP   ☐ Section 704(b) book
☐ Other (explain)

Part III Partner's Share of Current Year Income, Deductions, Credits, and Other Items		
1 Ordinary business income (loss) 25000	**15** Credits	
2 Net rental real estate income (loss)		
3 Other net rental income (loss)	**16** Foreign transactions	
4 Guaranteed payments		
5 Interest income 500		
6a Ordinary dividends		
6b Qualified dividends		
7 Royalties		
8 Net short-term capital gain (loss)		
9a Net long-term capital gain (loss)	**17** Alternative minimum tax (AMT) items	
9b Collectibles (28%) gain (loss) 500		
9c Unrecaptured section 1250 gain		
10 Net section 1231 gain (loss)	**18** Tax-exempt income and nondeductible expenses	
11 Other income (loss) 500		
	19 Distributions	
12 Section 179 deduction		
13 Other deductions	**20** Other information	
14 Self-employment earnings (loss)		

*See attached statement for additional information.

For IRS Use Only

For Privacy Act and Paperwork Reduction Act Notice, see Instructions for Form 1065.   Cat. No. 11394R   Schedule K-1 (Form 1065) 2006

Figure 4.2. Sample Schedule K-1

Figure 4.2. Sample Schedule K-1 (continued)

LLC Taxes: Employment and Payroll Taxes

Limited liability companies that employ workers must withhold employment taxes and must file employment-related tax forms, aka payroll taxes. If your LLC has employees, you will have important tax-withholding responsibilities and employment tax-reporting responsibilities. You will be deducting taxes from wages, forwarding them to the IRS, and then reporting quarterly on Form 941, *Employer's Quarterly Federal Tax Return*. The checklist below provides a summary and overview of employment taxation responsibilities.

Withholding is a serious responsibility with serious consequences if it's mishandled. Keep in mind that LLCs shield their owners from most liabilities, but not from mishandling employee tax withholding. Generally speaking, submitting money withheld on behalf of employees should be the top-priority payment for an LLC. I am familiar with many cases in which an LLC or a corporation failed to make its withholding payments and the IRS charged the unpaid sums to the accounts of individual owners of the business. The IRS is well within its rights to do so.

Great Resource

A great resource to learn more about business taxes at the federal level is the IRS Publication 334, *Tax Guide for Small Business*.

How to Handle Employment Taxes: Payroll Services

Employment taxes are a large responsibility and a significant paperwork burden. The best way to handle payroll taxes and federal employment reporting is to use one of the many electronic payroll services. These services specialize in preparing checks and reports for employees, making deposits with the federal tax authorities, and submitting quarterly tax reports for employers. Traditionally, the large data service company ADP (Automatic Data Processing) served as the world's largest provider of payroll services to small business. Computers and powerful software now enable other companies to compete with ADP. Even Intuit, the maker of the Quicken line of financial software products, operates a payroll service now. Payroll services are very economical, costing as little as $200 per year for a small business.

Employer Tax Responsibility Checklist

The following checklist sets forth a brief summary of an LLC employer's basic tax responsibilities. Because the circumstances for LLCs can vary greatly, responsibilities for withholding, depositing, and reporting employment taxes can differ.

Upon Hiring New Employees

❑ Verify the work eligibility of employees.

❑ Record employees' names and SSNs from Social Security cards.

❑ Ask employees to complete Form W-4.

Each Payday

❑ Withhold federal income tax based on each employee's Form W-4.

❑ Withhold employee's share of Social Security and Medicare taxes.

❑ Include advance earned income credit payment in paycheck if employee requested it on Form W-5, *Earned Income Credit Advance Payment Certificate*.

❑ Deposit: withheld income tax.

❑ Deposit withheld and employer Social Security taxes.

❑ Deposit withheld and employer Medicare taxes.

Note: Due date of withholding deposits generally depends on your deposit schedule (monthly or semiweekly).

Quarterly (by April 30, July 31, October 31, and January 31)

❑ Deposit FUTA tax if undeposited amount is over $500.

❑ File Form 941, *Employer's Quarterly Federal Tax Return*; pay tax with return if not required to deposit.

Annually (by January 31)

❑ File Form 944, *Employer's Annual Federal Tax Return*, if required; pay tax with return if not required to deposit.

Annually (check calendar for due dates)

❑ Remind employees to submit new Form W-4 if they need to change their withholding.

❑ Ask for new Form W-4 from employees claiming exemption from income tax withholding.

❑ Reconcile Form 941 (or Form 944) with Form W-2, *Wage and Tax Statement*, and Form W-3, *Transmittal of Wage and Tax Statements*.

❑ Give each employee a Form W-2.

❑ File Copy A of Forms W-2 and the transmittal Form W-3 with the Social Security Administration.

❑ Give each other payee a Form 1099 (e.g., Forms 1099-R—*Distributions from Pensions, Annuities, Retirement or Profit-Sharing Plans, IRAs, Insurance Contracts, etc.*—and 1099-MISC—*Miscellaneous Income*).

❑ File Forms 1099 and Form 1096, *Annual Summary and Transmittal of U.S. Information Returns*.

❑ File Form 940, *Employer's Annual Federal Unemployment (FUTA) Tax Return*.

❑ File Form 945, *Annual Return of Withheld Federal Income Tax*, for any nonpayroll income tax withholding taxes with Form 941.

Three Languages for Three Types of Business Entities

Because LLCs, corporations, and partnerships differ fundamentally as business entities, basic concepts are expressed in different terms for each entity. For example, LLCs have *members*, not *shareholders* or *partners*. They have *membership interests*, not *shares* like corporations. Calling an LLC member a "shareholder" is not technically incorrect. Nevertheless, the legislators, lawyers, administrators, and judges who govern the body of law surrounding LLCs will universally use the proper terminology.

The following table shows how the terms for key concepts differ with respect to partnerships, corporations, and LLCs.

Concept	Partnership	Corporation	LLC
Owners	Partners	Shareholders	Members
Ownership share	Partnership interest or percentage interest	Shares or stock certificates	Membership interest, percentage interest, membership unit, or unit
Charter Document Filed with State	For general partnership (optional): Statement of Partnership; For limited partnerships: Certificate of Limited Partnership	Articles of Incorporation or Certificate of Incorporation	Articles of Organization or Certificate of Organization
Operating/Governing Document	Partnership Agreement	Bylaws	LLC Operating Agreement
Company organizer	Organizer, founding partner	Incorporator	Organizer
Managers	For limited partnership: general partners	Directors and Officers	Managers or managing members

PART TWO

The Limited Liability Company Players

CHAPTER 5

Promoters, Organizers, Managers, Officers, and Agents

This chapter will serve as a scorecard of sorts, identifying the various roles that are played in a limited liability company and describing the responsibilities and duties of each player.

For many limited liability companies, one person may wear different hats. One person may serve as manager, officer, and owner as well as promoter and organizer. Which hat you wear at any point in time could be significant in determining whether or not you could have personal liability for entity actions. The common theme that will always arise in a personal liability inquiry is separateness between owner and entity. LLCs that operate with one person wearing all hats are always more likely to face personal liability.

This chapter will expand on concepts introduced in the preceding chapter concerning managers, officers, and owners. Later chapters will cover managers' and members' meetings.

Promoters

A promoter is anyone who acts or claims to act for or on behalf of an LLC prior to its formal organization. For example, you want to start a business and you plan on organizing it as an LLC. Prior to organizing, you talk with potential investors—hopefully, in compliance with securities law requirements—suppliers, and customers.

During these preorganization activities, you are a promoter. As a promoter, you are personally liable to any third party for preorganization activities, such as contracting with suppliers or others. You will also be personally liable for your torts, such as fraud, misrepresentation, or negligence.

> ### Expert Tip
>
> Because promoters are personally liable for their preorganization activities, ask for a written acknowledgment from potential suppliers, customers, or investors that clearly states you are acting on behalf of the LLC and only the LLC is liable in the event of a dispute.

Although the LLC, once formed, can agree to indemnify you from this preorganization liability (reimburse your cost, expenses, and liability), the third party can still look directly to you and your personal assets for any recovery unless he or she agrees, in writing, to look only to the LLC for recovery. In contract terms, this substitution of a contract with an LLC for a contract with an individual is called a *novation*.

As a promoter, you must deal fairly with the LLC. This requires full and fair disclosure of all aspects of a transaction between you and the LLC.

Here's an example. You own a piece of real estate. You have owned it for five years. Recently, you and John Doan decide to start a business together and form an LLC. Your real estate property would be perfect for the LLC. After full and fair disclosure to John Doan, you may sell the real estate to the LLC for its fair market value.

Now assume that you do not own any real estate. After you and John Doan decide to go into business, you locate a piece of property that would be perfect for your LLC. You recognize that the real estate is grossly undervalued. You purchase the real estate for $100, even though it is worth at least $10,000. You must sell the real estate to the LLC for $100. Otherwise, you would be making a secret profit and not dealing fairly with the LLC.

When do you become a promoter? As lawyers say, that is a question of fact based on all the facts and circumstances of a particular case. If you are uncertain, consider these questions:

- When was the idea to form the LLC conceived?
- When did you begin any action related to the proposed LLC's business?

If you engage in an act (such as acquiring property) prior to deciding to form an LLC, you are not a promoter. However, it is not always easy to tell when an idea was conceived. If your activities relate directly to the business of an LLC formed later, there is a stronger possibility that your actions will be considered those of a promoter.

Organizers

An organizer is the person or entity that organizes an LLC and files its articles of organization. The organizer enjoys limited powers. He or she can act as a promoter, as described above, and he or she can present and file the articles of organization with the secretary of state. Whether the organizer has a further role depends on state law. LLC articles of organization, depending on the state, generally require that the articles of organization name a member or a manager. Also, even in states that do not require the disclosure of an initial manager or member, an organizer may include such a disclosure at his or her option. Either way, if the articles of organization set forth either a member or a manager or both, the power of the organizer is extinguished upon the filing of the articles of organization. This organizer's power is assumed by the manager or member.

Alternatively, some states (e.g., California and Delaware) do not require that the articles of organization disclose a member or a manager. In such states, the organizer's power extends to assisting the members with the organization of the LLC, but thereafter the organizer's role ends.

An organizer is the limited liability company equivalent of an incorporator in the corporate setting. However, an incorporator typically enjoys far greater powers than an organizer. An incorporator has the right to approve initial bylaws and appoint directors. The role and powers of an LLC organizer are relatively limited. When an attorney forms an LLC on behalf of a client, he or she serves as organizer. If you intend to use this book to guide you with your organization, you will be serving as the organizer.

Managers, Board of Managers, and Committee of Managers

First, let's recall that LLC managers are optional. Only manager-managed LLCs have a manager or managers. Member-managed LLCs do not have managers; the members act as managers. Whether or not your LLC has appointed managers is a choice that you make when you organize your LLC. Of course, you can always convert a member-managed LLC to a manager-managed LLC or a a manager-managed LLC to a member-managed LLC.

This choice carries personal liability considerations. Manager-managed LLCs offer their owners greater personal liability protection; we discuss that topic in Chapter 12: How to Effectively Manage Your LLC to Maximize Liability Protection. You should carefully review that section before either choosing to form or continuing to operate a member-managed LLC.

If your LLC is manager-managed, then managers are the elected representatives. Managers enjoy broad powers; those powers will be outlined in state statutes and modified by the operating agreement. Essentially, managers have full powers to operate the LLC on a day-to-day basis.

A comparison with corporations is useful here. By law, corporations typically have taller management structures than LLCs. The shareholders of corporations elect directors, who in turn elect officers. These officers run a corporation's everyday business, while the directors guide policy and make long-range decisions. Manager-managed LLCs have flatter management structures: the members elect managers, who run the LLC's everyday business. Member-managed LLCs have the flattest management structure—they are run by the members themselves.

LLCs typically do not have officers, but there is no reason that LLCs cannot have officers. (We'll discuss LLC officers below.) Typically, they have one or more managers who run the LLC. Tasks typically within the manager's authority include:

- Running the business on a day-to-day basis
- Signing contracts in the name of the LLC
- Hiring and firing employees
- Approving purchases of inventory and supplies
- Meeting with customers and vendors
- Voting on acquisitions and mergers
- Approving large purchases of real estate and capital equipment

How Many Managers Do You Need?

You must first decide the number of managers for your LLC. The major factor to keep in mind when deciding on the number of managers is that owners of single-manager LLCs are more subject to personal liability risks. Alter ego liability, discussed below, can attach to members of an LLC that commingles personal and LLC assets or does not observe a meaningful separation of LLC and owners. A sole manager with boundless authority is more likely to disregard important formalities and more likely to behave independently of the LLC's owners. Conversely, a multi-manager LLC is more likely to reach decisions through discussion, consensus, and vote.

As we have seen, there are many opportunities in the planning and operation of an LLC to improve the personal liability protection of LLC owners by imposing separateness between owners and the LLC. Put another way, the personal liability protection of an LLC's owners is greater if they do not have total control over the LLC. Any layer of management between owner and LLC (i.e., managers and officers) serves to separate the owners from total control over the entity. If the intervening layer of management is more than one person, that number serves to separate LLC owners from total control over the LLC. Also, if the intervening managers and/or officers are independent (i.e., not owners or immediate relatives of owners), that independence serves to separate the owners from total control over the LLC..

The number of managers for an LLC should be determined by the degree of risk that the enterprise undertakes. LLCs owners are allowed by state laws to operate their LLCs with little formality, without representative management, or with a single manager. This erodes the independence of an LLC and therefore creates liability risk. When you evaluate the number of managers to run your LLC, you should consider how risky your line of business is. Low-risk enterprises should be well served with only one manager. High-risk enterprises (such as enterprises in the building trades, skateboard parks, day-care facilities, etc.) should strongly consider appointing two or three managers, of whom at least one should be independent.

The number of managers will also be determined by the number of owners. If an LLC has three equal owners, typically all three will want a say in the management. So, for such an entity, three managers is a perfect number. Except for very small LLCs, the most suitable number of managers will be three. Two managers may also be suitable for a smaller LLC, but if the managers disagree on a policy decision and cannot resolve the conflict, it may lead to deadlock that may require resolution by action of members or, worse, in court. LLCs with only one manager may have difficulty attracting investment.

Managers should always avoid conflicts of interest and abstain from votes in which they have a personal interest. For example, if an LLC is considering purchasing a piece of property, it is improper for a manager to vote on it if he or she has an ownership interest in the property. If an LLC has only one manager, he or she cannot abstain from such a vote, because a board cannot act without at least one vote. This is another disadvantage of a single-manager LLC.

Where Do Managers Come From?

Most often, managers are also members of the LLC. If a manager is also a member or officer of the LLC, he or she is called an *inside* manager. If the manager has no other role with the LLC, he or she is an *independent* manager, sometimes called an *outside* manager. Outside managers are often attorneys, accountants, insurance agents, prominent business or civic leaders, or business educators. You should consider using one or more independent managers. Because they are neither members nor regular employees, independent outside managers can bring an objective perspective to your LLC. You may also benefit from an outside manager's knowledge and experience. Non-owner employees also often serve as managers. Employees, while still interested parties due to their employment relationship with the LLC, are more independent than members because they have no ownership interest in the enterprise. If independent management is important to your enterprise, you should strongly consider appointing employees as managers.

How Are Managers Appointed?

Managers are appointed by members in a manner consistent with state law and the LLC's operating agreement. In an LLC's "chain of command," members are at the top. Members appoint managers, who then serve at the will of the members. Members can usually remove managers at any time, unless there are unusual provisions in the LLC operating agreement. Similarly, if an LLC has officers, the managers appoint the officers, who then serve at the will of the managers.

Managers are initially appointed in the LLC's operating agreement. The sample manager-managed LLC operating agreements that we include in this book state that the managers named in the document are to serve as managers and then names them in a table or list at the end of the document. That initial appointment, however, will take effect only when the members approve the operating agreement. Thereafter, the managers will be appointed periodically by the members, either at annual meetings of the members or at special meetings of the members called for the purpose of electing managers. We'll discuss the mechanics of meetings and voting below in Chapter 9: Members' Meetings.

How Do the Managers Take Action?

How the managers take action will be outlined in the operating agreement. LLCs are very flexible entities, so the manner in which the managers will act may differ greatly among LLCs. The managers conduct meetings at regularly scheduled intervals (usually annually) or at special meetings called by a manager, a senior officer, or one or more members. For more information on noticing, calling, and conducting managers' meetings, refer to Chapter 8.

Unless the articles or operating agreement require a higher percentage, if a majority of managers is present at a meeting, that constitutes a quorum, and a majority of the quorum is sufficient to authorize the LLC or particular officers or agents to act on behalf of the LLC. These authorizations or directives usually appear in the form of a corporate resolution.

Good to Know

Under some circumstances a minority of managers can successfully pass a vote. Here's how it works. Assume that an LLC has 13 managers. At a managers' meeting, only seven managers show up, which constitutes a quorum of more than 50 percent of the sitting managers. With a quorum, the board can vote. If four of the seven vote to pass a resolution, it passes. Thus, four of 13 managers can bind the LLC.

How Long Do Managers Serve?

The articles or operating agreement should provide the answer to this question. Managers commonly serve a one-year term, subject to reelection by the members or removal by the members or in some cases by other managers. The terms of managers are sometimes staggered, much in the way the U.S. House of Representatives rotates one-third of its members every two years. The staggering of managers promotes continuity.

For example, TonoSilver, Inc. has nine managers. If it chooses, the members could select nine managers each year for one-year terms or select three managers each year for three-year terms. Staggering ensures that at least some of the managers will have prior experience and there will be some continuity.

Can the Managers Delegate Authority?

Managers can delegate authority to officers, employees, and others. Managers sometimes create committees consisting of managers and non-managers to focus on specific issues for the LLC. A manager can't delegate all of his or her power and authority. Also, managers cannot vote by proxy.

Managers are required to bring their independent business judgment to their office; this judgment can't be delegated. For example, the managers can authorize an officer or committee to study the feasibility of selling the business or merging with another business. However, the managers can't delegate the ultimate decision of whether or not to sell or merge.

Duties of Due Care and Loyalty

Managers have several duties to the LLC and its members. If a manager fails to fulfill these duties, he or she may be personally liable to the LLC or to the members. There are four duties that the law imposes on representative managers: the duty of due care, the duty of loyalty, the duty of fair dealing, and a duty to act in good faith. The duties of due care and loyalty are the most significant.

The Manager's Duty of Due Care

A manager must exercise ordinary care. This means he or she must act as any ordinary prudent person would under the same circumstances and use his or her best business judgment in reaching a decision. Some independent investigation of the matters being considered is required, because if a manager merely rubber-stamps the recommendations and actions of other managers without further investigation and follow-up, he or she may later be liable for failing to exercise proper duty of due care.

For example, John, Jane, and Joan are the only managers of TonoSilver, LLC. The LLC has more than a dozen members located in several states.

John and Jane have formed several other LLCs on the side. These LLCs supply TonoSilver, LLC with the raw materials it needs to make its widgets. Joan has no interest in these other LLCs. The contracts between these LLCs and TonoSilver, LLC bind TonoSilver, LLC for a long term to purchase materials at an exorbitant rate.

Joan attends managers' meetings and is aware that John and Jane have an interest in these other LLCs.

Joan does not investigate the fairness of these contracts. She simply goes along with John and Jane. Without question, John and Jane have breached their duty of loyalty (described below) to TonoSilver, LLC. Also, Joan has breached her duty of due care to TonoSilver, LLC by failing to investigate the fairness of the transactions and failing to use any judgment in deciding to approve the transactions.

To satisfy the duty of care, a manager must:

- Act in good faith and in the best interests of the LLC
- Exercise good business judgment
- Use ordinary care
- Make an independent investigation and determination of matters presented to the managers

Managers may rely on reports of company officers or outside experts where it would be reasonable to do so. For example, if the managers receive a recommendation from outside attorneys or accountants to take certain action to avoid a major tax liability, it would probably be reasonable for the managers to rely on such a report. However, if the report was prepared by the company president, who stands to profit from the proposed transaction, it would not be reasonable for the managers to rely on the report without further investigation.

Free Resource

learnaboutlaw.com maintains online question-and-answer forums operated by several practicing attorneys. Follow the links to "forums"; you can post questions for free and practicing lawyers will answer your questions or you can search the listed topics.

The Manager's Duty of Loyalty

A manager is also required to give his or her undivided loyalty to the LLC. To fulfill this duty, he or she must fully and fairly disclose all material facts in any proposed transaction with the LLC in which there's a potential conflict of interest for him or her. A manager should not profit personally from inside information.

Conflicts of interest involving officers and managers and the LLC are common. For example:

- An officer or manager owns an interest in a competitor or a supplier.
- The officer or manager owns real estate which the LLC is seeking to lease or buy.
- The officer or manager's family member has an interest in a supplier, a competitor, or real estate the company is considering leasing or buying.

In these situations, full disclosure of the relationship should be made. Although the interested manager may wish to participate in the discussion, he or she should abstain from voting on whether or not to approve the transaction.

Another aspect of the duty of loyalty is known as the *corporate opportunity doctrine*. Under this theory, a manager or officer may not independently pursue a business opportunity related to the LLC's business without first offering the LLC the chance to pursue it.

Here is a three-part test to determine whether or not there is a corporate opportunity:

- Is the LLC financially able to undertake the opportunity?
- Is the opportunity in the LLC's line of business (either actual or reasonably foreseeable)?
- Is the LLC interested in the opportunity?

If the answer to these questions is yes, the manager or officer must disclose the opportunity to the other managers and allow the LLC the first chance to pursue it. If in doubt, always disclose.

To illustrate, John, Jane, and Joan are the officers and managers of TonoSilver, LLC. The LLC sells MP3 players at retail stores it owns. In the past the company has explored the possibility of manufacturing its own MP3 players for resale but has not acted on the idea. John learns that Sonic Gadgets, Inc., an MP3 player manufacturer, is for sale. Unbeknownst to Jane and Joan, John forms a separate LLC and buys the assets of Sonic Gadgets, Inc. Has John breached his duty of loyalty to TonoSilver, LLC? If the company was financially able to pursue the purchase of Sonic Gadgets, Inc., the answer is probably yes. To be safe, John should have presented the information about Sonic Gadgets, Inc. to the TonoSilver, LLC managers and let the managers decide whether or not to pursue the opportunity.

Statutory Sources of Liability for Managers

In addition to the duties described above, several statutes also impose personal liability on managers or officers in certain circumstances, such as the following:

- The failure to file articles of organization or an application for certificate of authority
- Wrongful declarations or payment of dividends or unlawful distribution of entity property
- False statements made in articles, annual reports, or similar items
- Failure to pay required taxes

Expert Tip

A manager should be willing to vote against the majority of the members or even resign if a suggested course of conduct is unlawful or ill-advised.

Advisory Boards

Some LLCs use an advisory board of managers as well as a regular board of managers. Advisory board members are selected by the LLC's board of managers. They are not elected by members and any actions of the advisory board are not binding on the LLC. Advisory board members do not vote; they only advise.

An advisory board can provide useful advice and information for the elected board. One advantage to the advisory board is that its members are not subject to the same standards of conduct ordinarily imposed upon elected managers. Business leaders may be unwilling to serve on an elected board because of liability concerns. There are no such concerns for advisory managers.

An advisory board can include any number of people. Good candidates include your LLC's banker, lawyer, accountant, and insurance agent. Other possibilities include representatives of a key supplier or a customer group.

Officers

LLCs differ from corporations in an important respect: LLCs do not always have officers. In most states, LLCs are not required by law to have officers. Corporations, on the other hand, are required by law to have at least one officer, such as a president, treasurer, or secretary. Because LLCs are not required to have officers, whether or not to appoint officers is a decision you should make based on your needs. An important consideration, however, is that banks typically require a duly appointed officer, such as a president or secretary, to open the bank account and sign checks.

The following passage, from California's LLC statute, makes clear that LLCs are empowered to appoint officers.

> 17154. (a) A written operating agreement may provide for the appointment of officers, including, without limitation, a chairperson or a president, or both, a secretary, a chief financial officer, and any other officers with such titles, powers, and duties as shall be specified in the articles of organization or operating agreement, or determined by the managers or members. An officer may, but need not, be a member or manager of the limited liability company, and any number of offices may be held by the same person.

All of the model LLC operating agreements in this book, both manager-managed and member-managed, allow for the appointment of officers. Officers are appointed by members in a member-managed LLC and appointed by managers in a manager-managed LLC. In both cases, they serve at the pleasure of the members or managers and can be removed at will.

If Officers Are Not Required, Why Appoint Them?

There are a few reasons why you might want to appoint officers, even though there is no legal requirement.

First, banks and other financial institutions still speak the language of corporations. Bankers are not as legally sophisticated as you might think. When you go to open a bank account, the banker is not going to be a lawyer. The bank will likely have application forms that ask for the name of the company's president and treasurer. It's easier to simply have a president open the account than engage in a debate over whether a president is required or not in your state of organization.

Another reason to have officers is that it helps when dealing with customers and vendors. When you tell a customer that you are the president of your company, the customer understands and knows that the president is the boss, with authority over all the other employees. On the other hand, if you tell the customer you are the "managing member," he or she will not necessarily understand that term, even though it would be legally accurate.

A further reason for an LLC to have officers is that it helps employees understand and follow your organization's internal hierarchy. It helps establish roles and responsibilities. Again, "president" means "boss": employees will know what a president is and what a president does. Also, if you create vice president or other officer positions, you can reward employees by placing them into those positions. This may serve to motivate employees.

The following discussion outlines the common types of officers for LLCs, with a brief description of each position. Remember, however, that you may need only a president and a secretary and also that you can create any officer's job description to fit your LLC's needs.

A good operating agreement will empower an LLC to have a president, a secretary, and a treasurer/chief financial officer. These are the three core officer positions that state LLC laws tend to require. The operating agreement may authorize the board of managers to appoint a chairperson of the board of managers, one or more vice presidents, and one or more assistant secretaries or assistant treasurers. This flexibility may prove useful in later years.

For example, a long-standing president who no longer wishes to devote full-time energies to the LLC but who still is of value to the LLC could be designated chairperson of the board of managers. Similarly, a valued employee could be named as a vice president or assistant secretary without significantly changing his or her job responsibilities. This form of recognizing your employees could be invaluable in promoting goodwill among your key employees.

Officer Job Descriptions

Chairperson: If there is a chairperson of the board, he or she ordinarily presides over managers' meetings. Like all officers, the chairperson can perform any other duties assigned by the board or operating agreement. If your LLC's board has only one manager, then that person is the chairperson.

President: The president is usually the chief executive officer of the company, responsible for managing day-to-day operations. If there is no chairperson, the president presides over managers' and members' meetings. Occasionally, this position is "president and chief executive officer." In other LLCs, president and chief executive officer are separate offices, occupied by different individuals.

Vice President: The vice president, if any, does what most vice presidents do—fills in when the president is unavailable. Vice presidents also can have specifically designated duties, such as a "Vice President of Marketing." Unlike the president of the United States, corporate vice presidents do not automatically become president if the president dies or is removed from office.

Secretary: An LLC secretary is not a clerical position. The secretary is responsible for maintaining required LLC records, such as minutes, member lists, and financial records. Many LLC secretaries record minutes of managers' and members' meetings. Secretaries also send out notices of such meetings when required by the operating agreement. They conduct elections at members' meetings and track such things as voter eligibility, proxies, and vote tabulations.

Treasurer/Chief Financial Officer: The treasurer or chief financial officer keeps and maintains books of account, including records of assets, liabilities, gains, losses, and other financial and tax information. The treasurer, sometimes called the chief financial officer, may or may not be involved with the daily recording of financial entries for the LLC. Bookkeepers or company-employed accountants usually perform these tasks, but the treasurer would oversee them.

Assistant Secretaries or Treasurers: The usual reason to have an assistant secretary or an assistant treasurer is that the LLC has grown too large for one person to perform all the required tasks. For example, many documents require the signature of the company president or vice president and a secretary or assistant secretary. If an LLC has offices in a number of locations, it is time-consuming to ship documents around to find people who can sign them. As a result, each location may employ persons who are named as vice presidents or assistant secretaries. Modern transmission services, such as telecopy machines and overnight delivery, reduce the need to have LLC officers at each business location.

Becoming an Officer

LLC officers are appointed by the board of managers and serve at the pleasure of the managers. Officers can be terminated at any time by the managers, with or without cause. If termination is in breach of an employment agreement between the LLC and the officer, the LLC may be liable for damages, but the officer may still be removed.

Small LLCs often have very few members and managers. So, it is not uncommon for an LLC to have one person who is the sole member, sole manager, and president. Prudence dictates that an LLC have at least a second person to serve as secretary, because this officer is charged with witnessing the signature of the president.

These tasks are typically within the scope of an officer's authority:

- Manage the LLC from day to day
- Hire and fire employees

- Negotiate and sign contracts
- Deal with customers and vendors
- Maintain the LLC's records

Indemnification and Insurance for Managers and Officers

The ULLCA and other limited liability company acts permit an LLC to indemnify its managers, officers, employees, and agents under certain circumstances. This is an important concept. Without indemnification, your LLC could have a difficult time attracting competent and qualified officers and managers. This is especially true for outside managers, whose only connection with the LLC is that they serve on the board of managers.

Indemnification is a legally enforceable promise to reimburse an officer or manager for expenses, claims, fees, and/or judgments incurred by him or her. Assume that an officer or manager is sued and, as a result of the lawsuit, has a judgment entered against him or her that he or she pays. If the officer or manager is eligible for indemnification, the LLC would reimburse his or her costs, expenses (possibly including legal fees), and judgment paid. Articles and operating agreements may limit the type of expenses or costs that can be reimbursed or limit the aggregate amount of the reimbursement.

Indemnification is optional; except in rare instances, LLCs need not provide for it. If indemnification is available, managers and officers must act in good faith and reasonably believe that their conduct is in the best interest of the LLC. If indemnification is permitted, it includes all costs, expenses, or liabilities, including any attorneys' fees.

Under the ULLCA, your LLC is required to indemnify any officer or manager who is brought into a claim solely because he or she is an officer or manager and not because of any active wrongdoing on his or her part. To be eligible, an officer or manager must be successful in his or her defense of the claim. No indemnification is permitted an officer or manager if the claim proceeding determines that the officer or manager is liable to the LLC or the manager or officer is charged with receiving an improper personal benefit.

To further protect your LLC and its managers, officers, and employees, the LLC should acquire insurance. There are many different types of insurance available to meet most risks faced by modern businesses. A good insurance agent, like an accountant and a lawyer, is a valuable and necessary part of your business team.

Insurance can help you meet the needs of your business through liability insurance (coverage for claims against the LLC resulting from its acts), fire insurance, health insurance for employees, errors or omissions insurance (to protect against employee theft or other dishonesty), and officers and managers insurance. Various forms of life and disability insurance are also available to fund stock redemptions or to provide money for recruiting and hiring a replacement for a key employee who dies.

Members

Members are the owners of the LLC. In a member-managed LLC, members operate the LLC just like a partnership. In a manager-managed LLC, members vote to elect managers and members vote on fundamental matters, such as mergers, dissolutions, and major asset purchases. In certain situations, such as a merger or a sale of assets, members may be able to demand that an LLC purchase their shares.

As a general rule, members are not liable for the debts and responsibilities of the LLC; however, this rule is not absolute. As you will learn in Chapter 12, members who dominate and control LLC activities increase their exposure to personal liability for LLC acts.

Unlike officers and managers, members ordinarily owe very little duty to the LLC or fellow members. Increasingly, however, large members owning a controlling interest of an LLC are required to avoid activities intended to oppress the voting rights of minority share interests.

Although members may avoid personal liability, it remains important to distinguish the capacity in which one acts. In small, closely held LLCs, the same individual is often a member, an officer, and a manager, so it's crucial for that person to know which hat he or she is wearing when acting for or on behalf of the LLC.

Principles of Agency Law

If you do business in the LLC form, you and the persons with whom you do business need to know who can act on behalf of the LLC. This is vitally important to your LLC because an LLC can act only through its agents. To understand the importance, you need to know some basic principles of *agency law*.

An *agent* is a person or entity that performs an act for or on behalf of another person or entity, known as the *principal*. For example, the real estate broker who sold your house acted as your agent and you were the principal. Sports and entertainment figures hire agents to negotiate lucrative contracts for them. Your business lawyer and accountant act as your agents for all matters for which you retain their services.

Agents are not always individuals. Partnerships and LLCs can also be agents.

In most instances, agents have the authority to act, authority that comes from the principal. In the case of an LLC, the authorization usually comes from the board of managers or the president. As you will see, not all acts taken on behalf of an LLC are authorized, yet some unauthorized acts by LLC employees or consultants may still be binding on the LLC.

Express or Implied Authority

Without question, anyone authorized by name or office to perform an act on behalf of the LLC has authority. This is known as *express* authority.

When the LLC seeks to borrow from a bank, the board of managers will customarily pass a resolution authorizing the president to negotiate the loan within certain parameters defined by the board and to sign off on the loan documents. The resolution should use language such as "John Doan, company president," rather than authorizing merely "John Doan" or the "company president."

A person or agent with express authority normally has the *implied* authority to perform all acts necessary to carry out the express authority.

Apparent Authority

A more dangerous type of authority for LLCs and others is *apparent* authority. Apparent authority is based on the perception of persons dealing with the LLC.

For example, an LLC's president is presumed to have authority to perform acts that are related to the LLC's ordinary business. A salesperson for that same LLC would not ordinarily have any apparent authority to perform any act on behalf of the LLC.

Apparent authority can exist even when express authority has been withdrawn.

For example, John Doan was employed as purchasing agent for your LLC. John switches jobs within the LLC and is no longer involved in purchasing. The LLC should notify its suppliers that John Doan is no longer authorized to purchase items for the LLC. Without this notice, John Doan still retains apparent authority to purchase on behalf of the LLC and bind the LLC.

Apparent authority may exist as the result of prior dealings or a course of business. For example, if your LLC has always paid for shipping services ordered by your warehouse clerk, it is reasonable for the shipper to conclude that the shipping clerk is authorized to perform this task. If this changes, you should notify the shipper.

Similarly, determine whether the individuals with whom your LLC does business are, in fact, authorized to act. You may request a copy of a board resolution authorizing the specific action or a letter from the company president indicating that a particular agent has authority to bind the business.

Ratification Authority

The final type of authority is called *ratification* or *estoppel* authority.

Technically, this is not a form of authority, since this is the result of events that occur after a transaction. For example, your LLC's board of managers could approve the unauthorized purchases made by John Doan in the preceding example, thereby ratifying the purchases. For ratification authority to apply, the board must be made aware of all of the terms and conditions of the transaction. The LLC could also use the goods and thereby be precluded from later challenging the purchases on grounds that the purchases were unauthorized.

Expert Tip

Language in your business contracts stating that an agreement is not binding on the LLC until executed by the LLC's president will eliminate many agency problems, so long as the president is in fact authorized to execute that particular agreement.

Final Thoughts on the Players

There are many hats worn in the LLC world and many roles to be played. In small businesses, it isn't uncommon for one person to serve as organizer, promoter, manager, officer, and member.

Which hat you're wearing at any point may determine your exposure to personal liability. Promoters are generally personally liable for all of their activities, whereas members are usually not liable to outsiders for claims against the LLC. Any blending of LLC roles is a factor that courts and administrative agencies will consider when deciding whether to impose personal liability on LLC managers, officers, and members.

It is important that, whatever role you are filling, you hold yourself out to others as acting on behalf of the LLC. Equally important, make certain that those with whom you do business know who has authority to obligate your LLC. If that authority should change, notify these businesses of the change immediately to avoid disputes down the road.

PART THREE

Handling Ownership and Ownership Units

CHAPTER 6

LLC Ownership and LLC Stock

In this chapter and the next, we will address issues surrounding the ownership of your LLC. Every business has one or more owners. We will analyze how ownership in your LLC works in a legal sense and how it works on a practical level. We will cover how to issue ownership to the company's founders and how to issue ownership to subsequent owners joining your business. We will also address how to transfer ownership from one party to another and how to extinguish ownership.

Before we begin to discuss LLC ownership, we'll need to discuss terminology for LLCs and corporations, which we mentioned briefly in Chapter 1. Company ownership is an ancient concept and the terminology and methodology are rooted in corporations, not in limited liability companies. So, there are some conceptual and language differences we'll need to touch on.

A corporation issues shares of stock to its owners as part of the organization process. Shares of stock represent the ownership of the corporation; shareholders are the owners of a corporation. LLCs, on the other hand, issue *membership units*, *membership shares*, or *members' interest*. There are also lesser-used phrases, such as *percentage interest*, *percentage share*, or *LLC share*. All of these phrases are legally and technically acceptable. The ownership methodology and terminology of LLCs are more akin to those of partnerships, where the ownership is expressed in terms of *percentage interest* or *percentage share*, rather than in a defined number of shares of stock. In the business and legal world, you might hear the phrases *LLC stock* or *equity*. Those phrases are not necessarily incorrect: they are just a bit awkward in the context of LLCs. Throughout this book, we use several terms for LLC shares.

There is one very important fundamental difference in how ownership is *counted* in LLCs and in corporations. In corporations, the owners own a *numerical* amount of *shares*. For example, I might own 150 shares of Pizza in a Cup Corporation. LLCs do not issue shares; they issue *percentage interests*. I would own a 15 percent interest in PizzaOnline, LLC.

If I won 150 shares of Pizza in a Cup Corporation, that number tells me nothing of my percentage interest in the corporation; that depends on the number of shares the company has issued. If Pizza in a Cup has 3,000 shares outstanding, for example, I would own 5 percent of the corporation.

Shares are a particularly corporate concept and the notion of shares does not fit with the methodology and logic of LLCs. There is one rare exception to the general rule that LLCs do not issue shares. That exception is that rarely some larger and highly capitalized LLCs issue *units* to investors; these units are counted much like shares in a corporation would be. But again, units can always be expressed as percentage interests, just like shares. Thus, it would probably just be easier and certainly more normal to manage your LLC with percentage interests rather than with units.

Equity, Ownership, Stock, and Securities Laws

Securities laws are the state and federal laws that govern the offering, issuance, and transfer of ownership in companies. The term "security" is a formal legal term for any of the following: stock, equity interest, partnership interest, and LLC membership, as well as bonds, stock options, and a wide range of other investment instruments. So, when corporations issue shares of stock, when partnerships issue partnership interests, and when LLCs issue membership interests or shares, they are all issuing securities.

Both federal and state governments regulate securities through a complex array of laws and regulations. They control and regulate both the offer to sell and the purchase and sale of securities. You should consult with an attorney who works extensively in securities law to help you with securities law questions. The following discussion highlights some points you should know.

Why Are There Securities Laws?

Most securities laws trace their origins to the Great Depression of the 1930s. Large fortunes and family savings were lost by millions who invested in the largely unregulated stock of the early 20th century. Congress responded to the Great Depression with the Securities Act of 1933 and the Securities and Exchange Act of 1934. Securities laws require that securities be registered with the Securities and Exchange Commission and/or state securities departments prior to their offer or sale or that companies obtain an exemption. The rules are hopelessly technical and require strict compliance. All securities laws contain anti-fraud provisions designed to promote full and fair disclosure of all material information relevant to an underlying company. There are no exemptions from the anti-fraud provisions.

Securities laws compel full and accurate disclosure of all material terms of a proposed securities offering. Information about the persons promoting the offering, the business of the issuer, the proposed use of funds, and financial details is provided so that an investor can make a rational and informed decision about whether or not to invest.

In practice, many offering circulars amount to little more than a long list of risk factors and reasons why someone should not invest in the security. Nonetheless, securities are bought and sold each day.

What Is a Security?

As mentioned above, the term "security" is broadly defined to include notes, stock, treasury stock, preorganization subscriptions, voting trust certificates, lease or investment contracts, and certificates of interest or participation in oil, gas, or mining titles. (Loans are generally excluded from the definition of securities if the loans are documented by a promissory note or loan agreement. The sale or exchange of promissory notes is a sale or exchange of securities. If in doubt, it is probably a security.) More to the point here is that LLC interests are a security.

What Does Registration of Securities Involve?

Registration is a formal process by which an issuer—an LLC or any other entity proposing to sell securities—provides the federal or state securities agency with information about the company, its business, its officers and managers, and the use of proceeds to be raised as well as the marketing plan and detailed financial information. Much of this information will be contained in a prospectus or offering circular, which is included as part of the registration materials. Registration can be a time-consuming and expensive process. You will need a securities attorney to assist you in this process. To learn more about the laws governing securities or for examples of registration forms for securities, visit the web site of the Securities and Exchange Commission at *www.sec.gov*.

Are There Any Exemptions from Registration?

If the securities regulation seems overly burdensome and alarming, remember that the owners of a company are nearly always free to invest in their own enterprise without concern for securities laws. It is only when an LLC seeks *outside* investment that the rights of investors must be considered. In other words, the securities laws won't apply when you invest in your own company.

Because registration is so burdensome, our securities laws allow for exemptions for smaller offerings and some intrastate offerings. Generally, the less money involved and the fewer persons to whom the securities are offered, the more likely an exemption is available. The most notable and useful exemptions are for "private placements." A private placement is simply an offering and/or sale of securities of a limited amount made to a small number of private individuals.

Common exempt transactions include the following:

- Sheriff's sales or other court-approved sales
- Preorganization subscriptions involving a limited number of investors, usually a maximum of 15 to 25
- Sales to institutional investors, such as banks or insurance companies
- Sales pursuant to federal or state securities regulations that outline the private placement of securities

To learn more about state securities laws, you can check with the securities regulation department of your state or the state where the stock is being offered or sold. Make these inquiries before taking any investment monies or offering any membership interests for sale.

How Does an LLC Issue Ownership to Founders and Outside Investors?

Small companies often issue ownership and stock in stages. In almost all cases, the first round of stock goes to the founders—*founders' shares*. Founders often pay a pittance for their ownership, less than what follow-on investors pay for ownership. Smaller companies might have only one round of *equity issuance*— a round of equity (ownership interest) issued to one or more founders. Larger companies that ultimately wind up on the national securities exchanges will go through dozens of offering rounds, ending with their initial public offering.

A corporation or LLC promoter will often locate prospective outside investors. In a small business, the promoter is usually the founder and the prospective outside investors will include friends and relatives of the founder. If these investors wish to purchase company equity, the company and the investor sign a contract called a *subscription agreement*, similar to the sample equity subscription agreement found at the end of this chapter. The term *subscription* comes from the word *subscribe*, which means to enter into a contract to invest in a company. The equity subscription agreement is an irrevocable offer to purchase shares; it is not effective until the LLC is formed and the LLC management accepts the subscription.

> ## Definition: Friends and Family
>
> In the early stages of small business formation, seeking investment from close friends and family is so common that the terms "friends and family offering" and "friends and family round" developed to describe this common early investment stage.

The subscription agreement will set forth a particular price for a particular slice of ownership. For example, 1 percent of an LLC's ownership might be offered for $1,000. Of course, the founders never offer 100 percent of a company's ownership—to do so would mean that the founders would retain zero ownership. The founders will offer 10 percent, 20 percent, or as much as 80 percent of their company to investors, depending on the needs of the company and the wishes of the founders. Of course, if the founders sell more than 50 percent of the company's ownership to outside investors, the founders lose their voting control of the company and will operate at the whim of their investors. For this reason, most founders try to retain more than 50 percent of the company ownership at all times.

The price at which company ownership is offered and sold is fixed by the LLC managers, at their discretion. By a written resolution, the LLC will authorize one or more members or managers to issue a certain percentage of interest shares to one or more parties in exchange for payment of a stated sum of money. Equity can also be issued for property; in that case, the managers set the value being assigned to the property. Absent fraud or other unusual circumstance, the manager's determination of value is conclusive and not subject to second-guessing by disgruntled minority owners or the courts.

Can Membership Be Sold to Different People at Different Prices?

This is a common question in company building. The answer is mixed.

First of all, as a company (whether corporation or LLC) grows, it will bring in new owners periodically. Typically, the founders are the first owners; other investors buy ownership after the LLC has developed a bit. Just as typical is the stepladder pricing of ownership: founders pay a pittance for their shares and follow-on investors pay a premium. Take Apple Computer as an example. Its founders acquired tens of millions of shares in the late 1970s at par value, about one-tenth of a cent per share. Several years later, the initial public offering purchasers paid $22.00 per share. As time passed, the price of ownership rose. This example illustrates the completely common and completely legal practice of changing the price of ownership as time passes.

In this example, the founders (who retained some voting power and influence in Apple's affairs) would not have been within their rights to purchase discounted ownership for themselves *at the same time* as they were offering shares to the public at $22.00. If Apple sold discounted stock to anyone, especially insiders with control, whoever purchased shares at $22.00 could either go to court to rescind the discounted stock purchases or demand at the next shareholders' meeting that the management rescind the discounted insider sales.

The key is timing: each offering should be a distinct event, with a beginning and an end. Each offering can begin at a new price. This is fairest to investors and legally sound.

After the managers have passed the authorizing resolution, the LLC's secretary (if one is appointed) or a manager should deliver a copy of the authorizing resolution to each new member. Because stock certificates are rarely used in LLCs (and certainly unnecessary), the resolution can serve as evidence of ownership in the LLC.

The following sample resolution illustrates an LLC action whereby the managers of an LLC issue membership interests to an individual and to another LLC. Note that the two ownership grants in the resolution differ slightly. In the first membership grant, the consideration given to the LLC is cash. In the second membership grant, the consideration given to the LLC is services.

RESOLUTION OF THE MANAGERS OF ALLERGY IMMUNOLOGICAL TECHNOLOGIES, LLC TO ISSUE MEMBERSHIP SHARES TO NEW INVESTORS

The undersigned, who constitute the appointed Managers of Allergy Immunological Technologies, LLC, a California LLC (the "LLC"), acting pursuant to Article III of the operating agreement of the LLC, and pursuant to the California LLC Act, hereby adopt and approve the recitals and resolutions set forth below, which shall have the same force and effect as if adopted and approved at a duly held meeting.

The purpose of this resolution is to issue membership shares of the company.

RESOLVED, that the LLC has entered into subscription agreements and received investments in cash and services from various parties. The LLC therefore must issue membership interests in connection with the subscription agreements.

1. Issuance of membership interest to Dave Marker, Sr.
The LLC and the following party:

Dave Marker, Sr.
701 Riford Road
Glen Ellyn, IL 60604

are parties to a subscription agreement dated on or about 8/31/07. Pursuant to the agreement, the LLC shall hereby issue 13 percent of its membership interest in consideration for cash of $22,000.00.

2. Issuance of membership interest to Dave Marker Ventures, LLC.
The LLC and the following party:

Dave Marker Ventures, LLC
223 Williams Road, Suite 103
Mooresville, NC 28117

are parties to a consulting agreement dated on or about 8/31/07. Pursuant to the agreement, the LLC shall hereby issue 13 percent of its membership interest in consideration for consulting services of $22,000.00.

> RESOLVED FURTHER: That all membership shares issued by this resolution shall be sold without the publication of any advertising or general solicitation.
>
> RESOLVED FURTHER: That all membership shares issued by this resolution shall be sold and issued only under exemption from both federal and state securities laws: the officers and managers of this LLC shall take such action as may be necessary or desirable to effect such exemption, and the LLC's membership shares shall be issued in accordance with the conditions thereof.
>
> Witness our Signatures to be effective on: 8/31/07
>
> _____
> Bob Emmett
>
> _____
> Larry Emmett

What Can Be Accepted in Payment for Equity?

Membership interests may be granted only if something of value is given in return. Money or property is always an acceptable form of payment for membership interests. If the LLC is willing to accept your prize hog in exchange for a membership share, the LLC may do so. Past services are almost always acceptable as well. For example, TonoSilver, LLC can issue a 5 percent or 10 percent ownership interest in the LLC to you in exchange for your computer programming services. However, the exchange of a future promise to pay money or the promise of future services for equity is not allowed in most states. Typically, the aggressive, pro-corporate states like Wyoming, Nevada, and Delaware allow LLCs to issue ownership for future services, and the pro-minority shareholder states like New York and California do not. You should check with an attorney or review your state's LLC act if your LLC intends to receive anything other than cash, property, or past services in exchange for membership interests.

Are Stock Certificates or Unit Certificates Required?

Briefly, no. First of all, as mentioned earlier, stock and stock certificates are for corporations, not LLCs. Even so, stock certificates are an abstraction: some people think stock is akin to currency, but it is merely *evidence* of ownership, more akin to a diploma certificate, for example. In fact, in several states, including Delaware, stock certificates are not even legally required as evidence of ownership in a corporation. And so, unit certificates for LLC ownership are not required and your LLC will suffer no fault for failing to issue certificates.

What is required, however, is a well-maintained and accurate *ownership ledger*. An ownership ledger can be called by several names: *transfer ledger, membership ledger, equity ledger, percentage ownership ledger,* or *LLC ledger.* An ownership ledger is simply a written table showing the names of an LLC's owners and the percentage interest held by each. The ownership ledger also records transfers and other dispositions of an LLC's membership shares. Responsibility for maintaining the ledger usually vests with the LLC's secretary, if one has been appointed.

Here is a sample ownership ledger below. It shows an original issuance of ownership to Peter Wilson and John Wilson of 65 percent and 35 percent, respectively. A few years later, John Wilson transfers his ownership to his daughter, Deirdre, and his 35 percent is reduced to zero.

Date of Original Acquisition of Ownership Interest	Owner Name	Percentage Interest	Disposition of Shares (transferred or surrendered stock certificate)
1/1/2003	Peter Wilson	65%	
1/1/2003	John Wilson	~~35%~~ 0%	On 6/1/2007, owner transferred his ownership to his daughter, Deirdre Wilson.
6/1/2007	Deirdre Wilson	35%	

Characteristics and Classes of Membership Interests

Membership interest, like stock in a corporation, is personal property. It can be bought, sold, mortgaged, given away, or disposed of in the same way as any other personal property—subject, of course, to the ever-present securities laws and regulations.

Membership interest also creates rights for its holder. These rights arise by virtue of the member's ownership and through state law, both statutory law and case law. A member of an LLC has a right to vote, a right to inspect the books and records of the LLC, a right to the equal division of dividends and assets of the LLC, and a right to insist that the operating agreement and articles of organization of the LLC be followed.

These ownership rights, however, can be restricted if the membership of the LLC is divided into multiple classes in a manner like a corporation—and if the newly admitted member of the LLC is advised at the time the ownership is granted. In most LLCs, the articles of organization authorize the issuance of one class of membership—common membership with voting rights—and the members vote according to their membership interests. So, a 60 percent owner can outvote a 40 percent owner. Some corporations have common voting stock and additional classes of preferred stock. Similarly, LLCs can have a class of voting membership and a preferred class of membership with rights and preferences that differ from the voting membership.

Although multiple classes of ownership are more common with corporations and especially with larger organizations, LLCs are also allowed to create multiple classes of membership. Secondary classes of membership appear in infinite varieties. However, all classes of membership can be broadly categorized into two groups: common and preferred.

Preferred membership interest is a class of membership that is secondary to common membership. It often carries no voting rights. It typically entitles its holder to a monetary priority or preference over the voting classes of membership; this is by far the most common use of preferred ownership in both corporations and LLCs. The practical use is simple: the founders and operators of an entity hold the voting class of ownership and the preferred membership owner is the investor who brought the bulk of the capital to fund the enterprise. Preferred membership interest might entitle the holder to priority in receiving dividends and, if the entity is liquidated, asset distributions. As such, the preferred membership owner will have the right to be paid back from his or her initial investment before the founders enjoy the right to share in substantial profits. In other words, the common membership holders bear the full risk of the entity's failure: if the business goes bust, the preferred membership owners will have distribution and dividend preference, so they get paid first and then the common membership holders get anything that's left over.

Preferred membership interest can have other characteristics: although usually nonvoting, it can be voting and even supervoting. Supervoting preferred membership interest entitles the holder to greater voting power than a company's other class or classes of ownership. Many states allow the authorization and issuance of supervoting membership. Such stock can have ten times voting power, 100 times voting power, or 1000 times voting power: there is no legal limit in states that allow it. Supervoting membership interest is a powerful device for whoever wishes to maintain voting control of a LLC. Of course, new investors tend to frown on current owners enjoying unassailable majority control. It all depends on your needs.

Expert Tip

A powerful device for maintaining control of a LLC is supervoting preferred membership interest, in a state that allows it, such as Nevada or Delaware. Here's how to do it. When you draft your articles of organization, authorize a common membership interest and a supervoting preferred membership interest—but indicate clearly that "the supervoting membership interest shall enjoy, as a class of interest, 80 percent of the total voting power of the LLC on all matters, while the common membership interest shall enjoy 20 percent of the total voting power of the LLC." With this device, the holders of the supervoting membership will always enjoy 80 percent voting power. A warning: this device is sophisticated and you should seek the help of an attorney to use it.

Expert Tip

Without a rich or passive investor, one class of voting common membership is probably all your LLC will require. Remember, you can always amend your articles later to accommodate investors who wish to have additional rights or preferences.

If you own an LLC membership interest, you enjoy the right to participate in the LLC's activities as an owner. Your participation can be nearly passive or very active, depending on the LLC. At a minimum, all members enjoy the right to vote for managers and to approve fundamental LLC changes. Membership includes another important right: the right to participate on a pro rata basis in dividend distributions made periodically or distributions made pursuant to dissolution of the LLC. This right to participate, however, may vary among classes of ownership. If an LLC has multiple classes, usually one class enjoys a right to dividends and distributions in preference to other classes. The other classes get what remains after the classes with priority enjoy their distribution.

What Characteristics Should You Give Your LLC Membership Interest?

The answer to this question depends largely on your current and future needs, how badly your LLC needs the cash or other property to be invested, and the bargaining strength of the prospective investor. For example, if you require only a small equity investor, you may not need to surrender significant voting control of the LLC: you can simply issue a small amount of voting membership to the investor. Or, your investor may have particular interests, such as an immediate return on his or her investment, so he or she might desire preferred membership interest, which would pay a fixed dividend over time and perhaps offer a preference on liquidation.

Where Are Stock Characteristics Described?

If you wish to create different classes of ownership with different rights or privileges, you will designate and describe the classes in your LLC operating agreement. This is an important difference between LLCs and corporations— corporations must designate all classes of stock in their charter document, the articles of incorporation. This gives LLCs an important advantage, because amending an LLC operating agreement is easier than amending a charter document, which requires a filing with the secretary of state and a filing fee.

Expert Tip

Don't issue multiple classes of ownership unless you have a clear need. Consider this decision carefully. Multiple classes of ownership create a lot of complexity, increase operating costs, and are usually appropriate only for larger entities. My clients often ask me to create and issue multiple classes of ownership when it really isn't necessary. Nearly as often, they later regret that they did not take my advice to authorize only one class of ownership.

Put yourself in the shoes of a prospective investor. What will he or she require to put money at risk in your LLC? The answer may involve some combination of a fixed return in the form of preferred membership interest, some voting rights (certain classes of ownership can vote on some LLC issues, but not all), and some ability to compel redemption or conversion from one class of ownership to another.

Contract Law Applies

The issuance of ownership creates a contractual relationship between the LLC and its owners. Your LLC is bound by its articles of organization and its operating agreement to act consistently with the dictates of these governing documents. If the governing documents grant certain rights or preferences for a class of the LLC's owners, the holders of that class of ownership are entitled to receive those benefits. An important right is the right to receive dividends; we'll explore that next.

Dividends

A *dividend* is a periodic distribution of cash made to shareholders of a corporation or owners of an LLC, usually out of the net earnings and profits, on a pro rata basis to the holders of the class of ownership entitled to the dividend. Sometimes accountants and lawyers call dividends *distributions*. The term "distribution" is broader than "dividends" and generally includes dividends and one-time payments, such as liquidating distributions made when a company is dissolved.

Generally, the authority to declare a dividend or distribution is vested in the LLC's managers. However, they can never declare a dividend if the LLC lacks sufficient net earnings and profits; declaring a dividend in that financial situation is deemed to violate the rights of creditors. A distribution must come only from profits. The managers' discretion to declare dividends also depends on the rights and privileges of the classes of ownership. If an LLC has only one class of ownership, then statutory and common law rules will apply and the managers will have wide latitude to declare distributions from an LLC's profits. If, however, the LLC has a preferred class of ownership with special dividend rules, the managers may be obligated to issue dividends to the holders of the preferred class. Again, however, no distribution can be made if the LLC lacks sufficient net earnings and profits. Also, the LLC managers must treat all holders of the same class of ownership equally. Dividends must be paid on a pro rata basis to all members of the same class and not just to certain members. However, the LLC managers can treat holders of different classes of shares differently. For example, the managers could declare a dividend for holders of a nonvoting class of common shares but not for a voting class of common shares.

How Are Dividends Declared?

To authorize the declaration of a dividend, the LLC managers pass a resolution. The resolution will also state that a dividend or distribution will be paid. It will set a record date. A record date determines which shareholders or owners are eligible to receive a declared dividend or capital gains distribution. Only owners as of the record date are entitled to share in the distribution or dividend. The resolution will also set a pay date, a date that falls after the record date.

RESOLUTION OF MANAGERS OF TONOSILVER, LLC DECLARING DIVIDEND

RESOLVED, that the managers of Tonosilver, LLC, hereby declare a regular annual dividend of $14.00 per 1 percent membership interest in the LLC, which shall be paid on 6/1/08, to the LLC members of common stock on the record date of the close of business on 5/1/08.

Witness our Signatures to be effective on: 5/15/08

_____

Bob Emmett

_____

Larry Emmett

A cash dividend is expressed either in terms of a certain amount of money per percentage of membership (e.g., $100 per 1 percent of membership) or by an aggregate sum, which is then divided pro rata among all of the membership (e.g., $10,000 to be distributed pro rata to the LLC membership).

Expert Tip

If you purchase an LLC membership interest from an individual, your purchase agreement should provide that you are entitled to any dividends that are declared or paid following the closing of the sale. There may be a gap between the time you acquire the shares and the time the corporate records are revised to show you as a record holder. If a record date is established during this gap, the seller would likely receive the dividend, not you.

How Are Dividends Taxed and Can I Pay Myself in Dividends?

Cash dividends are taxable income for the owner who receives them; distributions are taxed the same way. However, because of tax law changes put in place in 2003, dividends are taxed at a maximum rate of 15 percent. Income, on the other hand is taxed at a maximum rate of 35 percent. If a light just went off in your head, you have correctly identified a common tax-saving device: if you, as an owner, take some of your company's profit in dividends rather than a salary, you can reduce your tax burden. And dividends offer another tax advantage beyond a lower tax rate: dividends are not subject to Medicare and Social Security taxes.

But be warned. First, the IRS knows this trick, and if you don't pay yourself a reasonable salary, they will call you on it and assess you additional taxes and a penalty. If you are working at the business full-time, you should be earning a reasonable salary: it's not considered reasonable to take all your earnings as dividends. Second, and very important, if you wish to avail yourself of this tax-saving device, you absolutely must secure the help of a qualified, experienced tax attorney or accountant.

What Are Cumulative Dividends?

Cumulative dividends are simply dividends that accumulate from quarter to quarter or year to year if they are not paid according to the terms of the cumulative preferred ownership under which they are granted. Unlike dividends on common membership that the LLC can pay out to owners under its discretion, dividends on cumulative preferred membership shares are an obligation, regardless of the earnings of the company. The unpaid accumulated preferred membership dividends must be paid before any common stock dividends are paid.

Pre-emptive Rights

Pre-emptive rights protect the interests of members by enabling them to maintain their percentage of ownership by pre-empting future sales of membership to third parties. Pre-emptive rights operate like a right of first refusal. If an LLC proposes to issue additional membership to new investors, current members have a right to acquire their pro rata share of the new issue. For example, if you own 10 percent of TonoSilver, LLC and the LLC proposes to issue a new 25 percent membership interest to a new investor, you would enjoy the right to acquire 10 percent (your pro rata share) of the new issue, or 2.5 percent of the LLC's ownership. Your percentage ownership would thus remain at 10 percent.

Stock Transfer Restrictions

One characteristic of LLC membership is that it is semitransferable property. Members can sell, mortgage, pass to heirs, or give away their ownership. For smaller businesses, however, several factors make membership shares less than fully transferable:

- There is usually no public market for small closely held LLC membership.
- Securities laws restrict the offer for sale and sale of stock and other securities. These restrictions severely limit an LLC member's ability to offer the stock publicly.
- It's hard to locate people interested in buying less than a controlling interest of the LLC. Very few investors will wish to buy a minority interest in a LLC unless the shares are highly liquid, as is the case with publicly traded companies.
- Even if a controlling interest is for sale, many purchasers will simply purchase the assets of the LLC and not interest in it. By acquiring a membership share, the buyer automatically assumes all the LLC's assets and liabilities, including unknown liabilities. Wiser buyers typically acquire all or part of an LLC's assets.
- Many LLC owners voluntarily enter into agreements that limit their ability to transfer shares. This is especially true for smaller businesses where LLC owners are active in the day-to-day operation.

Miscellaneous Stock Concepts

The following discussion covers a potpourri of stock-related concepts and defines terms that you are likely to encounter.

Basis. Basis is an important tax concept. It is used in determining gain or loss when an asset is sold. In the case of membership interest, basis is generally what you pay for your membership interest plus any additional capital contributions that you make to the LLC. Basis can also be decreased. For example, if a deduction or loss item passes through the LLC to you, individually, your basis will be decreased by the amount of that deduction or loss, but never to below zero. The concept can get painfully complicated, so consult with your personal tax advisor.

> ## Online Resource
>
> To get IRS forms and explanatory publications, visit *www.irs.gov/formspubs*.

Sample Equity Subscription Agreement

THESE MEMBERSHIP SHARES ARE OFFERED SOLELY TO ACCREDITED INVESTORS (PERSONS OR ENTITIES OF SUBSTANTIAL MEANS WHO MUST MEET STRICT AND SIGNIFICANT FINANCIAL QUALIFICATIONS AND CAN AFFORD A COMPLETE LOSS OF THEIR INVESTMENT). FOR MORE INFORMATION ON QUALIFICATION AS AN ACCREDITED INVESTOR, PLEASE READ THE SECTION ENTITLED "ACCREDITED INVESTORS" IN THE BODY OF THE MEMORANDUM OF WHICH THIS SUBSCRIPTION AGREEMENT IS A PART.

Instructions to Subscription Agreement

a. Investors wishing to subscribe to purchase membership shares of TonoSilver, LLC should complete and sign this Subscription Agreement.
b. CAREFULLY REVIEW THE MEMORANDUM OF WHICH THIS SUBSCRIPTION AGREEMENT IS AN EXHIBIT.
c. Completed Subscription Agreements with completed Investor Questionnaire and payment should be returned to:

TONOSILVER COMPANY, LLC

29893 Paint Brush Drive, Evergreen, CA 92130

d. Payment should be made to "TONOSILVER COMPANY, LLC."

Subscription Agreement

The undersigned hereby offers and subscribes to purchase the number of Membership Shares set forth herein of TONOSILVER COMPANY, LLC ("TonoSilver") at $0.50 per share. The undersigned understands that the Shares are being issued without registration under the Securities Act of 1933, as amended (the "Act"), in reliance upon the private placement exemption contained in Sections 3(b) and 4(2) of the Act, and Regulation D promulgated thereunder, and that such reliance is based on the undersigned's representations set forth below. To induce the Company to accept this subscription and issue and deliver the Shares, the undersigned agrees, warrants, and represents as follows:

1. This offer is subject to acceptance or rejection by TonoSilver in its sole discretion. This

Agreement shall not be binding upon either party until accepted by TonoSilver.

2. The undersigned is purchasing the Membership Shares for his or her own account. The undersigned has not offered or sold a participation in this purchase of Shares, and will not offer or sell the Shares or interest therein or otherwise, in violation of the Act.

3. The undersigned acknowledges that the Membership Shares have been offered to him or her in direct communication between himself or herself and TonoSilver, and not through any advertisement of any kind.

4. The undersigned acknowledges that he or she has read all the materials included in the Memorandum, that the offer and sale of Membership Shares to the undersigned were based on the representations and warranties of the undersigned in its Subscription Agreement, and that he or she has been encouraged to seek his or her own legal and financial counsel to assist him or her in evaluating this investment. The undersigned acknowledges that TonoSilver has given him or her and all of his or her counselors access to all information relating to the business that they or any one of them has requested. The undersigned acknowledges that he or she has sufficient knowledge and financial and business experience concerning the affairs and conditions of TonoSilver so that he or she can make a reasoned decision as to this investment in TonoSilver and is capable of evaluating the merits and risks of this investment.

5. The undersigned acknowledges that he or she is able to bear, and understands, the economic risks of the proposed investment and all other risks disclosed in the Memorandum under the caption RISK FACTORS.

6. The undersigned understands the following: THIS SECURITY HAS NOT BEEN REGISTERED WITH THE SECURITIES AND EXCHANGE COMMISSION UNDER THE SECURITIES ACT OF 1933, AS AMENDED (THE "ACT"), IN RELIANCE UPON THE EXEMPTION FROM REGISTRATION PROVIDED IN SECTION 4(2) AND REGULATION D UNDER THE ACT.

7. This Subscription Agreement has been delivered in and shall be construed in accordance with the laws of the State in which the Company is incorporated, which is [INSERT STATE OF INCORPORATION].

8. The Company hereby represents and warrants as follows:
(a) Neither the Company nor a predecessor of the Company; affiliated Company; officer,

director, or general partner of the Company; promoter of the Company presently connected with the Company in any capacity; beneficial owner of 10 percent or more of any class of equity securities of the Company; underwriter of the securities to be offered under this subsection; or any partner, director, or officer of such underwriter has, within five years of the date of this Agreement:

(i) Filed a registration statement that is the subject of a currently effective registration stop order entered by any state securities administrator or the Securities and Exchange Commission;

(ii) Been convicted of any criminal offense in connection with the offer, purchase, or sale of a security, or involving fraud or deceit;

(iii)Been subject to a state administrative enforcement order or judgment finding fraud or deceit in connection with the purchase, offer, or sale of any security;

(iv)Been subject to a state administrative enforcement order or judgment that prohibits, denies, or revokes the use of an exemption from registration in connection with the purchase, offer, or sale of a security; or

(v) Been subject to an order, judgment, or decree of any court of competent jurisdiction temporarily, preliminarily, or permanently restraining or enjoining such party from engaging in or continuing to engage in any conduct or practice involving fraud or deceit in connection with the purchase, offer, or sale of any security.

(b) The Company made no advertising or general solicitation in any way in connection with this offering.

(c) The Company is not a development stage company with no specific business plan or purpose or a development stage company that has indicated that its business plan is to engage in a merger or acquisition with an unidentified company or companies or other entity or person.

(d) The Company hereby makes this offering in good faith reliance that the offering qualifies for an exemption from registration under Rule 504 of the General Rules and Regulations promulgated under the Securities Act of 1933.

(e) The Company shall file a notice on Form D in the form prescribed by rule of the Securities and Exchange Commission, not later than the day on which the Company receives from any person an executed subscription agreement or other contract to purchase the securities being offered or the Company receives consideration from any person therefor, whichever is earlier.

(f) No compensation was or will be given or paid, directly or indirectly, to any person in connection with this offering and sale of the Shares.

9. THE UNDERSIGNED IS AN "ACCREDITED INVESTOR" UNDER THE INVESTOR SUITABIL-ITY STANDARDS IMPOSED BY RULE 501, SUBSECTION (A), OF THE GENERAL RULES AND REGULATIONS PROMULGATED UNDER THE SECURITIES ACT OF 1933. FURTHERMORE, THE UNDERSIGNED HAS SUCH KNOWLEDGE AND EXPERIENCE IN FINANCIAL AND BUSINESS MATTERS THAT IT IS CAPABLE OF EVALUATING THE RISKS AND MERITS OF AN INVESTMENT IN THE COMPANY AND HAS THE FINANCIAL ABILITY TO BEAR THE ECONOMIC RISKS OF ITS INVESTMENT.

Subscriber:

I, _____, hereby offer and subscribe to purchase _____ number of Membership Shares set forth herein of TONOSILVER COM-PANY, LLC at _____ per share. I have enclosed a check for the amount of the subscription written to TONOSILVER COMPANY, LLC.

_____
Subscriber Signature

_____
Subscriber Name

_____
Subscriber Address, City, State, ZIP

_____
Subscriber Entity Type (if not an individual)

TONOSILVER COMPANY, LLC

The above and foregoing Subscription accepted this _____ day of _____.

By: _____

its: _____

Sample Ownership Transfer Ledger

Date of Original Acquisition of Ownership Interest	Owner Name	Percentage Interest	Disposition of Shares (transferred or surrendered stock certificate)

Agreements to Control Ownership and Management

A common concern among founders of a small business is ensuring that the ownership or management of an LLC will never fall into the hands of outsiders—unless the present owners or managers consent or approve. Because LLC ownership is property, it can be passed in a will, sold, or given away.

Imagine a case where three LLC owners work to build a business. One of the owners declares bankruptcy and the bankrupt owner's membership share is awarded to a creditor in the bankruptcy proceeding. Now, the two partners are faced with an unwelcome and possibly hostile new owner, one who does not share their goals of building up the LLC into a thriving business.

To prevent this possibility, it is possible for founders to exert control over the manner in which LLC interests are passed to third parties. The device that members use for this purpose is the operating agreement. Remember: the operating agreement dictates the LLC's internal operating rules. In a sense, the operating agreement acts as a type of contract between or among the members of an LLC. As such, the operating agreement can dictate all manner of rules with respect to the manner in which membership interests are passed to third parties.

Restricting Admission of New Members

In most small LLCs, the founders will wish to maintain some control over the admission of new owners. Because all owners of an LLC enjoy both rights and voting power, a hostile or problematic owner can be a nuisance to other owners. A new owner can enter an LLC in either of two ways—by purchasing a membership interest by making a capital contribution or by receiving a transfer of ownership from an owner. Either way, in a closely held enterprise like a small LLC, the current owners will nearly always wish to maintain some control over membership.

By way of example, if we examine the short-form operating agreements at the end of Chapter 3 (for both member-managed and manager-managed LLCs), we can show how current members would admit a new member. If an LLC's operating agreement is silent as to the manner and quantity of vote required of the current members to approve a new member, then the vote required is a simple majority—over 50 percent. That's fundamental business law. The short-form operating agreements at the end of Chapter 3 are silent about voting to admit new members through a purchase of membership interest, so a simple majority vote is sufficient.

However, if the short-form operating agreements were silent with respect to the admission of a new member via transfer from a member, then the current members could not control the admission of the new member. This is because each member's LLC ownership interest is a transferable property right.

To control that possibility, the short-form operating agreements state that "no Member may assign such person's Interest in the Company in whole or in part except by the vote or written consent of the other Members owning more than fifty percent (50%) of the Interests." This "admission approval clause" operates to require approval by majority membership vote of any persons who might be admitted to the LLC through transfer.

You may wish to have admission to your LLC be more restrictive. You can restrict it by requiring a higher percentage vote of the current members to admit new members. In theory, an LLC's operating agreement can require a unanimous vote to admit new members—but that may be overly restrictive, since requiring a unanimous vote gives any member, no matter how small his or her interest, veto power over admitting a new member. A requirement of a two-thirds vote strikes an appropriate balance. The long-form operating agreements that appear in the supplemental forms in Appendix A require a two-thirds majority vote for admitting new members to the LLC.

With respect to the LLC selling new membership interest, the long-form operating agreements state that "the Members may admit additional Members to the Company only if approved by a two-thirds majority in interest of the Company Membership." Similarly, the long-form operating agreements require a supermajority vote for the admission of anyone seeking admission via a transfer of a current member's interest. The clause states, "In order to be permitted, a transfer or assignment of all or any part of a Membership Interest must have the approval of a two-thirds majority of the Members of the Company."

State LLC laws and the Uniform Limited Liability Company Act allow members to restrict admission to the LLC. If the members do not approve the new member following the transfer, he or she can be prohibited from admission to the LLC and his or her membership has no legal effect and is therefore worthless. He or she does not own an interest in the LLC and does not enjoy any rights as an owner. The would-be new member might lobby the current members to gain support for a membership vote. But without a two-thirds vote, he or she will not be admitted to the LLC.

Expert Tip

A word of warning is in order. Operating agreements are powerful. They can become complicated and involve complex legal issues, including tax and securities laws. These agreements should be carefully tailored to fit your situation. Work closely with your business attorney and accountant to put together an operating agreement that will work best for you.

Expelling Members from the LLC

In some instances, a member or members may wish to remove another member from the LLC. When a member is removed from the LLC, it is called an expulsion. There are three ways a member can be forcibly expelled from an LLC; Utah's LLC statute clearly describes each:

§ 48-2c-710. Expulsion of a member.

A member of a company may be expelled:

(1) as provided in the company's operating agreement;

(2) by unanimous vote of the other members if it is unlawful to carry on the company's business with the member; or

(3) on application by the company or another member, by judicial determination that the member:

(a) has engaged in wrongful conduct that adversely and materially affected the company's business;

(b) has willfully or persistently committed a material breach of the articles of organization or operating agreement or of a duty owed to the company or to the other members under Section 48-2c-807; or

(c) has engaged in conduct relating to the company's business which makes it not reasonably practicable to carry on the business with the member.

The LLC's operating agreement governs the rights of members to expel a co-member. Of course, not all operating agreements contain an expulsion clause. If the operating agreement contains no expulsion clause, the members must turn to state law to determine the manner in which a member can be expelled. In Utah, as we can see from the statute cited above, expulsion requires a unanimous vote of the membership. In some states, the LLC statute contains no provision for expulsion of a member by vote of the other members. If the LLC cannot meet the voting requirement imposed by either the state LLC act or the operating agreement, the LLC has two choices: as a last resort, the LLC can either close its doors and dissolve or go to court and ask a judge to expel the undesired member. But a judicial expulsion will require some proof that the undesired member caused some harm to the LLC or breached his or her obligations in some way.

The two short-form operating agreements in Chapter 3 do not contain clauses regarding expulsion of members. If you use either of them for your LLC, you'll need to look to your state's LLC statute if you ever wish to expel a member. If your state's LLC statute is silent, you may be forced to either dissolve your LLC or go to court and ask a judge to expel the undesired member. However, the long-form operating agreements in Appendix A contain an expulsion clause. The expulsion clause reads, "Any Member may be expelled from the Company upon a vote of two-thirds majority in interest of the Company Membership." The practical effect of this clause is that in an LLC with three equal members, two members always enjoy the power to expel a third.

Buying Back the Interests of Departing Members

As we have learned, a member can depart an LLC in several ways. The member may leave voluntarily. The member may be expelled by other members. The member may die and attempt to leave his or her ownership share in a will or trust. Regardless of the means by which a member leaves the LLC, he or she or his or her heir is entitled to receive the value of the LLC membership interest that he or she is giving up. As stated earlier, the other members have the right to refuse to admit a new member. If they do not approve the new member, then they must purchase the interest of the departing member. It would not be fair to deny the departing member the right to sell or bequeath his or her interest and at the same time fail to compensate the departing member or his or her estate for that property interest.

Consequently, the procedure by which ownership interests are valued becomes very important. Valuing a departing member's interest can be thorny. As you might imagine, the issue is most appropriately addressed in the operating agreement.

Free Resource

learnaboutlaw.com maintains online question-and-answer forums operated by several practicing attorneys. Follow the links to "forums"; there you can post questions and practicing lawyers will answer them at no charge or you can search the list of topics.

When a Member Seeks to Transfer His or Her Interest

The mechanics of evaluating and purchasing a transferring member's interest work as follows.

The member who wishes to make the transfer gives notice. A common procedure—and the procedure employed in the long-form operating agreements in Appendix A—is that a member who wishes to transfer his or her interest in the LLC to an outside party provides a written notice of that intent to the company.

The company has the option to purchase the share. The LLC has an option, a first right of refusal, to purchase the transferring member's interest according to the method of valuation set forth in the operating agreement. The LLC can either exercise the option to purchase the membership interest (in which case the membership interest is redeemed by the LLC and it extinguishes, thereby increasing the relative ownership of all remaining members) or choose not to elect to purchase the membership interest.

The member's share is valued. If the LLC elects to purchase the member's share, it must be valued. The LLC operating agreement sets forth a valuation procedure that we'll discuss below.

The members vote to approve or not. If the LLC elects not to purchase the membership share, the members must still approve the transfer to a third party. If they approve the transfer, the LLC takes on the new member and moves forward. If the members do not vote in favor of the transfer, the outgoing member can either choose to remain in the LLC or withdraw from the LLC. The next section outlines the procedure for valuing a departing member's share.

When a Member Departs from the LLC

As an alternative to transferring membership interest, the member may also consider simply leaving the LLC. Again, the departing member is entitled to compensation for his or her membership interest. The mechanics of evaluating and purchasing a departing member's membership interest work as follows. (Again, the procedure outlined here is the procedure set forth in the long-form LLC operating agreements that appear in Appendix A.)

The member who wishes to depart from the LLC gives notice. First, the departing member gives notice to the LLC that he or she wishes to leave the LLC membership.

Current members enjoy pro rata purchase option. This gets a little tricky. Each current member has the right to purchase the portion of the departing member's ownership that corresponds to the current member's present ownership percentage. If they choose to do so, here's how it works. Let's suppose that a 25 percent member departs, leaving two members, one with 50 percent ownership and one with 25 percent ownership. If the 50 percent owner and the 25 percent owner both choose to exercise the purchase option, then they share the option in the proportion to their current ownership: the 50 percent owner purchases 66.66 percent of the departing member's interest and the 25 percent owner purchases 33.33 percent of it. It's complicated, but fair: it distributes the option among the remaining members in proportion to their current percentage interests, thereby maintaining the balance of ownership. The purchase price is the value set forth in the LLC operating agreement.

The LLC purchases the remainder. If the current members do not purchase the departing member's interest, the LLC is forced to purchase his or her interest—or dissolve the LLC. The purchase price is the value set forth in the LLC operating agreement.

Valuing a Member's Interest

The purchase of a departing member's interest requires the valuation of that interest, whether the member's interest is purchased by the LLC or by the other members. There are four common methods for valuing LLC membership interest:

- Agreed value
- Book value
- Capitalization of earnings
- Appraisal

Most sophisticated operating agreements provide a means of pricing an outgoing member's share. The short-form operating agreements in Chapter 3 have no such provision; however, the long-form operating agreements in Appendix A include a method for doing so.

The method of valuation set out in the long-form operating agreements is an annual agreed valuation. Each year, at the annual meeting of members, the members agree to a value. This method of valuation will not work for all LLCs, but it has some benefits. First, this method is much simpler than the alternatives (discussed below), all of which require the input of an accountant and a fairly thorough analysis of the LLC's business performance. Second, this method offers a great degree of certainty: the members will always know, at any time, what their membership interest is worth. Third, because of the certainty, the members are left with no room for arguing over the valuation, as would be the case with some of the more subjective valuation methods. The disadvantage to the agreed value method is that if the members fail to agree on a valuation, they'll have to amend the operating agreement to adopt one of the other valuation methods.

A common method used to value a company is the book value method. Book value is the net asset value of a company, calculated by adding its tangible assets and subtracting its tangible liabilities. In other words, book value is the value that would be the bottom line of a balance sheet. Book value ignores future business, goodwill, and other intangible indicia of value. The advantage to book value as a valuation method is that it is simple and certain. A disadvantage is that the calculation requires the input of an accountant.

The supplemental LLC forms in Appendix A include an alternate paragraph (LLC Form 3: Alternative Provision for Use in Long-Form Operating Agreements: Book Value Method of Valuation) that can be used in a long-form operating agreement to adopt a book value method of valuation.

Another common method used to value a company and hence the value of a departing member's interest is the capitalization of earnings method. This is a means of valuing a business by determining the net present value of expected future profits. Unlike the agreed value method and the book value method, the capitalization of earnings method relies on forecasting, subjective estimates of future profits, and a little luck. The calculation is relatively simple: an accountant begins with the net profit for the previous fiscal year and applies a multiplier to that profit—usually two, three, four, or five. The resulting number is the net present value. So, a business that earned $100,000 in its last full fiscal year might be worth $300,000 or $400,000, depending on the multiplier. The multiplier is arbitrary; multipliers between three and five are most commonly used. This method follows the theory that a business's value is simply a reflection of the profit it earns. This method of valuation is used quite commonly in operating agreements and outright purchases of businesses. A big advantage to this method is that it's very simple and certain. In fact, you don't need an accountant to do the calculation.

The supplemental LLC forms in Appendix A include an alternate paragraph (LLC Form 4: Alternative Provision for Use in Long-Form Operating Agreements: Capitalization of Earnings Method of Valuation) that can be used in a long-form operating agreement to adopt a capitalization of earnings method of valuation.

Finally, another common method used to value a company and hence the value of a departing member's interest is a simple appraisal. The members agree to appoint an appraiser. If they cannot agree to a single appraiser, then each member appoints his or her own appraiser (this gets expensive) and the appraisers work together to establish a value. If the appraisers cannot agree on a value, the appraisers jointly select another appraiser who makes the final determination. Or alternatively, the members can jointly agree to name an appraiser when the operating agreement is executed. The problem with an agreed appointment is that the appraiser may move away, leave the business, or pass away.

I strongly prefer not to use an appraisal to value a business because it is the most costly method and is not likely to be significantly more accurate than book value or capitalization of earnings. Of course, neither book value nor capitalization of earnings gives much weight to intangibles such as a trade name or goodwill in the marketplace. And so, the best reason to adopt an appraisal method for valuing a business is if the value of the business is closely tied to intangibles.

Included in the supplemental LLC forms in Appendix A is an alternate paragraph (LLC Form 5: Alternative Provision for Use in Long-Form Operating Agreements: Appraisal Method of Valuation) that can be included in a long-form operating agreement to adopt an appraisal method of valuation.

LLC Formalities: Meetings, Minutes, and Resolutions of Managers and Members

PART FOUR

Manager's Meetings

LLCs are often touted as superior to corporations because they require "no formalities" or "no annual meetings." Certainly, LLCs do not bear the same burden of formalities as corporations. However, to say that LLCs need follow no formalities at all is untrue and irresponsible. Chapter 12, "How to Effectively Manage Your LLC to Maximize Liability Protection," explains how formalities are important to owners and managers of LLCs and how failing to follow formalities can have devastating consequences for owners of LLCs.

First, LLCs must follow formalities. Second, LLCs that go beyond the minimum formalities will enjoy "ironclad" liability protection. The LLC is decades old now and, as it moves into its adolescence as a business form, court decisions are starting to emerge that reveal that courts are more than willing to "pierce the LLC veil" to reach the owners behind an LLC if the LLC fails to maintain a vigilant separateness between entity and owner. So, you should read this chapter and Chapters 11 and 12 to learn how liability protection and LLC formalities go hand in hand. As you progress through Part Four, keep in mind the following principles regarding formalities:

You can and should always observe greater formalities than the statutory minimum. Your state's LLC statute will likely impose a very low degree of formality upon your entity. However, experienced lawyers know that judges may impose a higher standard on businesspersons whenever necessary—and judges have done so in recent LLC veil-piercing cases. If you follow a higher standard of conduct, you'll be safer in the long run.

Regardless of the statutory minimum, you must also consider the dictates of your LLC's operating agreement. This is a formal set of rules that your LLC has set for itself. If you and your co-owners fail to operate according to your agreement, a clever plaintiff's lawyer or regulator can use that failure.

Never make your operating agreement so burdensome that you cannot meet its requirements. Ideally, your operating agreement should impose a greater degree of formality on the LLC than the statutory minimum: that reflects care. Similarly, your conduct should always exceed the standard imposed by your operating agreement: that reflects a greater degree of care.

You are always free to formalize and document any LLC action, even if it does not necessarily warrant a formal vote of the managers or members. A smart lawyer once gave me some great advice when I asked her how to build a case for the possible firing of a problem employee. She said, "Fatten the file," meaning that my client should pepper the employee's file with conduct reports and any other ongoing information to support my client's case. You can "fatten" your LLC's minute book and resolution file by over-observing formalities. For example, if you hire an employee, call a meeting of managers and record a quick vote.

As mentioned earlier, your LLC may not have managers. If your LLC is managed by its members, then you obviously have no managers and thus you are not required to conduct meetings of managers—the subject of this chapter. A member-managed LLC conducts meetings of members, which we cover in the next chapter.

Most state statutes do not mandate that an LLC's managers meet once a year, but that's the minimum. Your managers should always, without exception, meet at least once a year. The interval is also usually expressed in the operating agreement or it may develop through custom and usage. In no event, though, should the managers meet *less* frequently than the operating agreement dictates. If they do so, they technically fall into noncompliance with their operating agreement. Managers also may meet at special meetings, which can be called anytime for any legitimate purpose.

Annual meetings are the cornerstone of an LLC's formality responsibilities. A court succinctly expressed this principle (in the corporate context, but the lesson is the same) with the quote, "Faithfulness to the formalities is the price paid to the corporation fiction, a relatively small price to pay for limited liability" (*Labadie Coal Co. v. Black*). We discuss the unfortunate effects of failing to follow LLC formalities in Part Five: LLC Lawsuits and Personal Liability Protection. The failure to maintain formalities can lead to a failure of an LLC's liability shield. Smaller LLCs, naturally, probably tend to meet less often than large LLCs, but should still strive to faithfully observe formalities.

It is not enough to hold meetings: the proceedings of meetings should be recorded. LLCs record their proceedings in documents called *minutes of meeting* or, more familiarly, *minutes*.

As an alternative to meeting, an LLC can take action by *written consent*—but only if certain conditions are met. When an LLC takes action by written consent, the LLC simply records the action in a written consent and saves it in the minute book.

The simplest and safest rule is as follows: record everything. It's no more complicated than that. Recording proceedings of annual and special meetings and other decisions in either minutes or written consents is vital to the success of your LLC, particularly with respect to maintaining liability protection. In this chapter, we'll discuss how and why to conduct meetings. Then, in Chapter 10, we discuss in detail how to simply and accurately record LLC decisions and meetings in minutes and written consents.

Is It a Regular Meeting or a Special Meeting?

Managers' meetings are described as *regular* or *special*.

Regular meetings are held at scheduled intervals as set forth in the operating agreement or according to custom and usage. An annual meeting is a regularly scheduled meeting, usually designated in the operating agreement. For example, the operating agreement might provide that the annual meeting is to be held on the second Tuesday in December of each year. Some LLC operating agreements do not require an annual meeting: this is the safest approach if you are not certain your organization will be disciplined enough to conduct meetings annually.

Special meetings are held when matters of particular importance, such as a proposed sale or merger of the business, arise between scheduled meeting dates. Special meetings could also be held to discuss matters raised at a regular meeting that are of significant importance or require greater time for discussion.

Special meetings can be called by anyone authorized to do so by the operating agreement. Ordinarily, any manager or any member should have this authority; however, the operating agreement may authorize additional parties, such as officers, to call a special managers' meeting.

Is Notice of the Meeting Required?

For regularly scheduled meetings, no additional notice is needed unless the operating agreement requires it. In any event, it is recommended that some notice of the time, date, and place of the meeting be provided, to make certain that a sufficient number of managers attend.

Special meetings require notice because they are not regularly scheduled. The operating agreement should specify whether or not the notice must be delivered personally or may be delivered by mail or fax. A time limitation must be honored. For example, the operating agreement may require that written notice of meetings be personally delivered to a manager or deposited in the mail no earlier than 14 days before the meeting and no later than 48 hours (with personal delivery) before the meeting. The sample operating agreement included in this book calls for notice of least ten days prior to the time of the meeting.

Notice requirements can be waived. Matters might arise that require the immediate attention of the managers. By attending the meeting, managers waive any objections to lack of notice, unless a manager states his or her objection at the beginning of the meeting.

Is There a Meeting Agenda?

It is a good idea to develop an agenda for each meeting to help keep the meeting moving, even if the limited liability company act, the articles of organization, and the operating agreement do not require it. Items for the agenda include the following:

- Call to order by the president or chairperson of the managers
- Approval of the minutes from the previous meeting
- The treasurer's report
- Old business (matters carried over from an earlier meeting, including committee reports)
- New business (matters not yet considered by the managers)
- Other new business and matters (items not previously considered and not set forth on the agenda)
- Adjournment

A sample agenda is shown on the next page.

Are Formal Procedures Required?

Most managers' meetings tend to be quite informal, especially for small LLCs. Managers openly discuss issues before them, trying to reach consensus on matters presented. The presiding officer, usually the president or the chair-

---

Sample Agenda for Managers' Meeting

TonoSilver, LLC

Managers' Meeting Agenda

February 14, 2009

1. Call to order and president's report.
2. Attendance/establishment of quorum.
3. Minutes of previous meeting.
4. Treasurer's report.
5. Reports (should be in writing and submitted in advance).
    a. Committee
    b. Managers
    c. Legal/accounting
    d. Others
6. Old business (matters previously considered but unresolved).
7. New business.
8. Miscellaneous news and announcements.
9. Selection of time, place, and location for next meeting.
10. Adjournment.

---

person, must control the tempo and substance of the discussion. He or she ensures orderly discussion by recognizing one manager at a time and not allowing arguments for or against an issue to be repeated.

Any proposal is presented in the form of a *resolution*. To approve a resolution, a manager makes a motion for the approval of a resolution, which is read aloud. The motion must be seconded by another manager. If there is no second, the motion dies. If the motion is seconded, the presiding officer or secretary reads back the motion. Then, the presiding officer asks if there is any further discussion of the motion. Discussions can range from little or no comment to a wide-ranging free-for-all. At the conclusion of the discussion, the motion is reread and the presiding officer asks three questions—All in favor? All opposed? Any abstentions? If the operating agreement requires or the managers agree, a vote could be held by secret written ballot, but this is rare and usually pointless.

Don't bother with secret written ballots unless there's a good reason.

During a discussion, it may become clear that the motion presented is going to fail and equally clear that it could succeed with minor modifications. The presiding officer can permit discussion to continue on the doomed motion, allowing it to fail, and then entertain a new motion containing the modifications. This new motion must be seconded and then discussed.

If the managers approve, the presiding officer could also ask the manager making the initial motion if he or she would consider withdrawing or amending it. If the motion is withdrawn, the process would begin anew for any later motion. If an amended motion is made, it must be seconded and discussed. The vote would be on the amended motion only.

Keep It Simple

The presiding officer bears the burden of keeping things simple. He or she should ensure that every motion is read prior to discussion and again prior to a vote. This procedure should eliminate confusion among the managers.

The managers do not have to approve or disapprove all matters presented to them and may defer an action to a later meeting, refer it to a committee for further study, or request additional information.

Any committee reports or additional information should be provided in advance of the next meeting to allow the managers the opportunity to study the material prior to the meeting. This approach will save time.

What's a Quorum?

A quorum is the minimum number of LLC managers necessary for a valid and binding vote or resolution. Unless the articles of organization or operating agreement require otherwise, a quorum is a majority of the managers. If there are ten managers, at least six are required for the managers to transact business. If there are five or fewer in attendance, the managers can discuss LLC matters generally, but can't authorize or approve any action.

If there are not enough managers in attendance to constitute a quorum, the operating agreement should authorize a majority of those present to adjourn the meeting and reschedule for a later date. As an alternative, the matter could be submitted to the members for approval. This approach may be feasible only when the managers' meeting precedes the annual members' meeting. Otherwise, the LLC will incur the expense of sending out notices to the members.

Expert Tip

Because managers cannot act unless there's a quorum, managers should be surveyed in advance of the meeting to make certain that enough will be present. In addition, modern LLC acts permit meetings to be conducted by conference telephone call, making it easier to ensure a quorum even though one or more managers are physically absent from the meeting location.

Are There Any Voting Requirements for the Managers?

Each manager holds one vote on all matters presented. Each manager must exercise his or her independent business judgment and act in a manner that he or she believes to be in the best interests of the LLC. Because managers are required to exercise their judgment, they may not, unlike members, vote through proxy or otherwise delegate their voting responsibility.

As mentioned earlier, unless the articles of organization or operating agreement impose a more stringent requirement, the affirmative vote of a majority of the managers present at a meeting is sufficient to authorize the matter presented, if there's a quorum. For example, if six managers out of ten are present at a meeting (that's 60 percent, a quorum), an affirmative vote by four of them can authorize action. In this example, a resolution is validly authorized by only 40 percent of the managers.

As you prepare your articles and operating agreement, consider which managers' acts should require a higher percentage or supermajority vote. Remember that with any fundamental change—amending LLC articles, the sale of the business, merger, or dissolution—the members will also have a say. For important changes that are not fundamental—such as executive compensation, purchasing assets of another business, or venturing into an unrelated business opportunity—you may wish to consider setting a higher quorum and/or voting requirement.

What If a Manager Has a Conflict of Interest?

Managers who have a conflict of interest should not vote on matters involving that conflict. The following are examples of conflict situations:

- Executive compensation payable to officers who serve as managers
- Managers or their family members who own property that the LLC seeks to purchase or lease
- Managers or their family members who serve as management to competitors or suppliers

If a conflict of interest arises at a meeting, the presiding officer must determine whether or not there is still a quorum of managers. For example, assume that six of ten managers attend a managers' meeting. One of those managers has a conflict on a matter presented at the meeting. If that manager abstains from voting on that matter, does a quorum still exist? The answer depends in part on whether or not the operating agreement permits the interested manager to be counted toward a quorum. If so, the conflict can be avoided if four of the other managers vote in favor of the matter. If not, the matter must be tabled until a quorum of disinterested managers can be assembled.

Expert Tip

Occasionally, a conflict may disqualify all of the managers or at least enough to prevent approval. In this situation, consider asking the members to approve the transaction.

Can Managers Act without a Formal Meeting?

In short, yes. Modern LLC statutes permit managers to act without having a meeting. If there is no meeting, all managers must sign their written consent to the LLC resolutions presented. We have given a few examples of written consent resolutions, and we will discuss taking resolutions by written consent at length in Chapter 10.

Who Serves as Managers?

Either your articles of organization or your operating agreement will establish the number of managers. The articles may also list the names and addresses of the initial managers, depending on your state. Thereafter, managers are typically elected by members at the annual meeting. If a vacancy occurs on the board of managers, most operating agreements permit the other managers to appoint someone to serve for the remainder of the term of the manager who has created the vacancy.

Expert Tip

Don't designate the number of managers in your articles of organization. If you later need to change the number of managers, you'll be forced to engage in the burdensome practice of amending your articles—you'll have to follow strict formalities, prepare amended articles, and pay a filing fee. You should designate the number of managers in your operating agreement, which is much easier to modify if you wish to make a change later on.

In small LLCs, the owners are often the managers: that's common and acceptable. Larger LLCs, however, sometimes seek out managers who are independent from the owners. Outside managers are useful because they bring expertise from other businesses or walks of life and because they are able to look at the LLC's activities more objectively. Some LLCs pay managers a fee for attending meetings and most will reimburse expenses incurred while traveling to and from meetings.

Manager Liability and the Business Judgment Rule

Managers can be held liable for mismanagement of LLCs that they serve. Courts recognize, however, that in a competitive business environment managers must be allowed wide latitude in fulfilling their duties. Thus, courts are reluctant to question a management decision. This rule, which originated in the context of corporations, is loosely termed the "business judgment rule." It holds that courts will not review managers' business decisions or hold managers liable for errors or mistakes in judgment so long as the managers meet the following standards:

- They were disinterested and independent.
- They were acting in good faith.
- They were reasonably diligent in informing themselves of the facts.

So, how does this rule apply in the real world? Well, imagine an LLC with five owners and one manager. The manager uses LLC funds to make a risky stock investment on a tip from a friend without even checking into the stock. The investment goes sour and causes the LLC to lose $50,000. This is a common hypothetical discussed in law school classes—the "reckless investor/manager."

In a state that follows the general business judgment rule (every state will have a slightly different rule), the manager would most likely be judged liable to the LLC or the owners. Losing money on an investment does not cause liability: the liability stems from the manager's degree of care or culpability in deciding to make that investment. Because he was not reasonably diligent in informing himself, he would likely be found liable for his error.

Final Thoughts on Managers' Meetings

The managers govern the general operation of the LLC, set goals, issue directives for the officers and employees to carry out, and meet at regularly scheduled intervals during the year. Managers' meetings must be properly called and the requisite notice provided. For the managers to take any action, a quorum must be present.

Managers must exercise due care and be careful to disclose all potential conflicts of interest. If a manager has a conflict of interest, he or she may not be eligible to vote on matters involving the conflict.

Modern limited liability company acts permit managers to meet by telephone, video conference, or similar means. Modern laws also permit consent resolutions whereby all the managers can authorize certain actions merely by signing a written resolution.

The following checklist could help you conduct an annual managers' meeting.

Annual Meeting of Managers Checklist

Use this checklist to be sure you conduct your annual meetings properly. If any issues remain unresolved by the end of the meeting, note who will be responsible for resolving them and by when.

Name of LLC: _____

Date and state of organization: _____

Date of meeting and location: _____

Notification procedures:

❏ Notices mailed

❏ Waivers received

❏ Consent resolutions instead of meeting?

Managers present at meeting:

_____

_____

_____

_____

_____

Attorney at meeting: _____

Accountant at meeting: _____

Insurance advisor at meeting: _____

Others present:

_____

_____

_____

_____

Check That Government Reports Have Been Filed

❑ Date(s) of last corporate state and federal tax returns: _____

❑ Have state franchise tax and annual reports been filed? _____

❑ Have annual pension/profit-sharing returns been filed with the IRS?

_____

❑ Any other filings to be made? _____

Check General LLC Operations

Review Minutes Book

❑ Are all minutes properly recorded? _____

❑ Are any additional minutes needed? _____

❑ Have mailing affidavits or waivers been filed? _____

❑ Have officers been appointed? _____

Review all employment agreements. _____

Check insurance coverages. _____

Check Ownership Records

❑ Is ownership ledger current? _____

❑ Have new members signed operating agreement? _____

Review Financial Status

Check financial statements for prior year-end, current year-to-date, and budget projections. The treasurer is responsible for gathering these reports, but they can be prepared by others, inhouse or outside.

Income, expenses, and salaries: _____

Cash available for pension/profit sharing? _____

Net profit: _____

Any dividends to be declared? _____

Review accounts receivable and uncollectible items—Any changes in collection required? _____

❑ Approve how to invest cash reserves.

❑ Review status of loans to officers or managers. _____

❑ Other? _____

Review Pension/Profit-Sharing Plan

The pension plan administrator provides this information. Since it is complicated, you may want to invite the administrator to join the meeting when this is to be discussed.

❑ Verify that new employees have been properly enrolled.

❑ Verify that beneficiary designations have been filed.

❑ Verify proper payment, allocations, and reports made for terminating employees.

❑ Verify dates for contributions.

❑ Review investment policy.

❑ Review investment gains, income, and losses.

❑ Review procedures to ensure that plans are being operated properly.

❑ Annual reports prepared.

❑ Are any amendments to plans required?

Review Other Fringe Benefit Programs

❑ Review and update insurance programs.

❑ Disability

❑ Health

❑ Life

❑ Review status of vacation, holiday and leave, and reimbursement policies.

❑ Any bonus payments required? _____

❑ Other? _____

Discuss Any Major Events

❑ Acquisitions or purchases?_____

❏ Sales or leases? _____

❏ Litigation? _____

❏ Changes in banking relationship? _____

❏ Loans or financing? _____

❏ Resignations or removals? _____

❏ Other? _____

Sample Waiver of Notice of Board of Managers' Meeting

The undersigned, a manager of TonoSilver, LLC, hereby waives notice of the meeting of the managers of TonoSilver, LLC to be held on _____ (date), 20____.

_____

John Doan, Manager

Date: _____

Members' Meetings

As explained earlier, LLCs can be managed by members or by managers. So, your members' meetings will come in two varieties. In a manager-managed LLC, most of its responsibilities are delegated to the managers; it leaves only core ownership responsibilities to the members, duties such as appointing managers, approving major changes to the LLC's line of business, and approving the sale of the LLC. In a member-managed LLC, in contrast, the members have all responsibilities and authority. The most helpful analogy to illustrate the difference between manager-managed and member-managed LLCs is that manager-managed LLCs make decisions like corporations and member-managed LLCs make decisions like partnerships.

The preceding discussion introduced concepts such as the importance of formalities, meeting notice, quorum, agenda, and procedures. We will not repeat those basic topics in the same detail in this chapter. As you read this chapter, you may wish to refer back to the preceding chapter and the sample operating agreement in Chapter 3.

Is Your Meeting Annual or Special?

An annual members' meeting is scheduled every year and involves all of the members. Unlike corporations, LLCs generally are not required by law to hold annual members' meetings. But, as discussed in the preceding chapter, LLCs that observe a greater degree of formality than the minimum imposed by law provide greater liability protection for their owners and less regulatory risk. In short, annual meetings are good governance.

Members commonly take care of the following matters at their annual meetings:

- Election of managers (for manager-managed LLCs)
- Review and approval of the LLC's annual budget
- Review of the LLC's past-year fiscal performance
- Discussion of the LLC's overall financial condition and the need for any capital contributions from members

This list is not exhaustive: members can discuss and decide nearly anything at their annual meeting. It all depends on the needs of the LLC—every company is different.

Any meeting that is not a periodic meeting is a special meeting. Special meetings are typically held for specific purposes, to take care of issues that arise. For example, the members of an LLC might call a special meeting to discuss the admission of a new member. If the LLC requires that the members approve the admission of any new member, the opportunity to admit a new member would necessitate a vote. Any matter for which a special meeting could be called could also be handled at an annual meeting; the only difference is timing. Special meetings are used when "something comes up" between annual meetings.

Who Can Call a Special Meeting?

The operating agreement should answer this question. In our sample operating agreements, the following persons can call a special meeting of members: "any Manager or a Member or Members owning, in the aggregate, at least 10 percent of the Interests." The preceding clause is fairly customary; the 10 percent minimum membership requirement ensures that members with very small holdings cannot call meetings, unless they can enlist the support of other members who agree that a meeting is warranted. By requiring a certain minimum percentage, you can be reasonably certain that any matter for which a special meeting is called is not frivolous.

Is Notice of the Meeting Required?

Notice is generally required for annual and special meetings of members. Even if it's not required, it's always a sound practice. Limited liability company acts often provide that notice of the meeting be given no more than 60 days or less than ten days prior to a meeting.

Notice of a meeting is usually prepared by a manager or an officer. Notice may be delivered personally or by first class mail to all members of record on the record date. As explained earlier, the record date is important: it's a date set by the LLC for the purpose of determining which members are eligible to vote at a meeting..

The record date can be crucial if a member transfers his or her shares close to the meeting date. Depending on the record date that is set, he or she may or may not be entitled to receive notice and to vote. If the managers do not set a record date, the limited liability company act or the operating agreement may do so. For example, the operating agreement could declare that the record date for any special meeting of members is 70 days prior to the scheduled meeting date. If no record date is designated, it would be the date the request for the special meeting is signed by the members requesting it.

A members' list should be prepared as of the record date, showing the name and address of each member as of that date and each member's percentage of ownership as of the record date. Percentages can change as frequently as members enter and exit an LLC. If different classes of ownership have been issued, the members' list should also identify the class of shares held and indicate whether or not that class has voting rights.

The members' list should be made available for inspection and copying by any member or his or her agent. Members might use the list to contact other members, solicit proxies, or simply to check its accuracy. The list should also be available at the members' meeting.

Expert Tip

It is good practice to send a notice of a meeting to each member of record, whether or not that member has voting rights. Include in the notice a description of all matters that you know will be presented. For special meetings, the voting is restricted to those topics described in the notice. In contrast, at annual meetings voting can cover issues not specified in the notice. For annual meetings, include in your notice the language, "and such other matters as may be properly presented."

Whoever prepares, mails, and/or delivers the notices should also prepare an affidavit attesting to the mailing or delivery of notices. This affidavit should be retained as a record. A sample form of notice and a sample affidavit attesting to the mailing of the notice are provided on the following pages.

Members can waive notice of a meeting. They do this by signing a written waiver of notice or by attending and participating in the meeting without voicing an objection. A sample form of waiver of notice appears at the end of this chapter.

Is a Quorum Required?

Yes, a quorum is required for a members' meeting. However, there's a common misconception about members' meetings and quorum.

To illustrate, TonoSilver, LLC has three members. John owns a 20 percent interest, Joan owns a 25 percent interest, and Jane owns a 55 percent interest. As those percentages show, no other membership interest is issued and outstanding. TonoSilver, LLC's operating agreement defines a quorum to be "a majority of the issued and outstanding membership interest." Notice that it is not "a majority of the members." So a quorum would not exist if at least two of the three members attend, unless one of the two is Jane. A quorum would exist only if Jane is present, because John and Joan together own only 45 percent of the issued and outstanding membership interests of TonoSilver, LLC. If Jane is not there in person or by proxy, there is no quorum. If only Jane attends a meeting, she constitutes a quorum, by reason of owning 55 percent membership interest.

The articles of organization or the operating agreement may require that a higher percentage than a simple majority of the issued and outstanding voting membership interest be present at a meeting to constitute a quorum.

Members, unlike managers, can be represented by others (a proxy) and need not be personally present at the meeting for quorum and voting purposes. We'll discuss proxies and proxy voting just below.

Who Can Vote at a Members' Meeting?

Any member owning voting membership interest on the record date can vote—assuming that the membership is in a class of ownership with voting privileges. Generally, a member can cast one vote for each percentage point of membership interest he or she holds. Members owning a nonvoting membership interest may be entitled to vote on any matters that would affect their class. For example, if a motion was proposed to amend the articles to eliminate nonvoting preferred membership interest, the holders of those membership interests would be permitted to vote on that issue—and that issue alone. Fundamental changes to the LLC (such as shutting it down) may also require the vote of nonvoting membership interest, depending on the dictates of state law.

What Is a Proxy?

A proxy is an authorization by a member giving another person the right to vote the member's membership interest. Proxy also refers to the document granting such authority. Proxy rules are typically outlined in state law and an LLC's operating agreement. Members may appoint a proxy to vote their membership interest at members' meetings.

To be effective, a proxy must be in writing and must designate the person or persons authorized to vote on behalf of the member. A designation of "my brother" is insufficient. "My brother Robert L. Doe" would be adequate.

Proxies are generally effective for up to 11 months unless earlier revoked; the length of effectiveness depends on the state law where the LLC is organized. Proxies are easily revoked. The last proxy in time prevails over any earlier proxy appointments. A proxy can also be revoked if the member shows up at the meeting and decides to vote his or her membership interest personally. Proxies can also be revoked upon the death or incapacity of a member; however, an LLC can honor a proxy until it learns of the member's death or incapacity.

You may occasionally hear the expression "coupled with an interest" in connection with a proxy. A proxy coupled with an interest is irrevocable because it is linked to an important right or obligation. For example, assume you own a membership interest in TonoSilver, LLC. You need to borrow money to pay off some personal loans. Your good friend Bob agrees to loan you the money, but only if you pledge your TonoSilver, LLC membership interest to him as security for repayment of the loan. Bob asks for an irrevocable proxy to allow him to vote your membership interest until the loan is repaid; he wants to ensure that his collateral isn't run into the ground by poor management. This combination of proxy and pledge is a proxy coupled with an interest. The proxy should state conspicuously on its face that it is irrevocable.

As the number of members grows, the use of proxy voting will become more common. A sample proxy is shown at the end of the chapter.

Can the LLC Reject a Proxy or a Member's Vote?

An LLC can reject the vote of a member or his or her proxy if the LLC has a good faith reason for doing so. For example, if the LLC believes that a signature on a proxy has been forged or the person presenting it can't provide adequate identification, it may reject the proxy. Similarly, if the name of the proxy appears to have been altered, the proxy may be rejected. These situations do not occur commonly.

What Is Cumulative Voting?

Cumulative voting is a technique used by some LLCs in the election of managers. It is intended to protect the interests of minority members by enhancing the ability of minority members to elect at least one LLC manager. Cumulative voting is complicated and applies, if at all, only to the election of managers, if a statement requiring cumulative voting is included in the articles of organization or the operating agreement.

Here's how it works. The articles of TonoSilver, LLC provide for three managers. John, Joan, and Jane are the only members of TonoSilver. John owns a 30 percent membership interest, and Joan and Jane each own a 35 percent membership interest. There are no other issued and outstanding membership interests.

At the annual meeting, three managers are to be elected. If cumulative voting were not mandatory, John would have only 30 of 100 votes, so his ability to retain a seat on the board would be substantially reduced. Without cumulative voting, Jane and Joan could outvote John, because they would use their greater voting power on each manager position individually.

Cumulative voting yields a different result. It gives each member the right to cast three votes (the number of managers to be elected) multiplied by the number of membership interests he or she owns. John would have 90 votes (three multiplied by 30) and Joan and Jane would each have 105 votes (three

---

Expert Tip

For larger boards of managers, you can reduce the impact of cumulative voting by staggering the terms of the managers. For example, each member of a nine-manager board could serve three-year terms, with one-third of the seats up for election each year. Such an approach provides continuity and ensures a carryover of experienced managers.

---

multiplied by 35). The votes can be distributed in any manner the members choose. Thus, cumulative voting gives minority members additional voting power. Presumably, John will cast all 90 votes in his favor to retain his seat on the board.

If cumulative voting applies to the election of managers, the meeting notice must conspicuously say so.

Election Inspectors

Election inspectors are individuals designated by the managers or members to make certain that members' meetings and votes at members' meetings are conducted in accordance with law and the operating agreement. Often a manager or LLC officer serves as the election inspector.

Election inspectors will:

- Determine the validity and authority of proxies
- Determine the existence of a quorum
- Hear challenges to voting rights or proxies
- Count ballots and announce results

Secret Ballots

Most matters presented to the members are determined by a show of hands or voice vote, at least with respect to uncontroversial or uncontested matters. If a matter is contested or controversial, a semi-secret ballot system should be used. Checks must be implemented to ensure that no one votes more membership interest than he or she owns. Because of these checks, the ballot may not be entirely secret. Election inspectors may learn the identity of members casting ballots to ensure that the percentage of membership interest voted is consistent with the percentage of membership interest owned.

If There Is No Quorum or the Meeting Ends with Unfinished Business

This process works equally well for situations where no quorum exists or where a quorum exists but not all business is completed. Adjourn the meeting and announce a time and date when the meeting will reconvene. Your operating agreement should permit a meeting to be adjourned and then continued later. Statutes usually permit this continuation and will not require the LLC to comply with the notice requirements a second time if the reconvened meeting is scheduled to take place within a certain time, generally within 120 days of the original meeting date.

> ## Expert Tip
> By adjourning and then reconvening a meeting later, an LLC can save the time and expense associated with formally calling a meeting and providing notice. The adjourned meeting is not considered a new meeting, but a continuation of the prior meeting.

Your operating agreement should provide that if no quorum exists, a majority of those present can adjourn the meeting and schedule a date to reconvene. Because of its obvious necessity, this is one of the few actions that can be authorized by less than a quorum.

Can Members Act without a Meeting?

Modern limited liability company acts permit members to act without a meeting by using consent resolutions. We covered consent resolutions in the previous chapter in the context of managers. The same issues, principles, and caveats are equally applicable to members.

If the members are all active in the business, consent resolutions may be an expeditious way to dispense with meetings. After all, each member is likely to be keenly aware of what the LLC is doing.

If members are not active in the business, a formal annual meeting is a good way for members to see and meet with management. Officers and managers can explain what the LLC has done over the past year and what its goals are for the coming year. A meeting is also an excellent public relations opportunity.

Consent resolutions are impractical if there are too many members or they're too geographically diverse. Formal meetings will be necessary. The same is true if there are members who tend to disagree with board proposals.

A checklist that will help members conduct their annual meeting is presented at the end of this chapter.

Sample Call for Special Meeting of Members

CALL FOR SPECIAL MEETING OF MEMBERS

To: The President of TonoSilver, LLC

The party or parties whose name appears below, the holder(s) of membership interests entitled to cast not less than 10 percent of the votes of TonoSilver LLC, do hereby call a special meeting of the members of the LLC to be held _____ (date) at _____ (time) for the purpose of considering and acting upon the following matters:

[Insert matters to be considered, such as "A proposal that John Jones be removed as an LLC manager."]

You are directed to give notice of this special meeting, in the manner prescribed by the LLC's operating agreement and by law, to all members entitled to receive notice of the meeting.

Date: _____

_____

_____

_____

Sample Notice of Special Meeting of Members

NOTICE OF SPECIAL MEETING OF MEMBERS OF TONOSILVER, LLC

Pursuant to a call made by members, notice is hereby given that a special meeting of the Members of TonoSilver, LLC be held at _____ (time) on _____ (date) at _____ (address), to consider and act on the following:

[Insert matters to be considered, such as "A proposal that John Jones be removed as an LLC manager."]

If you do not expect to be present at the meeting and wish your membership interest to be voted, you may complete the attached form of proxy and mail it in the enclosed addressed envelope.

Date:_____

_____
President

Sample Notice of Annual Meeting of Members

NOTICE OF ANNUAL MEETING OF MEMBERS OF TONOSILVER, LLC

To: The Members of TonoSilver, LLC

In accordance with the operating agreement of the LLC, please be advised that the annual meeting of members will be held at the principal office of the LLC located at 111 Main Street, Portland, Oregon at _____ (time) , PST, on _____ (day), _____ (date), to consider the following:

1. The election of managers to serve until the next annual meeting of members or until their successors are elected and qualified;

2. [Add any other issues.]; and

3. To transact such other business as may properly be brought before the meeting.

Respectfully submitted,

_____

LLC President

Sample Affidavit of Mailing of Meeting Notice

AFFIDAVIT OF MAILING OF MEETING NOTICE

State of _____, County of _____

The undersigned, being first duly sworn, states as follows:

1. The undersigned is the duly elected and acting manager of TonoSilver, LLC.

2. As manager, the undersigned caused to be deposited in the United States mail, postage prepaid, the meeting notice attached hereto and by this reference incorporated herein, properly addressed and mailed to the persons and at the addresses set forth in the attached list, which is by this reference incorporated herein.

3. The notices were deposited in the mail on _____, 20____.

Date: _____

_____
Manager

Sample Waiver of Notice of Members' Meeting

The undersigned, a member of TonoSilver, LLC, hereby waives notice of the meeting of members of TonoSilver, LLC to be held on _____ (date), 20____.

_____
John Doan, Member

Date: _____

Sample Appointment of Proxy for Annual or Special Members' Meeting

APPOINTMENT OF PROXY FOR [ANNUAL/SPECIAL] MEETING

TonoSilver, LLC

MEMBER: John Miller

PERCENTAGE OF MEMBERSHIP INTEREST HELD: _____

I, the undersigned, as record holder of the membership interest of TonoSilver, LLC described above, revoke any previous proxies and appoint the person whose name appears just below this paragraph in the box to the right as my proxy to attend the [ANNUAL/SPECIAL] members' meeting on _____ and any adjournment of that meeting.

THE BOARD STRONGLY RECOMMENDS THAT YOU RETURN THIS PROXY IF YOU DO NOT

INTEND TO APPEAR PERSONALLY AT THE [ANNUAL/SPECIAL] MEMBERS' MEETING.

The person I want to appoint as my proxy is: _____

The proxy holder is entitled to cast a total number of votes equal to, but not exceeding, the percentage of membership interest that I would be entitled to cast if I were personally present.

I authorize my proxy holder to vote and otherwise represent my interest with regard to any business that may come before this meeting in the same manner and with the same effect as if I were personally present.

I MAY REVOKE THIS PROXY AT ANY TIME. THIS PROXY WILL LAPSE THREE MONTHS AFTER THE DATE OF ITS EXECUTION.

ALL PROXIES MUST BE SIGNED. PLEASE SIGN EXACTLY AS YOUR NAME APPEARS ON YOUR MEMBERSHIP INTEREST CERTIFICATE. JOINT MEMBERS MUST EACH SIGN THIS PROXY. IF SIGNED BY AN ATTORNEY IN FACT, THE POWER OF ATTORNEY MUST BE ATTACHED.

IF YOU REQUIRE ASSISTANCE WITH THIS PROXY, PLEASE CONTACT LLC MANAGER: _____, AT 415-555-1212.

Please sign your name below; if you are signing for a business entity, please state your title:

DATE (IMPORTANT!):_____

_____
Name

_____
Title

Annual Meeting Checklist for Members

Basic Information to Document

Name of LLC: _____

Date and state of organization: _____

Date of meeting and location: _____

Notification procedures:

❏ Notices mailed _____

❏ Waivers in _____

❏ Consent resolutions instead of meeting? _____

Officers at meeting: _____

Attorney at meeting: _____

Accountant at meeting: _____

Insurance advisor at meeting: _____

Members at meeting: _____

Others present: _____

❏ Elect managers

❏ Any changes required for operating agreement or articles? _____

❏ Review membership interest purchase agreement. _____

❏ Any changes required to valuation in membership interest purchase
    agreement? _____

Discuss Any Major Events

❏ Acquisitions or purchases? _____

❏ Sales or leases? _____

❏ Litigation? _____

❏ Resignations or removals? _____

❏ Other? _____

CHAPTER 10

Minutes of Meetings, Resolutions by Consent, and More Paperwork

Articles of organization, operating agreements, member lists, proxies, membership ledgers, meeting notices, minutes, and waivers all constitute a substantial amount of paperwork. As this chapter will show, there's even more.

Keep in mind, however, that good record-keeping and adherence to certain commonsense formalities are important to every successful business. This is true whether your business is a corporation, an LLC, or a partnership. Payroll records, inventory lists, and billing records are examples of the types of records maintained by most businesses.

How important are good business records? They are vital. As you have seen, certain records are available for inspection by members, while others are available for inspection by auditors, including those working for the Internal Revenue Service, state unemployment divisions, and countless other government agencies. Your records are also subject to inspection by parties to a lawsuit involving your LLC. If an auditor is impressed with the thoroughness and accuracy of your records, the audit will be a much less painful experience.

Good record-keeping will also facilitate a sale of your business. Prospective purchasers will want to view your records to decide whether or not to purchase it and to determine the purchase price they will offer. Once again, good records are an indication that the business has been well run. To the prospective purchaser, the risk of hidden liabilities is reduced when records are complete and logically organized.

In the courtroom as well, good record-keeping practices pay off. Properly maintained business records can be admitted into evidence if it can be shown that the records were prepared in the ordinary course of business at or near the time of the event shown in the records. The ability to introduce evidence under the business records exception to the hearsay rule can save time and money in litigation.

Good record-keeping formalities are largely a function of common sense and developing good business habits. As you read this chapter, you will wonder why such commonsense information is included. Yet you will also learn that many business owners ignore these commonsense requirements and end up paying the consequences.

The following discussion covers many unrelated types of paperwork. The common thread is that each type could be important in preserving your LLC's status and shielding you from personal liability.

Recording Meetings of Managers and Members with Minutes

In Chapters 8 and 9, we discussed the importance of managers' and members' meetings. As promised, we will now examine how to properly memorialize your LLC's meetings.

This section applies to both annual meetings and special meetings. Annual and special meetings of members and of managers must be recorded. The written record of the actions taken at such meetings is called the minutes. Minutes are very simple to prepare and are often quite short. We have included sample minutes of the following "core" types of meetings at the end of this section:

- Minutes of Annual Meeting of Members
- Minutes of Special Meeting of Members
- Minutes of Annual Meeting of Managers
- Minutes of Special Meeting of Managers

All meetings are either meetings of managers or members and all meetings are either annual or special, so all of your minutes will fall into one of these four categories. We have also included sample minutes that cover a wider and more unusual variety of LLC actions by written resolutions in Appendix A; more are available by visiting www.learnaboutlaw.com. Keep in mind that you can always convert a written resolution to minutes and vice versa by changing the heading and the boilerplate portions of the text.

What Minutes Should Contain

Minutes of meetings should always contain the following information:

- The nature of the meeting, i.e., members' or managers' meeting, annual or special
- That either the meeting was called by notice or the persons voting waived such notice by executing a written waiver of notice
- Those present at the meeting
- The date, time, and place of the meeting
- The chairperson of the meeting
- Actions taken at the meeting, i.e., election of managers, issuance of membership interest, purchase of real estate, etc.

Legal Requirements for Minutes

One great misconception is that LLC minutes must meet strict legal requirements. That is not necessarily so. Articles of organization and operating agreements must be drafted very carefully. Minutes can be drafted far less formally. The presence of minutes—the fact that they were recorded and maintained—is far more important than the specific language they use.

Minutes should at the very minimum accurately record what took place at the meeting. The model minutes included in this book should meet 90 percent of your needs. When in doubt, simply record in the minutes all actions and decisions in plain, conversational English. The person recording the minutes should sign them, attesting to their accuracy. (There is no need to have each member sign the minutes.)

Let's take a look at some sample minutes and illuminate some important points.

Minutes of Annual Meeting of Members

What follows are fairly typical minutes of an annual meeting of members. For some small LLCs, not much may happen at an annual meeting of members. Typically, an annual meeting of members will address solely the election of managers for the upcoming year.

MINUTES OF THE ANNUAL MEETING OF MEMBERS OF ENVIROTEK, LLC

The members of ENVIROTEK, LLC, held their annual meeting on _____ (date), at _____ (time), at _____ (place).

The following members were present at the meeting, in person or by proxy, representing membership percentage interests as indicated:

      John Jones, 10 percent membership percentage interest

      John Smith, 10 percent membership percentage interest

      John Miller, 80 percent membership percentage interest

Also present were Michael Spadaccini, attorney to the LLC, and Lisa Jones, an employee of the LLC.

The president of the LLC called the meeting to order and announced that he would chair the meeting, that a quorum was present, and that the meeting was held pursuant to a written notice of meeting given to all members of the LLC. A copy of this notice was ordered inserted in the minute book immediately preceding the minutes of this meeting. The minutes of the previous meeting of members were then read and approved. The minutes were then inserted into the minute book of the LLC.

The chairperson then announced that the election of managers was in order. The chairperson called the matter to a vote, noting that each member had nominated himself to serve. Managers were then elected to serve until the next annual meeting of members and until their successors were duly elected and qualified, as follows:

> John Jones
> John Smith
> John Miller

The chairperson then announced a proposal to change the LLC's fiscal year from December 31 to June 30. The chairperson advocated the change because he felt that the June 30 fiscal year would more closely reflect the seasonality of the LLC's sales. While John Smith and John Miller agreed with this point, they noted that the administrative work associated with the change would strain the organization, so they would not support the change. Thus, the matter was not brought to a vote. The chairperson noted that the managers would bring the matter up at next year's meeting, and John Smith and John Miller agreed that was suitable.

There being no further business to come before the meeting, on motion duly made, seconded, and adopted, the meeting was adjourned.

I, the Secretary of the LLC, attest that the foregoing minutes are a true and accurate description of the matters and votes brought before the LLC at the above-captioned meeting.

_____

LLC Secretary

That's it—no more is required, unless of course additional votes came before the members at the annual meeting.

Let's examine the minutes to illustrate a few points. Note that in the preceding minutes there are certain formalities, such as a statement that the meeting was an annual meeting and that notice was made to members and a list of the parties who were present. Beyond such basic formalities, the minutes simply recite what took place. Typically, managers are elected for one-year terms, but your LLC may differ. Your operating agreement will dictate the term for which managers serve.

Minutes of a Special Meeting of Members

Special meetings of members, as we have learned, are not periodic, but are called when some matter of importance arises. The event that triggers a special meeting can be positive, but it is often negative. As an attorney, I attended a few contentious special meetings of shareholders in the corporate context. A common point of disagreement among members, and a common reason for special meetings, is the competency and performance of management. Remember: in manager-managed LLCs, members elect managers to run the companies. As such, their role doesn't typically go much farther than appointing or firing managers.

MINUTES OF A SPECIAL MEETING OF MEMBERS OF ENVIROTEK, LLC

The members of ENVIROTEK, LLC, held a special meeting on _____ (date), at _____ (time), at _____ (place).

The following members were present at the meeting, in person or by proxy, representing membership percentage interests as indicated:

      John Jones, 10 percent membership percentage interest

      John Smith, 10 percent membership percentage interest

      John Miller, 80 percent membership percentage interest

Also present were Michael Spadaccini, attorney to the LLC, and Lisa Jones, an employee of the LLC.

The president of the LLC called the meeting to order and announced that he would chair the meeting, that a quorum was present, and that the meeting was held pursuant to a written notice of meeting given to all members of the LLC. A copy of this notice was ordered inserted in the minute book immediately preceding the minutes of this meeting.

The chairperson then announced that the meeting had been called by John Jones in his capacity as member, as allowed by the operating agreement of the LLC. John Jones had called the meeting to remove the presently sitting manager, Lisa Knowles. John Jones noted that Ms. Knowles had moved out of the state, abandoned her position as manager, and failed to honor her employment obligations to the LLC. The other members agreed and a vote was taken. The vote was unanimous that Ms. Knowles be removed as manager and John Jones be substituted in her place.

There being no further business to come before the meeting, on motion duly made, seconded, and adopted, the meeting was adjourned.

I, the Secretary of the LLC, attest that the foregoing minutes are a true and accurate description of the matters and votes brought before the LLC at the above-captioned meeting.

_____

LLC Secretary

Here again, the regular formalities are noted in the minutes. This sort of special meeting is typical. A manager has abandoned her responsibilities and the meeting was called to replace her.

Minutes of Annual Meeting of Managers

As we have discussed, an LLC should always hold annual meetings of managers: it's a sound practice. However, it may be that the managers have very little to discuss at the annual meeting other than the election of officers—if the LLC has officers. But, even so, you should always hold an annual meeting and minutes should be prepared to memorialize the meeting.

Typically, an annual meeting of managers will address solely the election of officers for the upcoming year. The sample minutes that follow address that typical circumstance.

MINUTES OF ANNUAL MEETING OF THE MANAGERS OF ENVIROTEK, LLC

The managers of ENVIROTEK, LLC held an annual meeting at _____ (time), on _____ (date), at _____ (place) _____.

The following managers were present at the meeting:

John Jones

John Smith

John Miller

Also present were Michael Spadaccini, attorney to the LLC, and Lisa Jones, employee of the LLC..

The chairperson called the meeting to order and announced that the meeting was held pursuant to the operating agreement of the LLC and was held without notice.

It was then moved, seconded, and resolved to dispense with the reading of the minutes of the last meeting.

The managers considered the election of officers to serve until the next annual meeting of managers. The managers unanimously voted to elect the following persons to the corresponding positions:

John Jones, President and CEO

John Smith, Treasurer and CFO

John Miller, LLC Secretary

There being no further business to come before the meeting, the meeting was duly adjourned.

_____
LLC Secretary

The preceding minutes of an annual meeting of managers are typical of 90 percent of all annual meetings of managers. The operating agreement generally establishes that officers be elected at the annual meeting of managers and the preceding minutes address that requirement.

Minutes of a Special Meeting of Managers

Special meetings of managers can typically be called for any purpose. Special meetings are quite common; conducting regular meetings is a sound practice. Our sample operating agreement, which is very typical, states that special meetings of the managers for any purpose may be called at any time. We discussed above in Chapter 8 the sorts of events that would typically trigger a special meeting of managers. Typical minutes memorializing a special meeting of managers follow.

MINUTES OF SPECIAL MEETING OF THE MANAGERS OF ENVIROTEK, LLC

The managers of ENVIROTEK, LLC held a special meeting at _____ (time), on _____ (date), at _____ (place) _____.

The following managers were present at the meeting:

John Jones

John Smith

John Miller

Also present were Michael Spadaccini, attorney to the LLC, and Lisa Jones, employee of the LLC.

The chairperson called the meeting to order and announced that the meeting was held pursuant to the operating agreement of the LLC and was duly noticed by mailing notice to all managers.

The managers then considered the acceptance of resignation of John Jones as LLC secretary. The managers, with John Jones abstaining from the vote, voted to accept the resignation of John Jones.

The managers then considered the appointment of John Miller as LLC secretary. The managers, with John Miller abstaining from the vote, voted to appoint John Miller to the position of LLC secretary.

The managers next considered the acquisition of NEWCORP, LLC by ENVIROTEK, LLC. The managers voted to execute an agreement of purchase of NEWCORP, LLC.

> There being no further business to come before the meeting, the meeting was duly adjourned.
>
> _____
> LLC Secretary

A few points are worth noting here. First of all, of the four classes of meetings (managers or members, annual or special), the class that will vary most widely in scope or purpose is without a doubt a special meeting of managers, because they are responsible for running the LLC and much more likely to encounter significant challenges and decisions as varied as any in business. So, for special meetings of managers you will most likely be drafting minutes ad hoc, without necessarily being able to rely on a perfect model. However, if you simply follow the guidelines outlined herein, you should be able to draft competent minutes.

Our sample minutes just above cover a few separate LLC events. First, an officer is resigning and the managers are accepting that resignation. Then, the managers are appointing a replacement. Note that the officer to be appointed is also a manager and he is wisely abstaining from the vote. Finally, the managers vote to acquire another LLC.

An Alternative to Minutes: Written Consent Resolutions

Under modern business LLC laws, many smaller LLCs have replaced formal meetings with written consent resolutions. A consent resolution or written consent is a written LLC resolution that is enacted by signature of one or more managers or members. It serves as an alternative to a fully noticed meeting. Whoever signs consents to the adoption of the resolution as if the resolution had been formally presented or approved by the managers or, as the case may be, the members, at a noticed meeting.

The general rule states that, to be legally effective, a consent resolution must be signed unanimously by all the managers (if a manager resolution) or unanimously by all the members (if a member resolution). However, there are exceptions to the unanimity rule.

First, some states allow written consent resolutions by members or managers to be made by less than a majority. Second, your operating agreement may specifically allow written consent resolutions to be made by less than a majority. If you cannot determine whether resolutions can be adopted by less than a majority, it's probably just as easy to call a meeting and record the vote by minutes rather than by written consent.

Multiple copies of the consent resolution can be used, eliminating the need to have the signatures appear on the same piece of paper.

Whether member or manager action is the result of a formal meeting or a consent resolution, the action taken should be evidenced by an appropriate entry in the LLC minute book. Most auditors will begin their review of LLC records with the minute book. If the book is up-to-date and contains regular records of manager and member activity, the auditor will be favorably impressed. This good impression may aid the entire audit process.

What types of activity should be recorded in the minute book? Routine day-to-day business activities don't need to be included. For example, if TonoSilver, LLC manufactures and sells widgets, a separate resolution is not required to document each sale. The articles of organization or state statutes already provide managers or members the authority for this activity. However, if TonoSilver, LLC does something outside of the scope of its ordinary business, a resolution should be reflected in the LLC minutes. Also, a lender or supplier may request a copy of a resolution showing that a particular LLC officer has authority to contract with the lender or supplier.

List of Activities That Require a Resolution

On an ongoing basis your managers must formally act to resolve to take certain actions. The following is a list of most of the actions that require a formal resolution:

❑ Opening bank accounts or establishing borrowing authority with a bank (most banks will provide you with a form resolution, which you should use rather than try to compile your own)

❑ Acceptance of written employment agreements

❑ Member agreements, if the LLC is a party

❑ Tax elections

❑ A small business LLC election pursuant to Internal Revenue Code Section 1244 (optional)

❑ Amendments to the articles of organization or the operating agreement

❑ Purchase or sale of a business

❑ Purchase, sale, or lease of property to be used by the business (items outside of ordinary business activities, such as an office building, a computer system, or a company car)

❑ Loans, financing, issuance of bonds

❑ Reorganizations, including mergers

❑ Dividend declarations

❑ Approval of plans to merge, liquidate, or dissolve

❑ Employee benefit plans, including pension and profit-sharing plans and health insurance

❑ Settlement of lawsuits and claims

❑ Indemnification of officers and managers

❑ Issuance of stock to investors, founders, or employees

❑ Changes of registered agent or registered office

❑ Filling vacancies on the board of managers or vacancies in officer positions

❑ Authority to enter into certain contracts

❑ Establishing committees or appointing members to serve on committees

❑ Redemption or retirement of an LLC membership percentage interest

❑ Salary matters pertaining to LLC officers

❑ Resolutions ratifying prior LLC acts by officers or managers

---

Expert Tip

If a resolution involves a transaction between the LLC and an officer or manager, the resolution should spell out in great detail the terms and conditions of the transaction to show that there has been an arm's-length negotiation between the officer or manager and the LLC and that the value paid is fair. This process can avoid claims down the road.

Definition

An *arm's-length relationship* is a term used to describe the condition of a business transaction, indicating that the parties to the transaction are independent and have equal bargaining strength, in order to avoid any appearance of favoritism or a conflict of interest.

Annual and Periodic Reports

Every state requires domestic and foreign LLCs to file some sort of annual or semiannual report. Some states also require LLCs to pay an annual franchise tax for the privilege of doing business in the state, either in conjunction with the annual report or as a separate report. See the State Reference Information (accompanying CD) to determine the requirements in your state of organization.

An annual report generally requires this information:

- LLC's name and the state or country where it is organized
- Name and address of the registered agent and registered office
- Address of the principal LLC office
- Names and business addresses of the managers
- Code classification of the principal business activity
- Federal employer identification number

The secretary of state usually mails the report form to every LLC each year; however, failure to receive the form from the secretary of state does not excuse the LLC from its obligation to file the report in a timely manner. Blank forms are available on the internet from all but a handful of states. See the State Reference Information on this book's CD to learn where to obtain your form and when to file it. States change their rules frequently, so it's a good idea to check with the secretary of state's office to confirm the due date.

Important dates should be conspicuously marked on the calendars of appropriate LLC officers. The due date for the annual report would be one such date. Tax filing dates, annual meeting dates, and member record dates would also be important dates to mark.

If an LLC does any of the following, the secretary of state can revoke its charter or administratively dissolve it:

- Fails to file its annual report
- Fails to pay required annual fees or franchise taxes
- Fails to appoint and maintain a registered office or agent
- Makes a filing containing a materially false statement

Although most states will notify an LLC in case of a default and provide 45 days to cure, this is not always true. Efforts should be made to prepare and file reports on a timely basis. See the State Reference Information (accompanhing CD) or contact your secretary of state to learn the filing requirements and fees in your state.

LLC Record-Keeping

The beginning of this chapter emphasized the importance of good record-keeping. All LLC records and other documents should be organized in a logical and orderly manner.

Different documents may be required to be produced for different purposes. For example, most limited liability company acts describe the types of documents that are to be made available for members to inspect. Other documents may be produced in response to investigations by government agencies or by subpoena or a request to produce documents pursuant to litigation.

The only limitation on providing documents in a litigation context or pursuant to a government investigation is that the documents be relevant to the matter involved. This is not a difficult standard to satisfy. Keep your records in good order.

The ULLCA and other modern limited liability company acts require an LLC to maintain the following records:

- All minutes of member and board meetings and records of all action taken without a meeting by members, managers, or committees formed by managers
- Appropriate accounting records
- Current list of the members' names and addresses, with the number and class of membership percentage interest held by each member

- Current list of the names and business addresses of LLC managers and officers
- Articles of organization and all amendments
- Operating agreement and all amendments
- Resolutions of the board creating one or more classes of membership interest and fixing their relative rights, preferences, and limitations
- All written communications to members for the last three years

Records must be maintained in written form or a form that can be converted into written form, such as microfiche or in computers. Records should be kept at the principal office of the LLC or at the registered office.

The ULLCA also requires that LLCs provide certain financial information to their members, including the following:

- A balance sheet as of the fiscal year-end
- An income statement
- A statement of changes in member equity

Financial reports must include those from any accountant who prepared any reports as well as a statement by the accountant documenting his or her reasonable belief that the statements were prepared in accordance with generally accepted accounting principles. Financial statements must be mailed to members within 120 days following the close of the fiscal year.

If an LLC has indemnified or advanced expenses to an officer or manager during the fiscal year or if the LLC issues or authorizes the issuance of membership interest in exchange for the promise of future services, the ULLCA requires that this information be disclosed to members in advance of the next members' meeting.

Records may be inspected by members. To inspect, a member must:

- Make a written demand at least five business days prior to the proposed inspection
- Describe with reasonable particularity the business purpose for the inspection and the documents to be inspected

The records sought must be directly connected with the business purpose specified by the member. Members can't go on "fishing expeditions" hoping to dredge up evidence of LLC wrongdoing. The request must specify both the purpose and the documents requested.

LLC Identity and Integrity
Letterhead and Business Cards

To preserve your LLC integrity, your business cards, letterhead, invoices, and other forms of written identification should state the LLC name. Let your customers and suppliers know that they are dealing with an LLC and not you individually. Don't hold yourself out as "John Doan, purveyor of fine widgets." Hold yourself out as "TonoSilver, LLC, purveyor of fine widgets—John Doan, President."

If your LLC does business under a fictitious name (a name other than its legal name), you have several choices to consider.

First, include both the legal name and the fictitious name. For example, the letterhead could read "TonoSilver, LLC dba Widget World."

Second, the heading could be "Widget World, a division of TonoSilver, LLC." Of course, this choice would work best if TonoSilver, LLC were engaged in more than one line of business.

A third choice would be to use the heading "Widget World." If you have properly filed your fictitious name registration, the third choice will suffice. Not all states have a fictitious name statute. In these states, use the full LLC name.

Fourth, a foreign LLC that is unable to use its name in another state in which it is qualified might choose "TonoSilver, LLC, an Oregon LLC doing business in Idaho as Widget World." Regardless of the choice made, all signatures or business cards should show "John Doan, President."

If you are involved in several business operations, each should have a separate letterhead, business card, and similar items. It must be clear to suppliers, customers, and others which hat you are wearing when you are doing business with them. If there is confusion over your business identity, any claim or lawsuit that would otherwise involve only one of your business operations could involve others, even all.

You should be equally careful with telephone listings, advertisements, and web pages.

Whenever you hold your business out to the public, make it clear that the LLC is the legal entity operating the business.

Identification Numbers, Permits, and Licenses

Because your LLC is a legal entity, federal law requires that you obtain a Federal Employer Identification Number (FEIN or FEIN). Most banks will require you to provide an EIN before opening a bank account. You obtain your EIN by filling out Form SS-4, *Application for Employer Identification Number*, and mailing or faxing it to the IRS or by applying online. The online application is a recent and welcome simplification of the process. If you mail the form, expect to wait up to six weeks to receive your EIN. If you fax your form to a service center, you will receive your EIN in about five days. You can also obtain an EIN immediately by telephoning an IRS service center during business hours—but be prepared to dial a few dozen times to get through.

How to Apply for an EIN Online

In order to submit an SS-4 application online, visit *https://sa2.www4.irs.gov/sa_vign/newFormSS4.do*.

A form will appear that will take you through the process step by step. Simply follow the instructions and you will receive your EIN in a few minutes. Print and save a copy of the form with your entity's records.

How to Apply for an EIN by Telephone

You can obtain a PDF file from the IRS web site at *www.irs.gov* that you can print out. The IRS periodically updates its forms, so it's always a good idea to use the form posted on the web site.

To obtain your EIN immediately, do the following:

- Either print or tear the form from the end of this chapter or download the form from the IRS web site.
- Fill in the first page of the form according to the instructions.

- Call the IRS at (800) 829-4933 between 7:00 A.M. and 10:00 P.M. local time (Pacific Time for Alaska and Hawaii). You must be authorized to sign the form or be an authorized designee.
- An IRS representative will use the information from the form to establish your account and assign you an EIN.
- Write the EIN on the upper right corner of the form and sign and date it. Keep this copy for your records.
- If requested by an IRS representative, mail or fax the signed Form SS-4 (including any authorization) within 24 hours to the address provided by the representative.

Title to Assets

All property should be titled in the LLC's name. From real estate to vehicles, if the LLC owns it, there should be a deed, title, or bill of sale in the LLC's name indicating ownership. If you sell property to the LLC, provide the LLC with a bill of sale. Dates acquired and purchase price paid are important facts for establishing ownership and tax basis. If you give property to the LLC, the LLC should acknowledge the gift in an LLC resolution or a letter to you, describing the gift, the date it was made, and a value assigned to the property.

Insurance

All casualty and liability insurance should be in the name of the LLC. Don't give your insurance carrier an opportunity to avoid paying claims by carrying the policy in your name. Again, make certain that LLC property is titled in the LLC's name so that claims can be processed if property is stolen or destroyed.

Bank Accounts

You should have a separate bank account for each business you operate. Don't combine business monies with personal monies or monies generated by other businesses. You should pay bills for a business with checks drawn from the account of that business. If you get into the habit of paying business bills from personal funds, business creditors will come to expect that you will pay all bills personally. Similarly, if you pay the bills of TonoSilver, LLC from the account of John Doan Enterprises, LLC, a separate LLC, you create uncertainty as to who is responsible for paying bills and debts.

Don't divert LLC monies for personal purposes. Once again, you will cloud the issue of who owns the asset and who is liable for claims resulting from its use. Monies paid from the LLC to you should come to you as salary, repayment of properly documented debt, or dividends.

Chapter 12 discusses the drastic consequences resulting from commingling business and personal funds.

Document LLC Transactions with Officers and Managers

If your LLC loans money to an officer or manager or if it buys, sells, or leases property to or from an officer or manager, the transaction should be carefully documented to show that it is fair. Use promissory notes providing for repayment terms comparable to those offered by local banks and require security for loans. You must be able to demonstrate to your members and the Internal Revenue Service that these transactions are done on an arm's-length basis with no preferential treatment to the officer or manager.

An arm's-length transaction assumes equal bargaining strength. This is not always the case. When you negotiate a loan with your banker, you may feel as if you are at a disadvantage, but negotiating with the bank should lead to a loan with interest and terms comparable to those in the marketplace. Any loan by an LLC or a board member to one of the LLC officers or managers must be on terms and conditions comparable to those that the officer or manager could have obtained from the marketplace.

LLC Paperwork Checklist

Use this checklist as a guide to conduct your business as an LLC and monitor your paperwork.

General Checklist
❑ Have you reserved your LLC name with the secretary of state?
❑ Have you filed your articles of organization with the secretary of state?

❑ Has your LLC operating agreement been prepared and approved by members and managers?

❑ Do your articles state your LLC purposes?

❑ Do your articles list your registered agent and registered office?

❑ Do your articles provide for cumulative voting for members? If not, does the applicable limited liability company act grant these rights?

❑ Have you registered with the secretary of state any fictitious names your LLC will use in its business?

❑ Will your LLC engage in business in other states? If so, has it qualified to do business as a foreign LLC?

Annual Meeting, Special Meeting, and Written Resolution Checklist

❑ Have minutes or consent resolutions been included for each annual meeting of members and managers?

❑ Have minutes or consent resolutions been included for each regular or special meeting of managers or members?

❑ Has an accurate and current list of members been prepared and maintained?

❑ Have meeting notices been provided to each member?

❑ If a special meeting is called, does the meeting notice specify a purpose for the meeting?

❑ If a meeting is convened, are operating agreement requirements pertaining to notice satisfied?

❑ Has an agenda been prepared and followed for the meeting?

❑ Have a method been determined for conducting voting at any meeting of members?

❑ Is there an affidavit of the LLC secretary attesting to giving notice?

❑ Are there signed waivers of notice, if required?

❑ If consent resolutions are used, are they signed by all managers or members?

❑ Are there meeting minutes or consent resolutions to reflect major activities of the LLC, including the following?

   • opening bank accounts or establishing borrowing authority

- written employment agreements
- member agreements, if LLC is a party
- tax elections
- amendments to articles of organization or operating agreement
- authorizing the purchase or sale of the business
- authorizing the purchase, sale, or lease of property to be used by the business (items outside of ordinary business activities, such as an office building, a computer system, or a company car)
- LLC loans, financing authority, or bond issuance
- reorganizations, including mergers or consolidations
- dividend declarations
- plans to dissolve and liquidate
- approval or authorization of employee benefit plans, including pension and profit-sharing plans and health insurance
- settlement of lawsuits and claims
- indemnification of officers and managers
- issuance of stock
- changes of registered agent and registered office
- filling vacancies of managers or officers
- authority to enter into certain contracts, including ones for large amounts of money or inventory or contracts outside of the ordinary course of the LLC's business
- establishing committees or appointing members to serve on committees
- redemption or retirement of LLC membership interest
- salary matters pertaining to officers
- resolutions ratifying prior LLC acts by officers or managers
- resolutions fixing the value of membership interest pursuant to any agreement to purchase membership interest

Dividends Checklist

❑ If a dividend is declared, does the resolution authorizing it fix a record date and describe in detail how and when the dividend will be paid or distributed?

❑ If a cash dividend is declared, are there sufficient earnings and profits to pay for it?

❑ If there are preferred members, does their membership interest provide for cumulative or noncumulative dividend payments?

LLC Records Checklist

❑ Do the LLC records include the following?

- articles of organization and all amendments
- operating agreement and all amendments
- all minutes and consent resolutions of managers and officers
- all written communication to members for the last three years
- balance sheet as of the most recent fiscal year-end
- income statement
- statement of changes in members' equity
- membership interest purchase agreements
- members' list
- current list of names and addresses of officers and managers
- federal and state income tax returns for the last six years
- state franchise tax and annual reports
- copies of leases and bills of sale pertaining to LLC property
- insurance policies in LLC name
- copies of all contracts or agreements to which LLC is a party

PART FIVE

LLC Lawsuits and Personal Liability Protection

CHAPTER 11

Suing and Being Sued as an LLC

An LLC is a distinct legal entity. As long as an LLC follows requisite formalities and mechanics, anyone with a claim against it must look to the LLC for relief, not individuals. Owners (members), managers, officers, employees, and others are shielded from personal liability by the veil of the LLC. This is true in most instances, even if an LLC lacks sufficient assets to pay the claim.

Similarly, when the LLC has a claim against a third party, the LLC itself brings the claim. For example, if a supplier fails to deliver goods to an LLC in a timely manner according to the terms of its agreement with the LLC, the LLC can file a claim against the supplier. If a motorist drives his car into the LLC's delivery truck, the LLC may seek relief against the motorist.

The LLC Sues

This part is easy. If an LLC has a claim, it may file a lawsuit in its own name, as the plaintiff. The complaint must comply with applicable rules of court, particularly in terms of the time within which the complaint can be filed and service of process. If the LLC is suing in a state outside its home state, it may have to qualify as a foreign LLC in the other state prior to filing its complaint.

Of course, an LLC can't act by itself, so its interests in the complaint must be advanced by an agent. Unlike individuals, who may always represent themselves (known as appearing *pro se* or *in pro per*), many states and all the U.S. federal courts require that an LLC be represented by a licensed attorney in court appearances. LLC members, managers, officers, or employees may not appear on behalf of the LLC unless they are licensed as attorneys. This principle may apply to judicial proceedings and administrative matters as well. Check with the local bar association in your state.

The LLC Is Sued

Because it is a distinct legal entity, an LLC can be sued. Complaints can be filed and heard against an LLC in courts and in administrative proceedings. These suits and proceedings can be filed in any jurisdiction where the LLC is either chartered or engaged in business, regardless of where the LLC's principal place of business is located. Conversely, an LLC cannot be sued in a state where it is neither chartered nor engaged in business. This basic procedural protection shields the LLC from being sued in a place where it has no connection.

For example, TonoSilver LLC, an Oregon LLC, is engaged in business in Oregon, Washington, Idaho, and Maine. A complaint against the LLC could be filed in any of these states. Local court or administrative rules may be used on occasion to dismiss or transfer actions that are filed in a jurisdiction for the sole apparent purpose of inconveniencing the entity against which the claim has been filed.

When an LLC is sued or an administrative claim is filed against it, notice of the action and a copy of the complaint are served on an LLC manager or owner at the LLC's principal place of business or on the LLC's registered agent designated in its articles of organization. State and local court rules govern who can be served with the complaint and the manner and sufficiency of the service.

Owner Suits

It is not uncommon that a partial owner of an LLC finds it necessary to bring a lawsuit against the LLC. These types of actions are generally divided into two classes: *individual* suits and *derivative* suits.

Individual Suits

In an individual suit, an owner seeks redress against the LLC for a wrong that has been done to that owner. For example, if the LLC does not honor a contract that it has with that owner, the owner could file suit against the LLC. If successful, that owner would recover damages from the LLC for breach of contract. Similarly, an owner injured as a result of the negligence of an LLC employee engaged in LLC business could sue the LLC.

Individual suits are often filed to compel an LLC to issue a share certificate, permit a member to inspect its books and records, or enable a member to vote on LLC matters. With individual suits, the right to sue belongs to the individual owner wronged by an LLC action and any recovery belongs to the owner.

Derivative Suits

It is important to note that LLC derivative suits are not recognized by all the states, although the right of LLC owners to bring equivalent actions is firmly and universally established. The right of LLC owners to bring derivative suits is a fairly active and shifting area of the law. For LLCs, derivative suits involve a legal wrong done to the LLC that the LLC is unable to redress.

For example, assume that the officers and managers of TonoSilver, LLC misappropriate company funds. The LLC has been damaged by this action, but because the officers and managers control the daily operations of the business, the LLC by itself is unable to seek relief.

Expert Tip

Derivative suits are always brought by an owner who does not have voting control of the LLC. Why? It's because a majority owner with voting control can always protect his or her personal interests. Derivative suits are a way for minority owners to protect themselves against unfair acts by those controlling the LLC.

In such a situation, one or more owners could bring a derivative action against the officers and managers to seek relief. For procedural purposes, the owners would file a suit against the owners and managers and the LLC as well. Any recovery would be paid to the LLC.

Some states permit successful owners to recover attorney's fees in derivative actions.

Derivative actions can also be maintained when an officer or manager breaches any of the duties owed by the officer or manager to the LLC or otherwise pursues a course of conduct detrimental to the LLC.

The law imposes a number of additional procedural safeguards to deter the filing of derivative lawsuits by disgruntled owners. Without these safeguards, many more of these suits would be filed, at great expense to LLCs.

The safeguards include the following:

- The owner filing the action must have been an owner at the time of the alleged harm (unless he or she acquired ownership interest by operation of law from a deceased owner who held the membership interest at the time of the harm).
- The complaint must allege with particularity that the owner has made a demand on the managers or managing members for relief prior to filing the suit and that the demand was refused.

- If no demand was made, the complaint must state in detail why no demand was made or why the owner believes that any such demand would be futile.
- Once filed, the suit may be dismissed or settled only with approval from the court.
- In some jurisdictions, the owner filing the complaint must maintain his or her status as owner throughout the proceedings.

Final Thoughts on Lawsuits

This is a litigious society. Lots of reasons are offered for this state of affairs. Many blame it on lawyers; others attribute it to a lottery mentality in many people. As with other things in life, there are probably a lot of factors working in combination to cause this situation.

As a lawyer, I often tell my business clients, "Anybody can sue anyone at anytime for anything." And in my practice I often saw specific, egregious examples of abusive and meritless lawsuits. This philosophy doesn't bring a smile to many faces. It does, however, focus my clients' attention on prevention.

What can a businessperson do to minimize the risk of costly litigation? This book provides many answers for LLCs.

How to Effectively Manage Your LLC to Maximize Liability Protection

F aithfulness to the formalities is the price paid to the corporation fiction, a relatively small price to pay for limited liability."
—as quoted by the court in *Labadie Coal Co. v. Black*

Introduction

The most notable feature of the LLC is that it protects the owners from personal liability for the company's debts and obligations. This feature is valuable for businesspersons. LLCs and corporations share this vital feature. In fact, the corporation developed historically as a means by which individuals could pool their investments in order to finance large business projects while enjoying protection from liability. Without this liability shield, individuals would be less likely to invest in companies and the projects they undertake; it would be a very different world without corporations and LLCs.

Consider the following, from California's LLC statute:

No member of a limited liability company shall be personally liable … for any debt, obligation, or liability of the limited liability company, whether that liability or obligation arises in contract, tort, or otherwise, solely by reason of being a member of the limited liability company.

As you can see, the protection afforded to LLC members in California is strong—and typical of statutes nationwide. Of course, in law there are always exceptions.

Our corporation law has roots in the Roman Empire. But LLCs are a more recent invention. So, where did LLC law come from? Because the LLC lawmakers had no body of law to draw upon, they did the obvious thing: they borrowed doctrines, statutes, and concepts from corporation law. Because the liability shield laws of both corporations and LLCs are so closely related, they are discussed together.

Understand, though, that liability protection for LLC owners is not absolute. An LLC is a legal entity separate from its owners, who, as we will discuss, must maintain that separation vigilantly. Legal errors, personal dealings, ignoring formalities, failure to pay taxes, and other misdeeds and missteps can destroy the legal protection afforded to LLC owners, thereby exposing them to liability. There are a number of reasons for concern.

- LLC laws require articles of organization and operating agreements and set other requirements.
- Articles of organization and operating agreements form a contract between the LLC and its owners, obligating the LLC to act in accordance with its articles and operating agreements.
- Managers and members owe the LLC and co-owners a fiduciary duty to act in good faith, exercise due care, and act in the best interests of the LLC.

- Majority owners must act in good faith, in a manner not calculated to oppress the rights of minority owners.
- LLC formalities must be respected and observed to preserve the integrity of the LLC and to shield members and managers or related businesses from personal liability.

Without question, you want to focus on running your business. Yet paperwork is a part of every business. Like death and taxes, it is unavoidable. Get started on the right foot by building record-keeping into the routine of your business.

This chapter explores several legal theories that have been used to impose liability on individual owners of entities or parent entities. The term most often used to describe this process or concept is "piercing the corporate veil." Don't be confused by the reference to corporations in this section—the doctrine of piercing the corporate veil applies to LLCs as well. Because LLCs have been around for only a few decades, there simply hasn't been time for a thorough body of law to develop around the doctrine of piercing the LLC veil. In the past few years, however, some legal cases have emerged and the phrase is starting to take hold as a separate but equivalent doctrine alongside "piercing the corporate veil." We'll illustrate these doctrines with several legal cases later in this chapter. After reading these cases, you may be struck by the ways in which some business owners did not demonstrate the necessary formality or pay sufficient attention to details. Certainly, the cases will show how you should operate your LLC and preserve your liability protection.

Expert Tip

Separateness is the key to maintaining LLC liability protection. No single concept is more essential than the legal separation between owner and LLC.

Understanding the importance of formality and attention to detail and compliance with applicable statutes, articles, and your operating agreement will preserve your LLC status and shield you from personal liability. You must develop good record-keeping habits from the beginning. This is essential.

The cases presented also highlight the variety of contexts in which piercing-the-veil cases can arise. In effect, any type of claim that can be asserted against an LLC—whether it be contract, tort, government claim, or other—can be the basis of an attempt to pierce the LLC veil.

To help you avoid personal liability for LLC acts, a checklist of dos and don'ts is provided for your convenience at the end of this chapter.

The doctrines of alter ego liability and piercing the LLC veil give courts the power to disregard the LLC liability shield and impose liability on LLC owners in extraordinary cases of owner misconduct. These two doctrines (different in name, but essentially the same) will apply universally to corporations and LLCs. The states offer dozens of differing tests for alter ego liability. One common theme, however, is that a unity of interest and ownership between the entity and its owners can erode liability protection.

Definitions

Alter ego liability, as the name implies, means that a company's owner or owners have treated the company as indistinct from themselves. Without separateness between owner and company, the owner is liable for the company's obligations.

Piercing the LLC veil, as the name implies, means that in some cases a creditor can ask a court to ignore the company liability shield and reach its owners.

Disregarding the LLC Entity

As noted throughout this book, the acts of the owners and managers must recognize and acknowledge an LLC's separateness, treating it as a distinct entity.

Courts recognize the distinct legal status of the LLC and are reluctant to disregard an LLC's separate status to reach the property of its owners. However, although reluctant, courts will pierce the LLC veil in appropriate circumstances.

Various legal theories have been used to impose personal liability on individuals or, in the case of subsidiaries, parent entities. Some of these theories require that the court disregard the LLC entity or pierce the LLC veil. However, not all claims against individuals require that the LLC status be disregarded.

Claims can be asserted against managers and owners without disregarding the LLC veil. For example, federal and state tax laws generally impose personal liability on those individuals responsible for preparing and filing income and sales tax returns. The government agency in question can bring civil and criminal tax claims against the LLC or the responsible individual or both. In enforcing a specific personal liability, there is no reason to examine LLC formalities or attempt to disregard the LLC entity.

The same is true for criminal acts and intentional torts. (An intentional tort is a conscious and deliberate act by which one person causes harm to another, for which the victim may sue the wrongdoer for damages.) If a manager or owner has knowingly and voluntarily participated in any aspect of the crime or tort, he or she can be personally liable without piercing the LLC veil. Of course, an aggressive plaintiff's attorney will probably bring claims against the individuals and the LLC using a number of legal theories, including ones that would seek to pierce the veil.

It is also important to note that most piercing-the-veil cases involve corporations and LLCs where the owners are also the managers. Control of the entity is an important concept in these cases. Legal theories commonly used against owners or managers who are not owners or who own only small percentages of membership interest involve breach of the duties of due care or loyalty, duties described in Chapter 5.

Instrumentality/Alter Ego

The two most common theories used to justify imposing personal liability in disregard of the corporate or LLC entity are the alter ego theory and the instrumentality rule.

The alter ego theory says, in effect, that if the owners of an LLC disregard the legal separateness of the LLC or disregard proper formalities, then the law will also disregard the LLC form if required to protect individuals and creditors. This theory attaches liability to LLC owners in cases of commingling of assets and failure to observe corporate formalities.

The instrumentality rule historically applied only to parent/subsidiary situations, but it now seems to apply beyond that context as well. The instrumentality rule has three components:

1. The owner(s) must completely dominate the finances, policy, and business practices of the LLC to the extent that the entity at the time of the transaction had no separate mind, will, or existence of its own. Ownership of all or substantial percentage of the stock of the LLC, alone, is not complete domination.
2. The control or domination is used to commit fraud or wrong, to cause the violation of a statute, breach a legal duty, or commit a dishonest or unjust act in violation of the claimant's legal rights.
3. The domination and violation of legal rights must have proximately caused the injury to the claimant.

The instrumentality rule originally developed as a means to impose liability on a parent entity for the acts of its subsidiary. Often, subsidiaries have been grossly undercapitalized and effectively judgment-proof: a legal judgment against the subsidiary would have little effect, since it lacked the assets to pay the damages assessed. To remedy this injustice, the courts have permitted creditors of the subsidiary to pierce the veil of the subsidiary and bring claims against the parent entity.

Courts have blurred the distinctions between the alter ego and instrumentality theories; in fact, many cases use both terms interchangeably. For the purposes of this discussion, the factors examined by the courts in deciding whether to pierce the LLC veil are the same under either theory. In fact, many of the criteria examined are relevant for claims based on breach of fiduciary duty against managers or owners or on criminal law or tort theories.

Before looking at specific cases to illustrate these theories and the criteria used, it is worth recalling that courts are reluctant to pierce the LLC veil. However, courts will strain to permit the piercing whenever failing to do so could produce an unjust result. For example, if your undercapitalized business seriously injures a bystander, your business has no insurance to cover the injuries, and your business has insufficient assets to cover the damages, a court will work hard to impose personal liability on you personally. It is public policy that businesses should be adequately capitalized to meet the reasonable needs of the business, including all foreseeable claims.

Contract and Tort Claims

Courts are more apt to pierce the veil in a tort case than in a contract case. As mentioned earlier, a tort is any action or failure to act (when there is a duty to act) that causes damage to another. Examples of tort actions include personal injuries, fraud, misrepresentation, negligence, battery, assault, trespass, and invasion of privacy. In a general sense, any claim not based on a contract could be a tort claim.

Once again, a policy decision of the courts comes into play. It is presumed that contract creditors entered into a contract voluntarily with an opportunity to find out for themselves about the LLC. If a contract creditor was not diligent in protecting itself at the time of contract, courts are not likely to pierce the LLC veil unless the circumstances are extreme. In contrast, tort claimants are rarely involved voluntarily or rarely have an opportunity to find out about the corporation in advance. Thus, a stronger argument can be made in tort cases that the LLC veil be set aside. Of course, many contract claimants will include a claim for fraud and seek recovery directly from the individuals involved in the fraud. Thus, a stronger argument can be made in tort cases that the LLC veil be set aside.

As you review the cases described below, keep in mind that no single criterion is controlling. In almost every instance, the LLC has failed to satisfy a number of criteria. For example, the fact that one owns all the stock of the LLC is not in itself enough reason to expose to pierce the LLC veil. The same is true where one serves as sole officer and manager as well. The courts look for several factors working in combination, such as absence of LLC records or minutes, inadequate capitalization, a serious harm to third parties, commingling of personal and LLC assets, etc.

Taxicab Cases

Every law student studies two or three taxicab cases. These cases were an important part of the early battleground in American corporate veil jurisprudence. Most people react with a mixture of horror and amazement that businesses could be operated in such a manner. And yet, many cab companies still operate in the manner described below.

In *Mull v. Colt Co.*, the plaintiff, Mull, suffered serious injuries when he was struck by a cab driven by Fermaglick. Fermaglick had no assets and was judgment-proof, so Mull sued the owner of the cab, Colt Company. At the time of the accident, New York law required that cabs maintain at least $5,000 in liability insurance. The state intended that the $5,000 be a minimum amount, but—as might be expected—that was all any cab company carried. It certainly was not enough to cover the medical bills totaling $30,000.

In the course of the discovery phase of the suit, Mull learned that Ackerman and Goodman owned all the stock of Colt Company—as well as all the stock of 100 other corporations, each of which owned two cabs and a $5,000 liability insurance policy. All 200 cabs were garaged, maintained, and dispatched from a single location. Ackerman and Goodman had obviously devised a creative plan to shield themselves from liability, but the court saw right through it.

If the court had not permitted the corporate veil to be pierced, Mull, who spent 209 days in the hospital and endured 20 surgeries, could have only recovered a wrecked cab and $5,000. The court noted that the use of multiple shell corporations, each carrying the minimum statutory insurance, clearly perverted the legislative intent. The court held, "When the statutory privilege of doing business in the corporate form is employed as a cloak for the evasion of obligations, as a mask behind which to do injustice or invoked to subvert equity, the separate personality of the corporation will be disregarded."

Wallace v. Tulsa Yellow Cab Taxi & Baggage Co. also involved a plaintiff who was injured by a taxi. Wallace sued the cab company and recovered a judgment. Unfortunately for Wallace, by the time he tried to collect on the judgment, the cab company had gone out of business—or had it? The court permitted Wallace to recover from Tulsa Yellow Cab, a successor corporation. The judge relied on these factors:

- The taxi business is hazardous by nature (great potential for harm).
- The only asset of the new corporation was $1,000 of paid-in stock (inadequate capital).
- The new corporation leased cabs from the old corporation pursuant to a lease that could be terminated on 24 hours' notice (an unusual provision).
- Although the owners of the new corporation were different, they were former employees of the old corporation and financed the purchase of their stock with money loaned to them by the owner of the old company (an unusual procedure with no obvious legitimate business purpose).
- The management of the new corporation was the same as that of the old corporation, so, in effect, the two corporations were the same.

In both of these cases, the courts relied upon inadequate capitalization and control as key criteria for piercing the corporate veil. The severity of the harm to the claimants was also a significant factor.

Personal Injury Cases and Claims

Of course, not all personal injuries are caused by taxis. In *Geringer v. Wildhorse Ranch, Inc.*, a widow sued for the wrongful death of her husband and children, who were killed in a paddleboat accident on a Colorado ranch. The action was filed against Wildhorse Ranch, Inc. and its principal owner.

The court pierced the corporate veil and attached liability to the principal owner, noting the following:

- No corporation stock had been issued in the corporation and no record of the stock existed (absence of records and formality).
- No corporate minutes existed, even though the defendant testified that informal board meetings had been conducted (absence of records and formality).
- The principal owner operated several corporations out of one office (absence of separation among corporations).

- The debts of one corporation were frequently paid with funds of another corporation or from the principal owner's personal funds (commingling of funds, no arm's-length dealings).
- The principal owner had purchased the paddleboats with funds from another corporation (commingling, related party transaction).
- No record of loans or ledgers existed (no loan documentation).
- Corporate records were so muddled that no clear picture of accountability or organization could be shown (poor record-keeping).
- Business cards listed the principal owner as the "owner" of the corporation (improper way to hold corporation out to public).
- Employees of the corporation believed that the principal owner was in control (agency, public perception).
- The principal owner knew that the paddleboats leaked and became unstable and overruled employee recommendations that the boats be repaired (active wrongdoing on the part of owner).

Contract Creditors and Contract Claims

Although a court is more likely to pierce a corporate or LLC veil in a tort situation, it will pierce the veil in an appropriate contract situation. An illustrative example is *Stone v. Frederick Hobby Associates II, LLC*, one of the first cases applying the traditional corporation veil test to an LLC.

Here are the facts. Dr. Stone and Dr. Stone, husband and wife, were dissatisfied with the $3,300,000 home constructed and sold to them by the defendant, Frederick Hobby Associates II, LLC. The Stones charged that the defendant builder had breached the construction contract. As part of their legal claim, the Stones asserted that defendant Hobby II's LLC form should be disregarded so as to reach the assets of Hobby II's two owners and a related LLC, Hobby I. The Stones sought to hold Hobby II's two owners and Hobby I responsible for their losses. They argued that Hobby II was a shell company with no assets and no ability to pay any potential damage award.

The Connecticut court agreed with the Stones on the underlying contract claim against the owners of Hobby II and against Hobby I. The court further recognized that the corporate veil doctrine would also be applicable to the LLC. Connecticut law authorizes individuals to be held personally liable for entity obligations under either the "instrumentality rule" or the "identity rule." The court held that the criteria for applying both rules had been satisfied.

These are the facts that the court recognized when applying the instrumentality test:

- The LLC's two members each held a 50 percent ownership interest in Hobby II and had full authority to manage Hobby II's affairs.
- Hobby II's office was located in one owner's home, on a rent-free basis.
- Hobby II had no assets other than the residence it sold to the plaintiffs.
- The defendant's attorney had remarked during a meeting that the defendant had no assets.
- Several documents used by Hobby II in connection with the subject premises listed entities or individuals similar to and easily confused with Hobby II as the operative actors. (For instance, in the Connecticut real estate conveyance tax return, it is unclear whether the seller is Hobby II or its member, Frederick Hobby III.)
- The plaintiffs alleged that the defendants, shortly following the closing date on the Stones' new residence, had transferred substantially all of Hobby II's assets (including the sale proceeds) to the two members and Hobby I.

The court concluded that the members had complete control over the LLC, that the control was used as a shield to evade contractual obligations to plaintiffs, and that the plaintiffs' losses emanated, at least in part, from the control the defendant members exercised over Hobby II. Accordingly, the court imposed personal liability on the members.

Expert Tip

Don't use your name, initials, or other personal reference in the name of your LLC unless there is a good reason to do so. If liability protection is important to you, you want to appear separate from your LLC, not unified with it.

The case of *Labadie Coal Co. v. Black* is another illustrative example. There, creditors were able to pierce the veil of a trading corporation and recover against the controlling owners. The court examined these factors:

- The controlling owners owned all of the corporation stock and controlled corporation decisions.
- The corporation failed to maintain corporation minutes or adequate records, including articles of incorporation, corporation operating agreements, and a current list of directors.
- The corporation failed to follow formalities pertaining to the issuance of corporation stock.
- Funds were commingled with funds and assets of other corporations.
- Corporation funds were diverted to the personal use of the owners.
- The corporation and the owners used the same office for different business activities.
- The corporation was inadequately capitalized.

The court noted that fraud was not required to pierce the corporate veil. All that was required was the presence of an unjust situation. The court also stated: "Faithfulness to the formalities is the price paid to the corporate fiction, a relatively small price to pay for limited liability. Furthermore, the formalities are themselves an excellent litmus of the extent to which the individuals involved actually view the corporation as a separate being."

Government Claims

Government agencies can pursue many of the same claims as individuals and private entities. Tort claims and contract claims are not limited to the private sector.

For example, in *United States v. Healthwin-Midtown Convalescent Hospital and Rehabilitation Center, Inc.*, the government sought to recover excess payments of Medicare benefits paid to the hospital.

The hospital's corporate charter had been revoked for failure to pay required state taxes. The action was pursued against the owner of 50 percent of the hospital's outstanding stock. The court identified the following factors in ruling in favor of the government:

- The principal owner owned 50 percent of the hospital's stock and 50 percent of the interests of the partnership that owned the real estate on which the hospital was built and the furnishings used by the hospital.
- The principal owner served as president, a board member, and administrator of the hospital (control).
- Other board members did not attend board meetings. (Note the potential for a claim of breach of duty of care against the absent directors.)
- The principal owner had check-writing authority and controlled the affairs of the corporation.
- The corporation was inadequately capitalized, with liabilities consistently in excess of $150,000 and initial capitalization of $10,000.
- Regular board meetings were not conducted (lack of formality).
- Funds were commingled.
- Corporation assets were diverted from the corporation.
- The principal owner failed to maintain an arm's-length relationship when dealing with the corporation and the partnership. The corporation paid the partnership amounts due in full, to the detriment of corporation creditors.

In *Securities and Exchange Commission v. Elmas Trading Corp.*, the court provided a detailed list of factors to be considered by courts in determining whether or not to pierce the corporate veil. Presumably, these factors would also apply when analyzing an LLC's liability shield. In this case, 16 separate entities consisting of corporations and partnerships were disregarded. The court noted that no one factor was determinative. Rather, all of the facts and circumstances had to be considered in each case.

The criteria listed by the court included the following:

- Failure to observe corporate formalities
- Nonpayment of dividends
- Insolvency of the corporation at the time of the transaction
- Siphoning funds of the corporation by the dominant owner

- Nonfunctioning of other officers or directors
- Absence of corporate records
- Use of the same office or business location by the corporation and its individual owners
- Absence of corporate records
- Commingling of funds and other assets
- Unauthorized diversion of corporation assets to other business activities or personal accounts of the owners
- Failure to maintain minutes or adequate corporation records of separate corporation businesses
- Common ownership of stock between two or more corporations
- Identical persons serving as officers and/or directors of two or more corporations
- The absence of corporation assets
- Commingling of funds and other assets
- The use of a corporation as a mere shell, instrumentality, or conduit for a single venture or the business of an individual or another corporation
- The concealment and misrepresentation of the identity of the responsible ownership, management, and financial interest of a corporation or the concealment of personal business activities
- Failure to maintain an arm's-length relationship in transactions between related entities
- Use of a corporate entity to procure labor, services, or merchandise for another person or entity to the detriment of creditors
- Manipulation of assets and liabilities between entities so as to concentrate the assets in one and the liabilities in another
- Contracting with another with the intent to avoid performance by the use of an corporation as a subterfuge of illegal transactions
- Formation and use of a corporation to transfer to it the liability of another person or entity

Parent as Alter Ego of Subsidiary

When one LLC owns all or substantially all of the voting stock of another LLC, the LLC owning the stock is the parent corporation and the other LLC is the subsidiary. Historically, the instrumentality rule has been used to impose liability on the parent for activities of the subsidiary. The veil of the parent and subsidiary could potentially be pierced to impose liability on controlling owners.

In one case, *Miles v. American Telephone & Telegraph Company*, the court refused to pierce the veil and impose liability on the parent corporation. There, the parent and subsidiary maintained their relationship on an arm's-length basis. In another, *Sabine Towing & Transportation Co., Inc. v. Merit Ventures, Inc.*, the subsidiary's veil was pierced.

In *Miles v. American Telephone & Telegraph Company*, the plaintiff, Miles, filed a lawsuit against AT&T alleging tortious invasion of the plaintiff's privacy by Southwestern Bell, a subsidiary of AT&T. The court granted summary judgment in AT&T's favor, dismissing it from the lawsuit, noting that the subsidiary maintained a great degree of separateness from its parent corporation. Listed below are subsidiary activities deemed to be significant by the court in not piercing the corporate veil. The subsidiary:

- Selected its own banks
- Selected, trained, and supervised its own personnel
- Set its own rates with the Federal Communications Commission
- Prepared its own budget
- Determined its own construction contracts
- Prepared its own annual report
- Published its own employee newsletter
- Paid its own bills
- Purchased its own property and equipment
- Developed its own sales and marketing procedures

The court in *Miles* also found that:

- The parent and subsidiary were distinct and adequately capitalized financial units.

- Daily operations of the two corporations were separate, with formal barriers between the managements of the two corporations.
- Those dealing with the corporations were apprised of their separate identities.

In *Sabine Towing*, the court reached a different decision. There, a suit was filed against the parent corporation for breach of shipping agreements. In reaching its decision to pierce the corporate veil, the court considered the following factors:

- Common stock ownership of the parent and subsidiary corporations existed.
- Parent and subsidiary corporations shared the same owners and managers, making it impossible for the subsidiary board to act independently.
- The same corporate offices were used by both corporations.
- The subsidiary was inadequately capitalized.
- The same corporate offices were used by both corporations.
- The subsidiary was financed by the parent whenever the subsidiary ran short of capital.
- The parent existed solely as a holding company, with no independent active business of its own.
- The parent used the subsidiary's assets and property as its own.
- No formal documentation existed of loans between the parent and subsidiary.
- Subsidiary decisions were made by the parent.
- There were no records of meetings or other corporate records.
- Subsidiary assets were stripped by the parent to the benefit of the parent and the detriment of the subsidiary.

For parent/subsidiary LLCs, the criteria examined in *Miles* provide a better guide for appropriate behavior than the criteria described in *Sabine Towing*. Once again, common sense should point you in the right direction, but it is important that you begin good record-keeping habits early.

How to Sign Documents as an LLC Officer

You must represent yourself as an officer of your entity, not as an individual. When you sign contractual and other documents, use the following form:

By: Judy Doe (signature)

Name: Judy Doe

Title: President of Everclear Waters, LLC

The Seven Most Important Liability Protection Rules

In order to maintain liability protection for yourself and other owners, you should strictly abide by the following rules:

- Pay creditors before you make distributions to owners. LLCs, like corporations, owe an important obligation to pay creditors before distributing profits to owners. Universally, state law will force an LLC owner to give back distributions of profits made to entity owners in lieu of paying creditors.

- Always hold yourself out as an officer/manager of the entity—not as an individual. Sign documents in your capacity as a representative of the entity, not personally, i.e., "John Jones, President, OldeCraft, LLC." Do not allow any creditor any reason to argue that you personally guaranteed an obligation. Identify your LLC in advertisements, in correspondence, on invoices, on statements, on business cards, on your web site, etc.

- Follow your LLC operating agreements. A crafty attorney working for a creditor can have an easy time asserting alter ego liability if you do not follow your own entity's written procedures.

- Keep proper records. When owners and managers/officers meet, prepare minutes of the meetings. If the owners or managers/officers reach a decision, even informally, commit that decision to writing in the form of a written consent. Creditors wishing to pierce the liability veil will always seek to discover improper record-keeping.

- Obtain and maintain a business checking account in the name of the entity. Furthermore, always keep your personal assets and entity assets separate. Also, if you operate more than one entity (many people do), keep each entity's assets separate. Keep accurate business records for your entity.

- Always keep your company in good standing with the secretary of state. An LLC is subject to administrative dissolution if it fails to meet its ongoing responsibilities. This means that you must always file all tax returns, including franchise tax returns, and file all periodic reporting forms. Also, maintain close contact with your registered agent and always pay your agent's bills on time.

- Never allow a company that you own with debts outstanding to be administratively dissolved. These debts can be imputed to you personally if the company is dissolved. If you must dissolve a company, do it with the assistance of a lawyer and follow your state's formal dissolution procedures.

A Dead Company Offers Little Liability Protection

If an LLC is not in good standing or has been dissolved, its ability to shield its owners from liability can be undermined. An LLC is in good standing when it is in full compliance with the law, its taxes are paid, and all periodic reports have been timely filed. An LLC can be subject to an administrative dissolution by the secretary of state if its taxes are not paid and its periodic filings are not made on time. Dissolution ends an LLC's life. A dead LLC offers significantly reduced liability protection to its owners.

The following oversights by management can threaten an LLC's ability to shield its owners from liability:

- Managers or members fail to pay LLC and franchise taxes in the state of organization.

- Managers or members fail to file annual and periodic reports in the state of organization.

- Managers or members fail to notify the secretary of state of a change of address.

- Managers or members fail to pay the annual fees of the resident agent or fail to advise the resident agent of a change of address.

Liability Protection: Corporation vs. LLC

Does an LLC offer greater liability protection than a corporation? In short—but this is a generalization—yes. Of course, the LLC wins by just a hair.

The reason is that LLCs do not require such intensive periodic formalities (e.g., annual meetings) as corporations. Such formalities consume time and resources. Although it is not recommended, many small corporations fall behind on their formalities, especially annual meetings and elections of directors. Failing to observe these formalities weakens the corporation liability shield. Because LLCs are not subject to such intensive formalities, LLC liability protection cannot be as easily weakened by failure to follow formalities.

Final Thoughts on Liability Protection

Attention to detail, common sense, and good record-keeping are three most effective ways to work at preserving your LLC and protecting your personal assets. As these cases have illustrated, you cannot escape personal liability if you do not treat your LLC as a separate legal entity. Don't use your LLC as your personal playground. Use common sense, maintain good records, and pay attention to detail.

LLC Dos and Don'ts Checklist

Do:

- Maintain capital reserves sufficient to meet reasonably foreseeable needs of the LLC, including liability insurance coverage.
- Maintain active and independent managers or managing members.
- If you serve as a manager or managing member, be active and use your best independent business judgment, even if that requires you to disagree with other managers.
- Use business cards and letterhead that reflect the LLC name.
- Make certain that LLC letters and agreements are signed by the LLC.

- Distinguish between preorganizational LLC activities by a promoter and postorganizational LLC activities by officers or managers.
- Use formal loan documents, including notes and security agreements, for LLC loans, especially to owners and managers, and get a written resolution authorizing the transaction.
- Use written leases, purchase and sale agreements, and bills of sale in transactions involving owners and managers and get a member or manager resolution authorizing the transaction.
- Use separate offices for activities of separate businesses.
- Use separate telephone lines for each business.
- Use separate employees for each business.
- Allow each LLC to own its own assets or equipment or lease them pursuant to written lease agreements.
- Apply for all required permits, licenses, and identification numbers in the LLC name.
- Obtain necessary business insurance in the LLC name.

Don't:
- Commingle personal and LLC assets or assets among related LLCs.
- Divert LLC assets for personal use.
- Engage in any act for an illegal or improper purpose, such as to defraud creditors or oppress minority owners.
- Hold yourself out as the owner of the LLC; you may be an owner, officer, or manager, but the LLC should be held out as the legal entity.
- Engage in transactions between LLCs and their owners and managers on any basis other than an arm's-length.
- If you operate several LLCs, don't use the same people as owners and managers of each LLC.

Parent/Subsidiary/Successor Considerations Checklist

In addition to the dos and don'ts listed above, parent, subsidiary, and successor LLCs should be sensitive to the following issues:

Parent/Subsidiary LLCs

To avoid liability by the parent, the subsidiary should be as independent as possible. Answer these questions.

Who makes decisions for the other? _____

Who finances the subsidiary? _____

Does the parent have its own active business, doing more than acting as a holding company for other businesses? ❑ Yes   ❑ No

Who prepares the budget? _____

Is there an identity of owners and managers? That is, are they the same people in both parent and subsidiary? ❑ Yes   ❑ No

Is there common ownership? ❑ Yes ❑ No

If a parent LLC controls the decision-making processes of the subsidiary, finances the subsidiary, prepares the subsidiary's budget, shares a complete or partial overlap of officers or managers, and engages in no active business of its own, the parent LLC is more likely to be held responsible for the acts of the subsidiary.

Successor Employer or LLC

If you can answer yes to the first three questions below, the successor LLC may retain liability for acts of its predecessor.

Is there continuity in the work force? ❑ Yes ❑ No

Is there continuity in the management? ❑ Yes ❑ No

Is there continuity in the ownership? ❑ Yes ❑ No

What other items carry over? _____

Using Your Professional Team

Throughout *The Operations Manual for LLCs*, we have made reference to your business lawyer, accountant, and insurance agent. These individuals are important to you and your business. To be most effective, you should consider them as your professional team.

Most businesses use lawyers, accountants, and insurance agents; however, surprisingly enough, many business owners never bring these professionals together to work as a team. This is a mistake. The business world is complex and it is rare to find one individual who can handle your legal, accounting, and insurance needs. By bringing these experts together, you benefit from a broader range of experience and ideas and you can avoid the increased time and expense resulting from duplication of efforts.

What appears in this chapter is one lawyer's approach to using your business lawyer most effectively. Although written from a lawyer's perspective, this chapter is just as relevant to helping you use your accountant and insurance agent.

Guidelines for Selecting and Working with Your Pros

Here are guidelines to help you select and work with your professional advisors.

Select Good Professionals

You need to find experienced professionals who work regularly with business clients. Although direct hands-on experience within the same industry as your business is desirable, general business experience is probably sufficient.

Word-of-mouth referrals work best. Talk with others in your industry or community. If you have an accountant, ask him or her to recommend a lawyer. If you have a lawyer, he or she may know an accountant and an insurance agent. Your insurance agent may suggest a lawyer or an accountant.

You also need to find a professional who has the time and desire to attend to your business. Many lawyers are good at attracting clients, but the same lawyer may be too busy to service your needs adequately.

Expert Tip

Martindale-Hubbell publishes a national directory of lawyers, the *Martindale-Hubbell Law Directory*. Most lawyers are rated by other practitioners within their geographic area. Ratings, from lowest to highest, are "cv," "bv," and "av." The directory can be found at most city or county law libraries.

Start Early

Too often, business owners don't contact their professional advisors until a problem has arisen. It's not until they are sued or receive a notice from the Internal Revenue Service that they call their professional. This puts them in a defensive posture, circling their wagons to minimize the damage.

When you start your business, schedule a meeting with your professional team. Tell them what you would like to do and how you would like to do it.

Ask them for their suggestions and ideas to help you fine-tune your plan and avoid unknown pitfalls and traps. At this session, you can delegate tasks among your professionals and determine costs.

Getting started on the right foot may cost a little more at the outset, but it will save you time and money in the long run. You may also find that your professional team is willing to discount its usual charges for this type of session in order to get your business.

Learn What You Can Do Inhouse

Professionals can provide many services; however, you can do some of these services yourself. Talk with your professional team about the types of things you can do inhouse and ask your team to instruct your employees so that they can perform the service. For example, lawyers can help businesses develop contract and agreement forms, instruct businesses on obtaining a security interest in goods sold, and set up correct collection practices. If questions come up during these activities, call your professional for advice. By and large, however, you will be able to handle these tasks using your employees.

Expert Tip

Check out your attorney. state bar associations now commonly maintain online records of attorney discipline. Avoid attorneys with a history of discipline problems. Never hire a lawyer without making inquiries.

Keep Your Professionals Up-to-Date

Your professionals can't function as a team if they don't know what you're doing. Plan at least one meeting during the year with your team. This meeting could be held in conjunction with an annual members' meeting.

Use the meeting to tell your professionals what the business has done since the last meeting and what you anticipate the business will do over the next year. Include in the discussion financial results and projections, hiring needs, retirement ideas, personnel matters, equipment or real estate needs, and anything else that impacts the business. In exchange, your professionals can point out legal or tax issues that could affect your plans.

Don't be alarmed if your professional team members don't always agree.

More often than not, you will have to make a decision involving choices. Your team should tell you what your choices are and the pros and cons of each. For example, your accountant may feel that a particular choice has greater risk associated with it than your attorney thinks. Ultimately, you must weigh the choices, balance the risks, and make the choice. Your professionals should feel free to challenge one another in a cooperative working environment.

When you meet with your team, spend time talking with them about how to use the team most effectively. Look for new ways to bring professional services inhouse. Ask professionals which correspondence or documents they would like to receive for their files. Talk with your professionals about how to reduce professional fees, if possible.

Most important, use the session to talk about what you like and don't like about the professional services that you've received. Many smaller businesses find that their legal matters are being handled by a constantly changing mix of lawyers. No business client enjoys being shuffled around. If you're dissatisfied, say so. Like everyone else, professionals want to know if you're unhappy with their service. Finally, don't forget to praise your professional when appropriate.

Bring Several Matters up at One Time

Lawyers and accountants often bill by the hour. Hourly segments are broken down into six-, ten-, or 15-minute segments, depending upon the firm's billing practice. It is often more cost-effective for you to make one call and ask three or four questions than to make three or four separate phone calls to ask those questions.

If it can wait, let it wait until some other matter arises. Don't get carried away with saving fees, however. If the matter is serious or appears to be, make the call.

Ask Questions

Business lawyers spend time immersed in business law matters for many clients. One consequence of this is that the lawyer may take certain things for granted. There is no such thing as a stupid question. If you don't know the answer, ask the question—several at a time, if possible. If you don't understand the answer, that's the professional's problem, not yours. Tell the professional that you still don't understand.

You want to focus your time and energy on running your business. You need to understand the legal, accounting, tax, and insurance issues that impact your business. Ask away.

Question Billing Statements

Clients are often shocked when they get a bill. This generally results from poor communication between professional and client. Know upfront how you will be charged. Ask for estimates for projects that you assign to your professionals. If something looks out of line on your bill, ask about it.

People make mistakes. In addition, many professionals will reduce a bill to preserve the relationship with a client. Don't haggle over nickels and dimes on every bill. Your professional may fire you.

Remember That You Are Important to Your Professional

To the professional, you are a source of income. If the professional serves you well, you are a referral for additional business clients. You also provide the challenge and variety that make his or her job interesting. Your professional team wants to serve you and your business. Don't let poor communication get in the way.

Final Thoughts on Using Your Professional Team

You will need a business lawyer, accountant, and insurance agent. Too many businesses use their experts without allowing them the opportunity to work with those clients as a team. Each professional brings different skills and perspectives to the table. By teaming your professionals, you will become better informed and make better decisions for your business.

Conclusion

After reading *The Operations Manual for LLCs*, you have greater insight into LLC formality and why it is important for your LLC. If you come away with a better understanding of the issues discussed in this book, you have made good use of your time. Don't feel you need to memorize all of the specifics; simply use the book as a handy reference tool for future questions or situations.

To help you recall some of the book's important points, a brief list of tips is provided below.

- Remember that LLCs are distinct legal entities with specific rights, duties, and obligations. If you ignore this fact, you increase your chance of personal liability for LLC acts. Respect the separate identity of your LLC in all aspects of your business.
- LLCs are not rigid entities. On the contrary, they can offer you many opportunities for flexibility through your operating agreement and articles of organization.
- Make your LLC fit your needs and goals. There is no single model to follow; what works for someone else might not work for you. Know the range of choices you have and be creative; use this flexibility.
- Develop good habits for your LLC. Observe required formalities and maintain records of LLC activity. Once you've established your routine for maintaining good records, the rest should be easy.
- Choose your professionals wisely and use them as a team. Develop good working relationships with your lawyer, accountant, and insurance

agent to make the best use of their time and learn what you can do inhouse. Work together for the good of your LLC.

- Determine what works best for your LLC by reviewing this book's sample documents, checklists, and forms.
- The business environment is constantly changing. By reading trade journals and using your professional advisors, stay abreast of the changes that may have an impact on your LLC.
- Because LLC laws vary from state to state, talk with your business lawyer, accountant, and secretary of state before you undertake any action.

If there are other areas that you feel should be covered in later editions of *The Operations Manual for LLCs* or if you have questions, please visit us at *www.learnaboutlaw.com* and follow the links to "forums." You can post a message there and the LearnAboutLaw staff will help you get answers to your questions free of charge.

Supplemental LLC Forms

What follows are a series of documents dealing with the different legal aspects of operating your LLC. You can use these as models for creating similar documents and forms for your limited liability company. A list of the forms included with page numbers is on the next page.

List of Forms

LLC Form 1: Long-Form Operating Agreement for Member-Managed LLC
OPERATING AGREEMENT OF [INSERT NAME OF LLC], LLC

THIS OPERATING AGREEMENT (the "Agreement") is made and entered into on _____, 20___, and those persons whose names, addresses, and signatures are set forth below, being the Members of [INSERT NAME OF LLC], LLC (the "Company"), represent and agree that they have caused or will cause to be filed, on behalf of the Company, Articles of Organization, and that they desire to enter into an operating agreement.

The Members agree as follows:

ARTICLE I. DEFINITIONS

1.1. "Act" means the Limited Liability Company Law of the State in which the Company is organized or chartered, including any amendments or the corresponding provision(s) of any succeeding law.

1.2. "Affiliate" or "Affiliate of a Member" means any Person under the control of, in common control with, or in control of a Member, whether that control is direct or indirect. The term "control," as used herein, means, with respect to a corporation or limited liability company, the ability to exercise more than fifty percent (50%) of the voting rights of the controlled entity and, with respect to an individual, partnership, trust, or other entity or association, the ability, directly or indirectly, to direct the management of policies of the controlled entity or individual.

1.3. "Agreement" means this Operating Agreement, in its original form and as amended from time to time.

1.4. "Articles" means the Articles of Organization or other charter document filed with the Secretary of State in the state of organization forming this limited liability company, as initially filed and as they may be amended from time to time.

1.5. "Capital Account" means the amount of the capital interest of a Member in the Company, consisting of the amount of money and the fair market value, net of liabilities, of any property initially contributed by the Member, as (1) increased by any additional contributions and the Member's share of the Company's profits; and (2) decreased by any distribution to that Member as well as that Member's share of Company losses.

1.6. "Code" means the Internal Revenue Code of 1986, as amended from time to time, the regulations promulgated thereunder, and any corresponding provision of any succeeding revenue law.

1.7. "Company Minimum Gain" shall have the same meaning as set forth for the term "Partnership Minimum Gain" in the Regulations section 1.704-2(d) (26 CFR Section 1.704-2(d)).

1.8. "Departing Member" means any Member whose conduct results in a Dissolution Event or who withdraws from or is expelled from the Company in accordance with Section 4.3, where such withdrawal does not result in dissolution of the Company.

1.9. "Dissolution Event" means, with respect to any Member, one or more of the following: the death, resignation, retirement, expulsion, bankruptcy, or dissolution of any Member.

1.10. "Distribution" means the transfer of money or property by the Company to the Members without consideration.

1.11. "Member" means each Person who has been admitted into membership in the Company, executes this Agreement and any subsequent amendments, and has not engaged in conduct resulting in a Dissolution Event or terminated membership for any other reason.

1.12. "Member Nonrecourse Debt" shall have the same meaning as set forth for the term "Partnership Nonrecourse Debt" in the Code.

1.13. "Member Nonrecourse Deductions" means items of Company loss, deduction, or Code Section 705(a)(2)(B) expenditures which are attributable to Member Nonrecourse Debt.

1.14. "Membership Interest" means a Member's rights in the Company, collectively, including the Member's economic interest, right to vote and participate in management, and right to information concerning the business and affairs of the Company provided in this Agreement or under the Act.

1.15. "Net Profits" and "Net Losses" mean the Company's income, loss, and deductions computed at the close of each fiscal year in accordance with the accounting methods used to prepare the Company's information tax return filed for federal income tax purposes.

1.16. "Nonrecourse Liability" has the meaning provided in the Code.

1.17. "Percentage Interest" means the percentage ownership of the Company of each Member as set forth in the column entitled "Member's Percentage Interest" contained in Table A as recalculated from time to time pursuant to this Agreement.

1.18. "Person" means an individual, partnership, limited partnership, corporation, limited liability company, registered limited liability partnership, trust, association, estate, or any other entity.

1.19. "Remaining Members" means, upon the occurrence of a Dissolution Event, those members of the Company whose conduct did not cause its occurrence.

ARTICLE II. FORMATION AND ORGANIZATION

2.1. Initial Date and Initial Parties. This Agreement is deemed entered into upon the date of the filing of the Company's Articles.

2.2. Subsequent Parties. No Person may become a Member of the Company without agreeing to and without becoming a signatory of this Agreement, and any offer or assignment of a Membership Interest is contingent upon the fulfillment of this condition.

2.3. Term. The Company shall commence upon the filing of its Articles and it shall continue in existence until December 31, 2050, unless terminated earlier under the provisions of this Agreement.

2.4. Principal Place of Business. The Company will have its principal place of business at [INSERT ADDRESS OF PRINCIPAL PLACE OF BUSINESS] or at any other address upon which the Members agree. The Company shall maintain its principal executive offices at its principal place of business, as well as all required records and documents.

2.5. Authorization and Purpose. The purpose of the Company is to engage in any lawful business activity that is permitted by the Act.

ARTICLE III. CAPITAL CONTRIBUTIONS AND ACCOUNTS

3.1. Initial Capital Contributions. The initial capital contribution of each Member is listed in Table A attached hereto. Table A shall be revised to reflect any additional contributions pursuant to Section 3.2.

3.2. Additional Contributions. No Member shall be required to make any additional contributions to the Company. However, upon agreement by the Members that additional capital is desirable or necessary, any Member may, but shall not be required to, contribute additional capital to the Company on a pro rata basis consistent with the Percentage Interest of each of the Members.

3.3. Interest Payments. No Member shall be entitled to receive interest payments in

connection with any contribution of capital to the Company, except as expressly provided herein.

3.4. Right to Return of Contributions. No Member shall be entitled to a return of any
capital contributed to the Company, except as expressly provided in the Agreement.

3.5. Capital Accounts. A Capital Account shall be created and maintained by the
Company for each Member, in conformance with the Code, which shall reflect all
Capital Contributions to the Company. Should any Member transfer or assign all or
any part of his or her Membership Interest in accordance with this Agreement, the
successor shall receive that portion of the Member's Capital Account attributable to
the interest assigned or transferred.

ARTICLE IV. MEMBERS

4.1. Limitation of Liability. No Member shall be personally liable for the debts, obligations, liabilities, or judgments of the Company solely by virtue of his or her
Membership in the Company, except as expressly set forth in this Agreement or
required by law.

4.2. Additional Members. The Members may admit additional Members to the
Company only if approved by a two-thirds majority in interest of the Company
Membership. Additional Members shall be permitted to participate in management at
the discretion of the existing Members. Likewise, the existing Members shall agree
upon an Additional Member's participation in Net Profits, Net Losses, and
Distributions, as those terms are defined in this Agreement. Table A shall be amended
to include the name, present mailing address, taxpayer identification number, and
percentage ownership of any Additional Members.

4.3. Withdrawal or Expulsion from Membership. Any Member may withdraw at any
time after sixty (60) days' written notice to the company, without prejudice to the
rights of the Company or any Member under any contract to which the withdrawing
Member is a party. Such withdrawing Member shall have the rights of a transferee
under this Agreement and the remaining Members shall be entitled to purchase the
withdrawing Member's Membership Interest in accordance with this Agreement. Any
Member may be expelled from the Company upon a vote of two-thirds majority in
interest of the Company Membership. Such expelled Member shall have the rights of

a transferee under this Agreement and the remaining Members shall be entitled to purchase the expelled Member's Membership Interest in accordance with this Agreement.

4.4. Competing Activities. The Members and their officers, directors, managers, agents, employees, and Affiliates are permitted to participate in other business activities which may be in competition, direct or indirect, with those of the Company. The Members further acknowledge that they are under no obligation to present to the Company any business or investment opportunities, even if the opportunities are of such a character as to be appropriate for the Company's undertaking. Each Member hereby waives the right to any claim against any other Member or Affiliate on account of such competing activities.

4.5. Compensation of Members. No Member or Affiliate shall be entitled to compensation for services rendered to the Company, absent agreement by the Members. However, Members and Affiliates shall be entitled to reimbursement for the actual cost of goods and services provided to the Company, including, without limitation, reimbursement for any professional services required to form the Company.

4.6. Transaction with the Company. The Members may permit a Member to lend money to and transact business with the Company, subject to any limitations contained in this Agreement or in the Act. To the extent permitted by applicable laws, such a Member shall be treated like any other Person with respect to transactions with the Company.

4.7. Meetings.

(a) There will be no regular or annual meeting of the Members. However, any Member(s) with an aggregate Percentage Interest of ten percent (10%) or more may call a meeting of the Members at any time. Such meeting shall be held at a place to be agreed upon by the Members.

(b) Minutes of the meeting shall be made and maintained along with the books and records of the Company.

(c) If any action on the part of the Members is to be proposed at the meeting, then written notice of the meeting must be provided to each Member entitled to vote not less than ten (10) days or more than sixty (60) days prior to the meeting. Notice may be given in person, by fax, by first class mail, or by any other written communication, charges prepaid, at the Members' addresses listed in Table A. The notice shall contain the date, time, and place of the meeting and a statement of the general nature of this business to be transacted there.

4.8. Actions at Meetings.

(a) No action may be taken at a meeting that was not proposed in the notice of the meeting, unless there is unanimous consent among all Members entitled to vote.

(b) No action may be taken at a meeting unless a quorum of Members is present, either in person or by proxy. A quorum of Members shall consist of Members holding a majority of the Percentage Interest in the Company.

(c) A Member may participate in, and is deemed present at, any meeting by clearly audible conference telephone or other similar means of communication.

(d) Any meeting may be adjourned upon the vote of the majority of the Membership Interests represented at the meeting.

(e) Actions taken at any meeting of the Members have full force and effect if each Member who was not present, in person or by proxy, signs a written waiver of notice and consent to the holding of the meeting or approval of the minutes of the meeting. All such waivers and consents shall become Company records.

(f) Presence at a meeting constitutes a waiver of the right to object to notice of a meeting, unless the Member expresses such an objection at the start of the meeting.

4.9. Actions Without Meetings. Any action that may be taken at a meeting of the Members may be taken without a meeting and without prior notice, if written consents to the action are submitted to the Company within sixty (60) days of the record date for the taking of the action, executed by Members holding a sufficient number of votes to authorize the taking of the action at a meeting at which all Members entitled to vote thereon are present and vote. All such consents shall be maintained as Company records.

4.10. Record Date. For the purposes of voting, notices of meetings, distributions, or any other rights under this Agreement, the Articles, or the Act, the Members representing in excess of ten percent (10%) of the Percentage Interests in the Company may fix, in advance, a record date that is not more than sixty (60) or less than ten (10) days prior to the date of such meeting or sixty (60) days prior to any other action. If no record date is fixed, the record date shall be determined in accordance with the Act.

4.11. **Voting Rights.** Except as expressly set forth in this Agreement, all actions requiring the vote, approval, or consent of the Members may be authorized upon the vote, approval, or consent of those Members holding a majority of the Percentage Interests in the Company. The following actions require the unanimous vote, approval, or consent of all Members who are neither the subjects of a dissolution event nor the transferors of a Membership Interest:

(a) Approval of the purchase by the Company or its nominee of the Membership Interest of a transferor Member;

(b) Approval of the sale, transfer, exchange, assignment, or other disposition of a Member's interest in the Company and admission of the transferee as a Member;

(c) A decision to make any amendment to the Articles or to this Agreement; and

(d) A decision to compromise the obligation of any Member to make a Capital Contribution or return money or property distributed in violation of the Act.

ARTICLE V. MANAGEMENT

5.1. **Management by Members.** The Company shall be managed by the Members. Each Member has the authority to manage and control the Company and to act on its behalf, except as limited by the Act, the Articles, or this Agreement. The Members shall be empowered to appoint Members to the following officer positions: president, secretary, and chief financial officer. Further, the Members shall be empowered to delegate responsibilities among themselves in accord with such appointments. No such appointment, however, shall affect the voting power of such Members as outlined herein.

5.2. **Limitation on Exposing Members to Personal Liability.** Neither the Company nor any Member may take any action that will have the effect of exposing any Member of the Company to personal liability for the obligations of the Company, without first obtaining the consent of the affected Member.

5.3. **Limitation on Powers of Members.** The Members shall not be authorized to permit the Company to perform the following acts or to engage in the following transactions without first obtaining the affirmative vote or written consent of the Members holding a majority Interest or such greater Percentage Interest as may be indicated below:

(a) The sale or other disposition of all or a substantial part of the Company's assets, whether occurring as a single transaction or a series of transactions over a 12-month period, except if the same is part of the orderly liquidation and winding up of the Company's affairs upon dissolution;

(b) The merger of the Company with any other business entity without the affirmative vote or written consent of all Members;

(c) Any alteration of the primary purpose or business of the Company shall require the affirmative vote or written consent of Members holding at least sixty-six percent (66%) of the Percentage Interest in the Company;

(d) The establishment of different classes of Members;

(e) Transactions between the Company and one or more Members or one or more of any Member's Affiliates, or transactions in which one or more Members or Affiliates thereof have a material financial interest;

(f) Without limiting subsection (e) of this section, the lending of money to any Member or Affiliate of the Company;

(g) Any act which would prevent the Company from conducting its duly authorized business;

(h) The confession of a judgment against the Company.

Notwithstanding any other provisions of this Agreement, the written consent of all of the Members is required to permit the Company to incur an indebtedness or obligation greater than one hundred thousand dollars ($100,000). All checks, drafts, or other instruments requiring the Company to make payment of an amount less than fifty thousand dollars ($50,000) may be signed by any Member, acting alone. Any check, draft, or other instrument requiring the Company to make payment in the amount of fifty thousand dollars ($50,000) or more shall require the signature of two (2) Members acting together.

5.4. Fiduciary Duties. The fiduciary duties a Member owes to the Company and to the other Members of the Company are those of a partner to a partnership and to the partners of a partnership.

5.5. Liability for Acts and Omissions. As long as a Member acts in accordance with Section 5.4, no Member shall incur liability to any other Member or to the Company for any act or omission which occurs while in the performance of services for the Company.

ARTICLE VI. ALLOCATION OF PROFIT AND LOSS

6.1. Compliance with the Code. The Company intends to comply with the Code and all applicable Regulations, including without limitation the minimum gain chargeback requirements, and intends that the provisions of this Article be interpreted consistently with that intent.

6.2. Net Profits. Except as specifically provided elsewhere in this Agreement, Distributions of Net Profit shall be made to Members in proportion to their Percentage Interest in the Company.

6.3. Net Losses. Except as specifically provided elsewhere in this Agreement, Net Losses shall be allocated to the Members in proportion to their Percentage Interest in the Company. However, the foregoing will not apply to the extent that it would result in a Negative Capital Account balance for any Member equal to the Company Minimum Gain which would be realized by that Member in the event of a foreclosure of the Company's assets. Any Net Loss which is not allocated in accordance with the foregoing provision shall be allocated to other Members who are unaffected by that provision. When subsequent allocations of profit and loss are calculated, the losses reallocated pursuant to this provision shall be taken into account such that the net amount of the allocation shall be as close as possible to that which would have been allocated to each Member if the reallocation pursuant to this section had not taken place.

6.4. Regulatory Allocations. Notwithstanding the provisions of Section 6.3, the following applies:

(a) Should there be a net decrease in Company Minimum Gain in any taxable year, the Members shall specially allocate to each Member items of income and gain for that year (and, if necessary, for subsequent years) as required by the Code governing minimum gain chargeback requirements.

(b) Should there be a net decrease in Company Minimum Gain based on a Member Nonrecourse Debt in any taxable year, the Members shall first determine the extent of each Member's share of the Company Minimum Gain attributable to Member Nonrecourse Debt in accordance with the Code. The Members shall then specially allocate items of income and gain for that year (and, if necessary, for subsequent years) in accordance with the Code to each Member who has a share of the Company Nonrecourse Debt Minimum Gain.

(c) The Members shall allocate Nonrecourse Deductions for any taxable year to each Member in proportion to his or her Percentage Interest.

(d) The Members shall allocate Member Nonrecourse Deductions for any taxable year to the Member who bears the risk of loss with respect to the Nonrecourse Debt to which the Member Nonrecourse Deduction is attributable, as provided in the Code.

(e) If a Member unexpectedly receives any allocation of loss or deduction, or item thereof, or distributions which result in the Member's having a Negative Capital Account balance at the end of the taxable year greater than the Member's share of Company Minimum Gain, the Company shall specially allocate items of income and gain to that Member in a manner designed to eliminate the excess Negative Capital Account balance as rapidly as possible. Any allocations made in accordance with this provision shall taken into consideration in determining subsequent allocations under Article VI, so that, to the extent possible, the total amount allocated in this and sub-sequent allocations equals that which would have been allocated had there been no unexpected adjustments, allocations, and distributions and no allocation pursuant to Section 6.4(e).

(f) In accordance with Code Section 704(c) and the Regulations promulgated pursuant thereto, and notwithstanding any other provision in this Article, income, gain, loss, and deductions with respect to any property contributed to the Company shall, solely for tax purposes, be allocated among Members, taking into account any variation between the adjusted basis of the property to the Company for federal income tax purposes and its fair market value on the date of contribution. Allocations pursuant to this subsection are made solely for federal, state, and local taxes and shall not be taken into consideration in determining a Member's Capital Account or share of Net Profits or Net Losses or any other items subject to Distribution under this agreement.

6.5. Distributions. The Members may elect, by unanimous vote, to make a Distribution of assets at any time that would not be prohibited under the Act or under this Agreement. Such a Distribution shall be made in proportion to the unreturned capital contributions of each Member until all contributions have been paid, and thereafter in proportion to each Member's Percentage Interest in the Company. All such Distributions shall be made to those Persons who, according to the books and records of the Company, were the holders of record of Membership Interests on the date of the Distribution. Subject to Section 6.6, neither the Company nor any Members shall be liable for the making of any Distributions in accordance with the provisions of this section.

6.6. Limitations on Distributions.

(a) The Members shall not make any Distribution if, after giving effect to the Distribution, (1) the Company would not be able to pay its debts as they become due in the usual course of business, or (2) the Company's total assets would be less than the sum of its total liabilities plus, unless this Agreement provides otherwise, the amount that would be needed, if the Company were to be dissolved at the time of Distribution, to satisfy the preferential rights of other Members upon dissolution that are superior to the rights of the Member receiving the Distribution.

(b) The Members may base a determination that a Distribution is not prohibited under this section on any of the following: (1) financial statements prepared on the basis of accounting practices and principles that are reasonable under the circumstances, (2) a fair valuation, or (3) any other method that is reasonable under the circumstances.

6.7. Return of Distributions. Members shall return to the Company any Distributions received which are in violation of this Agreement or the Act. Such Distributions shall be returned to the account or accounts of the Company from which they were taken in order to make the Distribution. If a Distribution is made in compliance with the Act and this Agreement, a Member is under no obligation to return it to the Company or to pay the amount of the Distribution for the account of the Company or to any creditor of the Company.

6.8. Members Bound by These Provisions. The Members understand and acknowledge the tax implications of the provisions of this Article of the Agreement and agree to be bound by these provisions in reporting items of income and loss relating to the Company on their federal and state income tax returns.

ARTICLE VII. TRANSFERS AND TERMINATIONS OF MEMBERSHIP INTERESTS

7.1. Restriction on Transferability of Membership Interests. A Member may not transfer, assign, encumber, or convey all or any part of his or her Membership Interest in the Company, except as provided herein. In entering into this Agreement, each of the Members acknowledges the reasonableness of this restriction, which is intended to further the purposes of the Company and the relationships among the Members.

7.2. Permitted Transfers. In order to be permitted, a transfer or assignment of all or any part of a Membership interest must have the approval of a two-thirds majority of the Members of the Company. Each Member, in his or her sole discretion, may proffer or withhold approval. In addition, the following conditions must be met:

(a) The transferee must provide a written agreement, satisfactory to the Members, to be bound by all of the provisions of this Agreement;

(b) The transferee must provide the Company with his or her taxpayer identification number and initial tax basis in the transferred interest;

(c) The transferee must pay the reasonable expenses incurred in connection with his or her admission to Membership;

(d) The transfer must be in compliance with all federal and state securities laws;

(e) The transfer must not result in the termination of the Company pursuant to Code Section 708.

(f) The transfer must not render the Company subject to the Investment Company Act of 1940, as amended; and

(g) The transferor must comply with the provisions of this Agreement.

7.3. Company's Right to Purchase Transferor's Interest. Any Member who wishes to transfer all or any part of his or her interest in the Company shall immediately provide the Company with written notice of his or her intention. The notice shall fully describe the nature of the interest to be transferred. Thereafter, the Company, or its nominee, shall have the option to purchase the transferor's interest at the Repurchase Price as calculated in Section 7.7.

The option provided to the Company shall be irrevocable and shall remain open for (30) days from the Effective Date, except that if notice is given by regular mail, the option shall remain open for thirty-five (35) days from the Effective Date. At any time while the option remains open, the Company (or its nominee) may elect to exercise the option and purchase the transferor's interest in the Company. The transferor Member shall not vote on the question of whether the Company should exercise its option. If the Company chooses to exercise its option to purchase the transferor Member's interest, it shall provide written notice to the transferor within the option period. The notice shall specify a "Closing Date" for the purchase, which shall occur within thirty (30) days of the expiration of the option period. If the Company declines to exercise its option to purchase the transferor Member's interest, the transferor Member may then transfer his or her interest in accordance with Section 7.2. Any transfer not in compliance with the provisions of Section 7.2 shall be null and void and have no force or effect.

In the event that the Company chooses to exercise its option to purchase the transferor Member's interest, the Company may elect to purchase the Member's interest on the following terms:

(a) The Company may elect to pay the Repurchase Price in cash, by making such cash payment to the transferor Member upon the Closing Date.

(b) The Company may elect to pay any portion of the Repurchase Price by delivering to the transferor Member, upon the Closing Date, all of the following:

(1). An amount equal to at least 10% of the Repurchase Price in cash or in an immediately negotiable draft, and

(2) A Promissory Note for the remaining amount of the Repurchase Price, to be paid in 12 successive monthly installments, with such installments beginning 30 days following the Closing Date, and ending one year from the Closing Date, and

(3) A security agreement guaranteeing the payment of the Promissory Note by offering the Transferor's former membership interest as security for the payment of the Promissory Note.

7.4. **Occurrence of Dissolution Event.** Upon the death, withdrawal, resignation, retirement, expulsion, insanity, bankruptcy, or dissolution of any Member (a Dissolution Event), the Company shall be dissolved, unless all of the Remaining Members elect by a majority in interest within 90 days thereafter to continue the operation of the business. In the event that the Remaining Members to agree, the Company and the Remaining Members shall have the right to purchase the interest of the Member whose actions caused the occurrence of the Dissolution Event. The interest shall be sold in the manner described in Section 7.6.

7.5. **Withdrawal from Membership.** Notwithstanding Section 7.4, in the event that a Member withdraws in accordance with Section 4.3, and such withdrawal does not result in the dissolution of the Company, the Company and the Remaining Members shall have the right to purchase the interest of the withdrawing Member in the manner described in Section 7.6.

7.6. Purchase of Interest of Departing Member. The purchase price of a Departing Member's interest shall be determined in accordance with the procedure provided in Section 7.7.

(a) Once a value has been determined, each Remaining Member shall be entitled to purchase that portion of the Departing Member's interest that corresponds to his or her percentage ownership of the Percentage Interests of those Members electing to purchase a portion of the Departing Member's interest in the Company.

(b) Each Remaining Member desiring to purchase a share of the Departing Member's interest shall have thirty (30) days to provide written notice to the Company of his or her intention to do so. The failure to provide notice shall be deemed a rejection of the opportunity to purchase the Departing Member's interest.

(c) If any Member elects not to purchase all of the Departing Member's interest to which he or she is entitled, the other Members may purchase that portion of the Departing Member's interest. Any interest which is not purchased by the Remaining Members must be purchased by the Company.

(d) The Members shall assign a closing date within 60 days after the Members' election to purchase is completed. At that time, the Departing Member shall deliver to the Remaining Members an instrument of title, free of any encumbrances and containing warranties of title, duly conveying his or her interest in the Company and, in return, he or she shall be paid the purchase price for his or her interest in cash. The Departing Member and the Remaining Members shall perform all acts reasonably necessary to consummate the transaction in accordance with this agreement.

7.7. Calculation of Repurchase Price. The "Repurchase Price" shall be determined as of the date of the event causing the transfer or dissolution event (the "Effective Date"). The date that the Company receives notice of a Member's intention to transfer his or her interest pursuant to this paragraph shall be deemed to be the Effective Date. The Repurchase Price shall be determined as follows:

(a) Annual Agreed Valuation. For the purpose of determining the price to be paid for a departing Member's Percentage Interest on or before _____, 20__, the value of each percentage point of Percentage Interest is $___. The parties agree that the price represents the fair market value of each percentage point of Percentage Interest, including the goodwill of the LLC. The Members shall redetermine the value of the

LLC each year, beginning on or before _____, 20__, and thereafter within sixty (60) days following the end of each fiscal year. The value agreed upon shall be committed to a company resolution and signed by all members. If the Members and the LLC fail to make a redetermination of value in any year, then the prior year's valuation shall govern the valuation.

7.8. **No Release of Liability.** Any Member or Departing Member whose interest in the Company is sold pursuant to Article VII is not relieved thereby of any liability he or she may owe the Company.

ARTICLE VIII. BOOKS, RECORDS, AND REPORTING

8.1. **Books and Records.** The Members shall maintain at the Company's principal place of business the following books and records: a current list of the full name and last known business or residence address of each Member, together with the Capital Contribution, Capital Account, and Membership Interest of each Member; a copy of the Articles and all amendments thereto, copies of the Company's federal, state, and local income tax or information returns and reports, if any, for the six (6) most recent taxable years, a copy of this Agreement and any amendments to it; copies of the Company's financial statements, if any; the books and records of the Company as they relate to its internal affairs for at least the current and past four (4) fiscal years; and true and correct copies of all relevant documents and records indicating the amount, cost, and value of all the property and assets of the Company.

8.2. **Accounting Methods.** The books and records of the Company shall be maintained in accordance with the accounting methods utilized for federal income tax purposes.

8.3. **Reports.** The Members shall cause to be prepared and filed in a timely manner all reports and documents required by any governmental agency. The Members shall cause to be prepared at least annually all information concerning the Company's operations that is required by the Members for the preparation of their federal and state tax returns.

8.4. **Inspection Rights.** For purposes reasonably related to their interests in the Company, all Members shall have the right to inspect and copy the books and records of the Company during normal business hours, upon reasonable request.

8.5. **Bank Accounts.** The Members shall maintain all of the funds of the Company in a bank account or accounts in the name of the Company, at a depository institution or institutions to be determined by a majority of the Members. The Members shall not permit the funds of the Company to be commingled in any manner with the funds or accounts of any other Person. The Members shall have the powers enumerated in Section 5.3 with respect to endorsing, signing, and negotiating checks, drafts, or other evidence of indebtedness to the Company or obligating the Company money to a third party.

ARTICLE IX. DISSOLUTION, LIQUIDATION, AND WINDING UP

9.1. Conditions Under Which Dissolution Shall Occur. The Company shall dissolve and its affairs shall be wound up upon the happening of the first of the following: at the time specified in the Articles; upon the happening of a Dissolution Event and the failure of the Remaining Members to elect to continue, in accordance with Section 7.4; upon the vote of all of the Members to dissolve; upon the entry of a decree of judicial dissolution pursuant to the Act; upon the happening of any event specified in the Articles as causing or requiring dissolution; or upon the sale of all or substantially all of the Company's assets.

9.2. Winding Up and Dissolution. If the Company is dissolved, the Members shall wind up its affairs, including the selling of all of the Company's assets and the provision of written notification to all of the Company's creditors of the commencement of dissolution proceedings.

9.3. Order of Payment. After determining that all known debts and liabilities of the Company in the process of winding up have been paid or provided for, including, without limitation, debts and liabilities to Members who are creditors of the Company, the Members shall distribute the remaining assets among the Members in accordance with their Positive Capital Account balances, after taking into consideration the profit and loss allocations made pursuant to Section 6.4. Members shall not be required to restore Negative Capital Account Balances.

ARTICLE X. INDEMNIFICATION

10.1.Indemnification. The Company shall indemnify any Member and may indemnify any Person to the fullest extent permitted by law on the date such indemnification is requested for any judgments, settlements, penalties, fines, or expenses of any kind incurred as a result of the Person's performance in the capacity of Member, officer, employee, or agent of the Company, as long as the Member or Person did not behave in violation of the Act or this Agreement.

ARTICLE XI. MISCELLANEOUS PROVISIONS

11.1. Assurances. Each Member shall execute all documents and certificates and perform all acts deemed appropriate by the Members and the Company or required by this Agreement or the Act in connection with the formation and operation of the Company and the acquisition, holding, or operation of any property by the Company.

11.2. Complete Agreement. This Agreement and the Articles constitute the complete and exclusive statement of the agreement among the Members with respect to the matters discussed herein and therein and they supersede all prior written or oral statements among the Members, including any prior statement, warranty, or representation.

11.3. Section Headings. The section headings which appear throughout this Agreement are provided for convenience only and are not intended to define or limit the scope of this Agreement or the intent of subject matter of its provisions.

11.4. Binding Effect. Subject to the provisions of this Agreement relating to the transferability of Membership Interests, this Agreement is binding upon and shall inure to the benefit of the parties hereto and their respective heirs, administrators, executors, successors, and assigns.

11.5. Interpretation. All pronouns and common nouns shall be deemed to refer to the masculine, feminine, neuter, singular, and plural, as the context may require. In the event that any claim is made by any Member relating to the drafting and interpretation of this Agreement, no presumption, inference, or burden of proof or persuasion shall be created or implied solely by virtue of the fact that this Agreement was drafted by or at the behest of a particular Member or his or her counsel.

11.6. Applicable Law. Each Member agrees that all disputes arising under or in connection with this Agreement and any transactions contemplated by this Agreement shall be governed by the internal law, and not the law of conflicts, of the state of organization.

11.7. Specific Performance. The Members acknowledge and agree that irreparable injury shall result from a breach of this Agreement and that money damages will not adequately compensate the injured party. Accordingly, in the event of a breach or a threatened breach of this Agreement, any party who may be injured shall be entitled, in addition to any other remedy which may be available, to injunctive relief to prevent or to correct the breach.

11.8. Remedies Cumulative. The remedies described in this Agreement are cumulative and shall not eliminate any other remedy to which a Person may be lawfully entitled.

11.9. Notice. Any notice or other writing to be served upon the Company or any Member thereof in connection with this Agreement shall be in writing and shall be deemed completed when delivered to the address specified in Table A, if to a Member, and to the resident agent, if to the Company. Any Member shall have the right to change the address at which notices shall be served upon ten (10) days' written notice to the Company and the other Members.

11.10. Amendments. Any amendments, modifications, or alterations to this Agreement or the Articles must be in writing and signed by all of the Members.

11.11. Severability. Each provision of this Agreement is severable from the other provisions. If, for any reason, any provision of this Agreement is declared invalid or contrary to existing law, the inoperability of that provision shall have no effect on the remaining provisions of the Agreement, which shall continue in full force and effect.

11.12. Counterparts. This Agreement may be executed in counterparts, each of which shall be deemed an original and all of which shall, when taken together, constitute a single document.

IN WITNESS WHEREOF, this Agreement has been made and executed by the Members effective as of the date first written above.

_____

[Member]

_____

[Member]

_____

[Member]

Table A: Name, Address, and Initial Capital Contribution of the Members

Name, Address, and Tax ID of Member	Value of Initial Capital Contribution	Nature of Member's Initial Capital Contribution (i.e., cash, services, property)	Percentage Interest of Member

LLC Form 2: Long-Form Operating Agreement for Manager-Managed LLC
OPERATING AGREEMENT OF [INSERT NAME OF LLC], LLC

THIS OPERATING AGREEMENT (the "Agreement") is made and entered into on _____, 20__, and those persons whose names, addresses and signatures are set forth below, being the Members of [INSERT NAME OF LLC], LLC (the "Company"), represent and agree that they have caused or will cause to be filed, on behalf of the Company, Articles of Organization, and that they desire to enter into an operating agreement.

The Members agree as follows:

ARTICLE I. DEFINITIONS

1.1. "Act" means the Limited Liability Company Law of the State in which the Company is organized or chartered, including any amendments or the corresponding provision(s) of any succeeding law.

1.2. "Affiliate" or "Affiliate of a Member" means any Person under the control of, in common control with, or in control of a Member, whether that control is direct or indirect. The term "control," as used herein, means, with respect to a corporation or limited liability company, the ability to exercise more than fifty percent (50%) of the voting rights of the controlled entity, and with respect to an individual, partnership, trust, or other entity or association, the ability, directly or indirectly, to direct the management of policies of the controlled entity or individual.

1.3. "Agreement" means this Operating Agreement, in its original form and as amended from time to time.

1.4. "Articles" means the Articles of Organization or other charter document filed with the Secretary of State in the State of organization forming this limited liability company, as initially filed and as they may be amended from time to time.

1.5. "Capital Account" means the amount of the capital interest of a Member in the Company, consisting of the amount of money and the fair market value, net of liabilities, of any property initially contributed by the Member, as (1) increased by any additional contributions and the Member's share of the Company's profits; and (2) decreased by any distribution to that Member as well as that Member's share of Company losses.

1.6. "Code" means the Internal Revenue Code of 1986, as amended from time to time, the regulations promulgated thereunder, and any corresponding provision of any succeeding revenue law.

1.7. "Company Minimum Gain" shall have the same meaning as set forth for the term "Partnership Minimum Gain" in the Regulations section 1.704-2(d) (26 CFR Section 1.704-2(d)).

1.8. "Departing Member" means any Member whose conduct results in a Dissolution Event or who withdraws from or is expelled from the Company in accordance with Section 4.3, where such withdrawal does not result in dissolution of the Company.

1.9. "Dissolution Event" means, with respect to any Member, one or more of the following: the death, resignation, retirement, expulsion, bankruptcy, or dissolution of any Member.

1.10. "Distribution" means the transfer of money or property by the Company to the Members without consideration.

1.11. "Manager" means each Person who has been appointed to serve as a Manager of the Company in accordance with the Act, the Articles, and this Agreement.

1.12. "Member" means each Person who has been admitted into membership in the Company; executes this Agreement and any subsequent amendments, and has not engaged in conduct resulting in a Dissolution Event or terminated membership for any other reason.

1.13. "Member Nonrecourse Debt" shall have the same meaning as set forth for the term "Partnership Nonrecourse Debt" in the Code.

1.14. "Member Nonrecourse Deductions" means items of Company loss, deduction, or Code Section 705(a)(2)(B) expenditures which are attributable to Member Nonrecourse Debt.

1.15. "Membership Interest" means a Member's rights in the Company, collectively, including the Member's economic interest, right to vote and participate in management, and right to information concerning the business and affairs of the Company provided in this Agreement or under the Act.

1.16. "Net Profits" and "Net Losses" mean the Company's income, loss, and deductions computed at the close of each fiscal year in accordance with the accounting methods used to prepare the Company's information tax return filed for federal income tax purposes.

1.17. "Nonrecourse Liability" has the meaning provided in the Code.

1.18. "Percentage Interest" means the percentage ownership of the Company of each Member as set forth in the column entitled "Member's Percentage Interest" contained in Table A as recalculated from time to time pursuant to this Agreement.

1.19. "Person" means an individual, partnership, limited partnership, corporation, limited liability company, registered limited liability partnership, trust, association, estate, or any other entity.

1.20. "Remaining Members" means, upon the occurrence of a Dissolution Event, those Members of the Company whose conduct did not cause its occurrence.

ARTICLE II. FORMATION AND ORGANIZATION

2.1. Initial Date and Initial Parties. This Agreement is deemed entered into upon the date of the filing of the Company's Articles.

2.2. Subsequent Parties. No Person may become a Member of the Company without agreeing to and without becoming a signatory of this Agreement, and any offer or assignment of a Membership Interest is contingent upon the fulfillment of this condition.

2.3. Term. The Company shall commence upon the filing of its Articles and it shall continue in existence until December 31, 2050, unless terminated earlier under the provisions of the Act this Agreement.

2.4. Principal Place of Business. The Company will have its principal place of business at [INSERT ADDRESS OF PRINCIPAL PLACE OF BUSINESS], or at any other address upon which the Members agree. The Company shall maintain its principal executive offices at its principal place of business, as well as all required records and documents.

2.5. Authorization and Purpose. The purpose of the Company is to engage in any lawful business activity which is permitted by the Act.

ARTICLE III. CAPITAL CONTRIBUTIONS AND ACCOUNTS

3.1. Initial Capital Contributions. The initial Capital Contribution of each Member is listed in Table A attached hereto. Table A shall be revised to reflect and additional contributions pursuant to Section 3.2.

3.2. Additional Contributions. No Member shall be required to make any additional contributions to the Company. However, upon agreement by the Members that additional capital is desirable or necessary, any Member may, but shall not be required to, contribute additional capital to the Company on a pro rata basis consistent with the Percentage Interest of each of the Members.

3.3. **Interest Payments.** No Member shall be entitled to receive interest payments in connection with any contribution of capital to the Company, except as expressly provided herein.

3.4. **Right to Return of Contributions.** No Member shall be entitled to a return of any capital contributed to the Company, except as expressly provided in the Agreement.

3.5. **Capital Accounts.** A Capital Account shall be created and maintained by the Company for each Member, in conformance with the Code, which shall reflect all Capital Contributions to the Company. Should any Member transfer or assign all or any part of his or her membership interest in accordance with this Agreement, the successor shall receive that portion of the Member's Capital Account attributable to the interest assigned or transferred.

ARTICLE IV. MEMBERS

4.1. **Limitation of Liability.** No Member shall be personally liable for the debts, obligations, liabilities, or judgments of the Company solely by virtue of his or her Membership in the Company, except as expressly set forth in this Agreement or required by law.

4.2. **Additional Members.** The Members may admit additional Members to the Company only if approved by a two-thirds majority in interest of the Company Membership. Additional Members shall be permitted to participate in management at the discretion of the existing Members. Likewise, the existing Members shall agree upon an Additional Member's participation in "Net Profits," "Net Losses," and distributions, as those terms are defined in this Agreement. Table A shall be amended to include the name, present mailing address, taxpayer identification number, and percentage ownership of any Additional Members.

4.3. **Withdrawal or Expulsion from Membership.** Any Member may withdraw at any time after sixty (60) days' written notice to the company, without prejudice to the rights of the Company or any Member under any contract to which the withdrawing Member is a party. Such withdrawing Member shall have the rights of a transferee under this Agreement and the remaining Members shall be entitled to purchase the withdrawing Member's Membership Interest in accordance with this Agreement. Any

Member may be expelled from the Company upon a vote of two-thirds majority in interest of the Company Membership. Such expelled Member shall have the rights of a transferee under this Agreement and the remaining Members shall be entitled to purchase the withdrawing Member's Membership Interest in accordance with this Agreement.

4.4. Competing Activities. The Members and their officers, directors, managers, agents, employees and Affiliates are permitted to participate in other business activities which may be in competition, direct or indirect, with those of the Company. The Members further acknowledge that they are under no obligation to present to the Company any business or investment opportunities, even if the opportunities are of such a character as to be appropriate for the Company's undertaking. Each Member hereby waives the right to any claim against any other Member or Affiliate on account of such competing activities.

4.5. Compensation of Members. No Member or Affiliate shall be entitled to compensation for services rendered to the Company, absent agreement by the Members. However, Members and Affiliates shall be entitled to reimbursement for the actual cost of goods and services provided to the Company, including, without limitation, reimbursement for any professional services required to form the Company.

4.6. Transaction with the Company. The Members may permit a Member to lend money to and transact business with the Company, subject to any limitations contained in this Agreement or in the Act. To the extent permitted by applicable laws, such a Member shall be treated like any other Person with respect to transactions with the Company.

4.7. Meetings.

(a) There will be no regular or annual meeting of the Members. However, any Member(s) with an aggregate Percentage Interest of ten percent (10%) or more may call a meeting of the Members at any time. Such meeting shall be held at a place to be agreed upon by the Members.

(b) Minutes of the meeting shall be made and maintained along with the books and records of the Company.

(c) If any action on the part of the Members is to be proposed at the meeting, then written notice of the meeting must be provided to each Member entitled to vote not less than ten (10) days or more than sixty (60) days prior to the meeting. Notice may be given in person, by fax, first class mail, or any other written communication, charges prepaid, at the Members' address listed in Table A. The notice shall contain the date, time, and place of the meeting and a statement of the general nature of this business to be transacted there.

4.8. Actions at Meetings.

(a) No action may be taken at a meeting that was not proposed in the notice of the meeting, unless there is unanimous consent among all Members entitled to vote.

(b) No action may be taken at a meeting unless a quorum of Members is present, either in person or by proxy. A quorum of Members shall consist of Members holding a majority of the Percentage Interest in the Company.

(c) A Member may participate in, and is deemed present at, any meeting by clearly audible conference telephone or other similar means of communication.

(d) Any meeting may be adjourned upon the vote of the majority of the Membership Interests represented at the meeting.

(e) Actions taken at any meeting of the Members have full force and effect if each Member who was not present in person or by proxy signs a written waiver of notice and consent to the holding of the meeting or approval of the minutes of the meeting. All such waivers and consents shall become Company records.

(f) Presence at a meeting constitutes a waiver of the right to object to notice of a meeting, unless the Member expresses such an objection at the start of the meeting.

4.9. Actions Without Meetings. Any action that may be taken at a meeting of the Members may be taken without a meeting and without prior notice, if written consents to the action are submitted to the Company within sixty (60) days of the record date for the taking of the action, executed by Members holding a sufficient number of votes to authorize the taking of the action at a meeting at which all Members entitled to vote thereon are present and vote. All such consents shall be maintained as Company records.

4.10. Record Date. For the purposes of voting, notices of meetings, distributions, or any other rights under this Agreement, the Articles, or the Act, the Members representing in excess of ten percent (10%) of the Percentage Interests in the Company may fix, in advance, a record date that is not more than sixty (60) or less than ten (10) days prior to the date of such meeting or sixty (60) days prior to any other action. If no record date is fixed, the record date shall be determined in accordance with the Act.

4.11. Voting Rights. Except as expressly set forth in this Agreement, all action requiring the vote, approval, or consent of the Members may be authorized upon the vote, approval, or consent of those Members holding a majority of the Percentage Interests in the Company. The following actions require the unanimous vote, approval, or consent of all Members who are neither the subjects of a Dissolution Event nor the transferors of a Membership Interest:

(a) Approval of the purchase by the Company or its nominee of the Membership Interest of a transferor Member;

(b) Approval of the sale, transfer, exchange, assignment, or other disposition of a Member's interest in the Company, and admission of the transferee as a Member;

(c) A decision to make any amendment to the Articles or to this Agreement; and

(d) A decision to compromise the obligation to any Member to make a Capital Contribution or return money or property distributed in violation of the Act.

ARTICLE V. MANAGEMENT

5.1. Management by Appointed Managers. The Company shall be managed by one or more appointed Managers. The number of Managers shall be three (3) and the identity of each Manager is set forth in Table B, below. The Members shall elect and appoint the Managers (and also determine the number of Managers) who shall have the full and exclusive right, power, and authority to manage the affairs of the Company and to bind the Company, to make all decisions with respect thereto, and to do or cause to be done any and all acts or things deemed by the Members to be necessary, appropriate, or desirable to carry out or further the business of the Company. All decisions and actions of the Managers shall be made by majority vote of the Managers as provided in this Agreement. There shall be no mandatory annual meetings of the Members or Managers; annual meetings shall be optional. Managers shall serve at the pleasure of the Members and until his or her successors and are duly elected and appointed by the Members.

5.2. Limitation on Powers of Managers; Member Vote Required for Some Actions.

The Managers shall not be authorized to permit the Company to perform the following acts or to engage in the following transactions without first obtaining the affirmative vote or written consent of the Members holding a majority Interest or such greater Percentage Interest as may be indicated below:

(a) The sale or other disposition of all or a substantial part of the Company's assets, whether occurring as a single transaction or a series of transactions over a 12-month period, except if the same is part of the orderly liquidation and winding up of the Company's affairs upon dissolution.

(b) The merger of the Company with any other business entity without the affirmative vote or written consent of all Members;

(c) Any alteration of the primary purpose or business of the Company shall require the affirmative vote or written consent of Members holding at least sixty-six percent (66%) of the Percentage Interest in the Company;

(d) The establishment of different classes of Members;

(e) Transactions between the Company and one or more Members or one or more of any Member's Affiliates, or transactions in which one or more Members or Affiliates thereof have a material financial interest;

(f) Without limiting subsection (e) of this section, the lending of money to any Member or Affiliate of the Company;

(g) Any act which would prevent the Company from conducting its duly authorized business;

(h) The confession of a judgment against the Company.

Notwithstanding any other provisions of this Agreement, the written consent of all of the Members is required to permit the Company to incur an indebtedness or obligation greater than one hundred thousand dollars ($100,000.00). All checks, drafts, or other instruments requiring the Company to make payment of an amount less than fifty thousand dollars ($50,000.00) may be signed by any Member, acting alone. Any check, draft, or other instrument requiring the Company to make payment in the amount of fifty thousand dollars ($50,000.00) or more shall require the signature of two (2) Members acting together.

5.3. Optional Appointment of Officers. The Managers are empowered to undertake the appointment of officers, including, without limitation, a chairperson or a president, or both, a secretary, a chief financial officer, and any other officers with such titles, powers, and duties as shall be determined by the Managers or Members. An officer may, but need not, be a Member or Manager of the Company, and any number of offices may be held by the same Person. Officers, if any, shall be appointed by the Managers and shall serve at the pleasure of the Managers, subject to the rights, if any, of an officer under any contract of employment. Any officer may resign at any time upon written notice to the Company without prejudice to the rights, if any, of the Company under any contract to which the officer is a party.

5.4. **Fiduciary Duties.** The fiduciary duties a Member owes to the Company and to the other Members of the Company are those of a partner to a partnership and to the partners of a partnership.

5.3. **Liability for Acts and Omissions.** As long as a Member acts in accordance with Section 5.4, no Member shall incur liability to any other Member or to the Company for any act or omission which occurs while in the performance of services for the Company.

ARTICLE VI. ALLOCATION OF PROFIT AND LOSS

6.1. **Compliance with the Code.** The Company intends to comply with the Code and all applicable Regulations, including without limitation the minimum gain chargeback requirements, and intends that the provisions of this Article be interpreted consistently with that intent.

6.2. **Net Profits.** Except as specifically provided elsewhere in this Agreement, Distributions of Net Profit shall be made to Members in proportion to their Percentage Interest in the Company.

6.3. **Net Losses.** Except as specifically provided elsewhere in this Agreement, Net Losses shall be allocated to the Members in proportion to their Percentage Interest in the Company. However, the foregoing will not apply to the extent that it would result in a Negative Capital Account balance for any Member equal to the Company Minimum Gain which would be realized by that Member in the event of a foreclosure of the Company's assets. Any Net Loss which is not allocated in accordance with the foregoing provision shall be allocated to other Members who are unaffected by that provision. When subsequent allocations of profit and loss are calculated, the losses reallocated pursuant to this provision shall be taken into account such that the net amount of the allocation shall be as close as possible to that which would have been allocated to each Member if the reallocation pursuant to this section had not taken place.

6.4. Regulatory Allocations. Notwithstanding the provisions of Section 6.3, the following applies:

(a) Should there be a net decrease in Company Minimum Gain in any taxable year, the Members shall specially allocate to each Member items of income and gain for that year (and, if necessary, for subsequent years) as required by the Code governing minimum gain chargeback requirements.

(b) Should there be a net decrease in Company Minimum Gain based on a Member Nonrecourse Debt in any taxable year, the Members shall first determine the extent of each Member's share of the Company Minimum Gain attributable to Member Nonrecourse Debt in accordance with the Code. The Members shall then specially allocate items of income and gain for that year (and, if necessary, for subsequent years) in accordance with the Code to each Member who has a share of the Company Nonrecourse Debt Minimum Gain.

(c) The Members shall allocate Nonrecourse deductions for any taxable year to each Member in proportion to his or her Percentage Interest.

(d) The Members shall allocate Member Nonrecourse Deductions for any taxable year to the Member who bears the risk of loss with respect to the Nonrecourse debt to which the Member Nonrecourse Deduction is attributable, as provided in the Code.

(e) If a Member unexpectedly receives any allocation of loss or deduction, or item thereof, or distributions which result in the Member's having a Negative Capital Account balance at the end of the taxable year greater than the Member's share of Company Minimum Gain, the Company shall specially allocate items of income and gain to that Member in a manner designed to eliminate the excess Negative Capital Account balance as rapidly as possible. Any allocations made in accordance with this provision shall taken into consideration in determining subsequent allocations under Article VI, so that, to the extent possible, the total amount allocated in this and subsequent allocations equals that which would have been allocated had there been no unexpected adjustments, allocations, and distributions and no allocation pursuant to Section 6.4(e).

(f) In accordance with Code Section 704(c) and the Regulations promulgated pursuant thereto, and notwithstanding any other provision in this Article, income, gain, loss, and deductions with respect to any property contributed to the Company shall, solely for tax purposes, be allocated among Members, taking into account any variation between the adjusted basis of the property to the Company for federal income tax purposes and its fair market value on the date of contribution. Allocations pursuant to this subsection are made solely for federal, state, and local taxes and shall not be taken into consideration in determining a Member's Capital Account or share of Net Profits or Net Losses or any other items subject to Distribution under this agreement.

6.5. **Distributions.** The Members may elect, by unanimous vote, to make a Distribution of assets at any time that would not be prohibited under the Act or under this Agreement. Such a Distribution shall be made in proportion to the unreturned capital contributions of each Member until all contributions have been paid, and thereafter in proportion to each Member's Percentage Interest in the Company. All such Distributions shall be made to those Persons who, according to the books and records of the Company, were the holders of record of Membership Interests on the date of the Distribution. Subject to Section 6.6, neither the Company nor any Members shall be liable for the making of any Distributions in accordance with the provisions of this section.

6.6. **Limitations on Distributions.**

(a) The Members shall not make any Distribution if, after giving effect to the Distribution: (1) The Company would not be able to pay its debts as they become due in the usual course of business; or (2) The Company's total assets would be less than the sum of its total liabilities plus, unless this Agreement provides otherwise, the amount that would be needed, if the Company were to be dissolved at the time of Distribution, to satisfy the preferential rights of other Members upon dissolution that are superior to the rights of the Member receiving the Distribution.

(b) The Members may base a determination that a Distribution is not prohibited under this section on any of the following: (1) Financial statements prepared on the basis of accounting practices and principles that are reasonable under the circumstances; (2) A fair valuation; or (3) Any other method that is reasonable under the circumstances.

6.7. Return of Distributions. Members shall return to the Company any Distributions received which are in violation of this Agreement or the Act. Such Distributions shall be returned to the account or accounts of the Company from which they were taken in order to make the Distribution. If a Distribution is made in compliance with the Act and this Agreement, a Member is under no obligation to return it to the Company or to pay the amount of the Distribution for the account of the Company or to any creditor of the Company.

6.8. Members Bound by These Provisions. The Members understand and acknowledge the tax implications of the provisions of this Article of the Agreement and agree to be bound by these provisions in reporting items of income and loss relating to the Company on their federal and state income tax returns.

ARTICLE VII. TRANSFERS AND TERMINATIONS OF MEMBERSHIP INTERESTS

7.1. Restriction on Transferability of Membership Interests. A Member may not transfer, assign, encumber, or convey all or any part of his or her Membership Interest in the Company, except as provided herein. In entering into this Agreement, each of the Members acknowledges the reasonableness of this restriction, which is intended to further the purposes of the Company and the relationships among the Members.

7.2. Permitted Transfers. In order to be permitted, a transfer or assignment of all or any part of a Membership interest must have the approval of a two-thirds majority of the Members of the Company. Each Member, in his or her sole discretion, may proffer or withhold approval. In addition, the following conditions must be met:

(a) The transferee must provide a written agreement, satisfactory to the Members, to be bound by all of the provisions of this Agreement;

(b) The transferee must provide the Company with his or her taxpayer identification number and initial tax basis in the transferred interest;

(c) The transferee must pay the reasonable expenses incurred in connection with his or her admission to Membership;

(d) The transfer must be in compliance with all federal and state securities laws;

(e) The transfer must not result in the termination of the Company pursuant to Code Section 708.

(f) The transfer must not render the Company subject to the Investment Company Act of 1940, as amended; and

(g) The transferor must comply with the provisions of this Agreement.

7.3. **Company's Right to Purchase Transferor's Interest.** Any Member who wishes to transfer all or any part of his or her Membership Interest in the Company shall immediately provide the Company with written notice of his or her intention. The notice shall fully describe the nature of the interest to be transferred. Thereafter, the Company, or its nominee, shall have the option to purchase the transferor's interest at the Repurchase Price as calculated in Section 7.7.

The option provided to the Company shall be irrevocable and shall remain open for thirty (30) days from the Effective Date, except that if notice is given by regular mail, the option shall remain open for thirty-five (35) days from the Effective Date. At any time while the option remains open, the Company (or its nominee) may elect to exercise the option and purchase the transferor's interest in the Company. The transferor Member shall not vote on the question of whether the Company should exercise its option. If the Company chooses to exercise its option to purchase the transferor Member's interest, it shall provide written notice to the transferor within the option period. The notice shall specify a "Closing Date" for the purchase, which shall occur within thirty (30) days of the expiration of the option period. If the Company declines to exercise its option to purchase the transferor Member's interest, the transferor Member may then transfer his or her interest in accordance with Section 7.2. Any transfer not in compliance with the provisions of Section 7.2 shall be null and void and have no force or effect.

In the event that the Company chooses to exercise its option to purchase the transferor Member's interest, the Company may elect to purchase the Member's interest on the following terms:

(a) The Company may elect to pay the Repurchase Price in cash, by making such cash payment to the transferor Member upon the Closing Date.

(b) The Company may elect to pay any portion of the Repurchase Price by delivering to the transferor Member, upon the Closing Date, all of the following:

(1). An amount equal to at least ten percent (10%) of the Repurchase Price in cash or in an immediately negotiable draft; and

(2) A Promissory Note for the remaining amount of the Repurchase Price, to be paid in 12 successive monthly installments, with such installments beginning 30

days following the Closing Date, and ending one year from the Closing Date; and (3) A security agreement guaranteeing the payment of the Promissory Note by offering the Transferor's former membership interest as security for the payment of the Promissory Note.

7.4. Occurrence of Dissolution Event. Upon the death, withdrawal, resignation, retirement, expulsion, insanity, bankruptcy, or dissolution of any Member (a Dissolution Event), the Company shall be dissolved, unless all of the Remaining Members elect by a majority in interest within ninety (90) days thereafter to continue the operation of the business. In the event that the Remaining Members to agree, the Company and the Remaining Members shall have the right to purchase the interest of the Member whose actions caused the occurrence of the Dissolution Event. The interest shall be sold in the manner described in Section 7.6.

7.5. Withdrawal from Membership. Notwithstanding Section 7.4, in the event that a Member withdraws in accordance with Section 4.3, and such withdrawal does not result in the dissolution of the Company, the Company and the Remaining Members shall have the right to purchase the interest of the withdrawing Member in the manner described in Section 7.6.

7.6. Purchase of Interest of Departing Member. The purchase price of a Departing Member's interest shall be determined in accordance with the procedure provided in Section 7.7.

(a) Once a value has been determined, each Remaining Member shall be entitled to purchase that portion of the Departing Member's interest that corresponds to his or her percentage ownership of the Percentage Interests of those Members electing to purchase a portion of the Departing Member's interest in the Company.

(b) Each Remaining Member desiring to purchase a share of the Departing Member's interest shall have thirty (30) days to provide written notice to the Company of his or her intention to do so. The failure to provide notice shall be deemed a rejection of the opportunity to purchase the Departing Member's interest.

(c) If any Member elects not to purchase all of the Departing Member's interest to which he or she is entitled, the other Members may purchase that portion of the Departing Member's interest. Any interest which is not purchased by the Remaining Members must be purchased by the Company.

(d) The Members shall assign a Closing Date within sixty (60) days after the Members' election to purchase is completed. At that time, the Departing Member shall deliver to the Remaining Members an instrument of title, free of any encumbrances and containing warranties of title, duly conveying his or her interest in the Company and, in return, he or she shall be paid the purchase price for his or her interest in cash. The Departing Member and the Remaining Members shall perform all acts reasonably necessary to consummate the transaction in accordance with this agreement.

7.7. Calculation of Repurchase Price. The "Repurchase Price" shall be determined as of the date of the event causing the transfer or Dissolution Event (the "Effective Date"). The date that the Company receives notice of a Member's intention to transfer his or her interest pursuant to this paragraph shall be deemed to be the Effective Date. The Repurchase Price shall be determined as follows:

(a) Annual Agreed Valuation. For the purpose of determining the price to be paid for a Departing Member's Percentage Interest on or before _____, 20__, the value of each percentage point of Percentage Interest is $___. The parties agree that the price represents the fair market value of each percentage point of Percentage Interest, including the goodwill of the Company. The Members shall redetermine the value of the Company each year, beginning on or before _____, 20__, and thereafter within sixty (60) days following the end of each fiscal year. The value agreed upon shall be committed to a Company resolution and signed by all members. If the Members and the Company fail to make a redetermination of value in any year, then the prior year's valuation shall govern the valuation.

7.8. **No Release of Liability.** Any Member or Departing Member whose interest in the Company is sold pursuant to Article VII is not relieved thereby of any liability he or she may owe the Company.

ARTICLE VIII. BOOKS, RECORDS, AND REPORTING

8.1. **Books and Records.** The Members shall maintain at the Company's principal place of business the following books and records: a current list of the full name and last known business or residence address of each Member, together with the Capital Contribution, Capital Account, and Membership Interest of each Member; a copy of the Articles and all amendments thereto, copies of the Company's federal, state, and local income tax or information returns and reports, if any, for the six (6) most recent taxable years; a copy of this Agreement and any amendments to it; copies of the Company's financial statements, if any; the books and records of the Company as they relate to its internal affairs for at least the current and past four (4) fiscal years; and true and correct copies of all relevant documents and records indicating the amount, cost, and value of all the property and assets of the Company.

8.2. Accounting Methods. The books and records of the Company shall be maintained in accordance with the accounting methods utilized for federal income tax purposes.

8.3. Reports. The Members shall cause to be prepared and filed in a timely manner all reports and documents required by any governmental agency. The Members shall cause to be prepared at least annually all information concerning the Company's operations that is required by the Members for the preparation of their federal and state tax returns.

8.4. Inspection Rights. For purposes reasonably related to their interests in the Company, all Members shall have the right to inspect and copy the books and records of the Company during normal business hours, upon reasonable request.

8.5. Bank Accounts. The Managers shall maintain all of the funds of the Company in a bank account or accounts in the name of the Company, at a depository institution or institutions to be determined by a majority of the Members. The Managers shall not permit the funds of the Company to be commingled in any manner with the funds or accounts of any other Person. The Managers shall have the powers enumerated in Section 5.2 with respect to endorsing, signing, and negotiating checks, drafts, or other evidence of indebtedness to the Company or obligating the Company money to a third party.

ARTICLE IX. DISSOLUTION, LIQUIDATION, AND WINDING UP

9.1. Conditions Under Which Dissolution Shall Occur. The Company shall dissolve and its affairs shall be wound up upon the happening the first of the following: at the time specified in the Articles, upon the happening of a Dissolution Event and the failure of the Remaining Members to elect to continue, in accordance with Section 7.4, upon the vote of all of the Members to dissolve, upon the entry of a decree of judicial dissolution pursuant to the Act, upon the happening of any event specified in the Articles as causing or requiring dissolution, or upon the sale of all or substantially all of the Company's assets.

9.2. **Winding Up and Dissolution.** If the Company is dissolved, the Members shall wind up its affairs, including the selling of all of the Company's assets and the provision of written notification to all of the Company's creditors of the commencement of Dissolution proceedings.

9.3. **Order of Payment.** After determining that all known debts and liabilities of the Company in the process of winding up have been paid or provided for, including, without limitation, debts and liabilities to Members who are creditors of the Company, the Members shall distribute the remaining assets among the Members in accordance with their Positive Capital Account balances, after taking into consideration the profit and loss allocations made pursuant to Section 6.4. Members shall not be required to restore Negative Capital Account Balances.

ARTICLE X. INDEMNIFICATION

10.1. **Indemnification.** The Company shall indemnify any Member and may indemnify any Person to the fullest extent permitted by law on the date such indemnification is requested for any judgments, settlements, penalties, fines, or expenses of any kind incurred as a result of the Person's performance in the capacity of Member, officer, employee, or agent of the Company, as long as the Member or Person did not behave in violation of the Act or this Agreement.

ARTICLE XI. MISCELLANEOUS PROVISIONS

11.1. **Assurances.** Each Member shall execute all documents and certificates and perform all acts deemed appropriate by the Members and the Company or required by this Agreement or the Act in connection with the formation and operation of the Company and the acquisition, holding, or operation of any property by the Company.

11.2. **Complete Agreement.** This Agreement and the Articles constitute the complete and exclusive statement of the agreement among the Members with respect to the matters discussed herein and therein and they supersede all prior written or oral statements among the Members, including and prior statement, warranty, or representation.

11.3. **Section Headings.** The section headings which appear throughout this Agreement are provided for convenience only and are not intended to define or limit the scope of this Agreement or the intent of subject matter of its provisions.

11.4. Binding Effect. Subject to the provisions of this Agreement relating to the transferability of Membership Interests, this Agreement is binding upon and shall inure to the benefit of the parties hereto and their respective heirs, administrators, executors, successors, and assigns.

11.5. Interpretation. All pronouns and common nouns shall be deemed to refer to the masculine, feminine, neuter, singular, and plural, as the context may require. In the event that any claim is made by any Member relating to the drafting and interpretation of this Agreement, no presumption, inference, or burden of proof or persuasion shall be created or implied solely by virtue of the fact that this Agreement was drafted by or at the behest of a particular Member or his or her counsel.

11.6. Applicable Law. Each Member agrees that all disputes arising under or in connection with this Agreement and any transactions contemplated by this Agreement shall be governed by the internal law, and not the law of conflicts, of the State of organization.

11.7. Specific Performance. The Members acknowledge and agree that irreparable injury shall result from a breach of this Agreement and that money damages will not adequately compensate the injured party. Accordingly, in the event of a breach or a threatened breach of this Agreement, any party who may be injured shall be entitled, in addition to any other remedy which may be available, to injunctive relief to prevent or to correct the breach.

11.8. Remedies Cumulative. The remedies described in this Agreement are cumulative and shall not eliminate any other remedy to which a Person may be lawfully entitled.

11.9. Notice. Any notice or other writing to be served upon the Company or any Member thereof in connection with this Agreement shall be in writing and shall be deemed completed when delivered to the address specified in Table A, if to a Member, and to the resident agent, if to the Company. Any Member shall have the right to change the address at which notices shall be served upon ten (10) days' written notice to the Company and the other Members.

11.10. Amendments. Any amendments, modifications, or alterations to this Agreement or the Articles must be in writing and signed by all of the Members.

11.11. Severability. Each provision of this Agreement is severable from the other provisions. If, for any reason, any provision of this Agreement is declared invalid or contrary to existing law, the inoperability of that provision shall have no effect on the remaining provisions of the Agreement, which shall continue in full force and effect.

11.12.**Counterparts.** This Agreement may be executed in counterparts, each of which shall be deemed an original and all of which shall, when taken together, constitute a single document.

Table A: Name, Address, and Initial Capital Contribution of the Members

Name, Address, and Tax ID of Member	Value of Initial Capital Contribution	Nature of Member's Initial Capital Contribution (i.e., cash, services, property)	Percentage Interest of Member

Table B: Managers

Name of Managers	Address of Managers

IN WITNESS WHEREOF, this Agreement has been made and executed by the Members effective as of the date first written above.

_____   _____
[MEMBER]   [MEMBER]

_____
[MEMBER]

LLC Form 3: Alternative Provision for Use in Long-Form Operating Agreements: Book Value Method of Valuation

7.7. Calculation of Repurchase Price. The "Repurchase Price" shall be determined as of the date of the event causing the transfer or dissolution event (the "Effective Date"). The date that the Company receives notice of a Member's intention to transfer his or her interest pursuant to this paragraph shall be deemed to be the Effective Date. The Repurchase Price shall be determined as follows:

(a) Computation of Book Value. The book value of each percentage point of Percentage Interest shall be computed by the independent certified public accountant (CPA) regularly used by the Company or, if the Company has no CPA, by a CPA selected by the Company for this purpose. The book value shall be determined in accordance with the regular financial statements prepared by the Company and in accordance with generally accepted accounting principles, applied consistently with the accounting principles previously applied by the Company, adjusted to reflect the following:

(i) All inventory, valued at market value.

(ii) All real property, leasehold improvements, equipment, and furnishings and fixtures valued at the valuation appearing on the Company's books as adjusted for depreciation or, with a useful life of greater than live years, as defined for tax purposes on the Company's books, valued at their fair market value.

(iii) The amount of any cash surrender value of any insurance policies owned by the Company on the life of any person.

(iv) The face amount of any accounts payable.

(v) The face amount of any accounts receivable, with a reasonable reserve for bad debts.

(vi) Any accrued taxes or assessments, deducted as liabilities.

(vii) All usual fiscal year-end accruals and deferrals (including depreciation), prorated over the fiscal year.

(viii) The reasonable lair market value of any goodwill or other intangible assets.

To arrive at the value of each percentage point of Membership Interest, the book value computed according to this Section shall be divided by one hundred (100). The Company shall provide any information the CPA deems necessary or useful in determining the value of the Membership Interest.

LLC Form 4: Alternative Provision for Use in Long-Form Operating Agreements: Capitalization of Earnings Method of Valuation

7.7. Calculation of Repurchase Price. The "Repurchase Price" shall be determined as of the date of the event causing the transfer or dissolution event (the "Effective Date"). The date that the Company receives notice of a Member's intention to transfer his or her interest pursuant to this paragraph shall be deemed to be the Effective Date. The Repurchase Price shall be determined as follows:

(a) Computation. The purchase price of each percentage point of Percentage Interest shall be computed by the independent certified public (CPA) regularly used by the Company or, if the Company has no CPA, by a CPA selected by the Company for this purpose. The price of the Company's total Membership Interest shall be the sum of the Company's net profits for the most recent [TWO, THREE, FOUR, OR FIVE] years, divided by [TWO, THREE, FOUR, OR FIVE]. This average net profit shall be multiplied by [INSERT THE MULTIPLIER BY WHICH YOU DESIRE TO AMPLIFY ANNUAL NET PROFITS, TYPICALLY A FIGURE BETWEEN TWO AND FOUR] and the result shall be divided by the number of shares then outstanding. The Company's net profits shall be determined in accordance with the regular financial statements and in accordance with generally accepted accounting principles.

LLC Form 5: Alternative Provision for Use in Long-Form Operating Agreements: Appraisal Method of Valuation

7.7. Calculation of Repurchase Price. The "Repurchase Price" shall be determined as of the date of the event causing the transfer or dissolution event (the "Effective Date"). The date that the Company receives notice of a Member's intention to transfer his or her interest pursuant to this paragraph shall be deemed to be the Effective Date. The Repurchase Price shall be determined as follows:

(a) Selection of Appraiser. Within 10 days after the event triggering the valuation of Membership Interests, the Company and the selling Member shall mutually select a qualified appraiser to appraise the Company and set a value on its Membership Interests. If the Company and the selling Member cannot agree on a mutually acceptable appraiser, each party shall have five (5) days after the expiration of the previous period to appoint its own qualified appraiser. If either party fails to appoint a qualified appraiser within the five- (5-) day period, the other party's appraiser, alone, shall have twenty-one (21) days to appraise the value of the Company's Membership Interests. If both parties have each selected appraisers, these appraisers shall have twenty-one (21) days to appraise the value of the Company's Membership Interests. If the two appraisers cannot come to agreement on the appraised value of the Interests, they shall both select another qualified appraiser, who will then determine the value of the Interests.

(b) Considerations in Making Appraisal. The appraiser(s) shall consider the following factors in making their appraisals:

(1) The value of comparable companies, if known.

(2) The fair market value, or replacement value, as appropriate, of any real property, leasehold improvements, equipment, and furnishings and fixtures.

(3) The face amount of any accounts payable or other corporate liabilities.

(4) The face amount of any accounts receivable, with a reasonable reserve for bad debts.

LLC Form 6: Notice to Remaining Members by a Member Desiring to Withdraw from LLC

Scott Bess
123 Elm Street
San Francisco, CA 94107
415-555-1212

September 28, 2007

Dear Brian,

This is my formal notice that I will be withdrawing from my ownership and membership of PLASTICWORLD, LLC. Section 11 of the operating agreement states that:

"No Member may withdraw from the Company except by written request of the Member given to each of the other Members and with the unanimous written consent of the other Members, the effective date of withdrawal being the date on which the unanimous written consent of all of the other Members is given."

In accordance with that Section, I hereby give such notice. As required by our operating agreement, I hereby ask that you, as the remaining member, consent to my withdrawal.

Assuming you consent to my withdrawal, we must next discuss the valuation of my interest. I suggest that we speak informally first; if we can't come to some resolution, we can then trigger the appraisal rights under the operating agreement.

I'll await your response.

Yours,

Scott Bess

LLC Form 7: Notice to Withdrawing Member

Brian Bess
801 Minnesota Street
San Francisco, CA 94107
415-555-1212

September 30, 2007

Dear Scott,

I received your letter giving notice of your desire to withdraw your ownership and membership of PLASTICWORLD, LLC.

As you requested, I consent to your withdrawal.

I also agree that we should discuss the valuation of your interest before we seek an expensive appraisal.

Yours,

Brian Bess

LLC Form 8: Written Consent of Members to Expel Member from LLC

WRITTEN CONSENT OF MEMBERS TO EXPEL MEMBER FROM LLC

The undersigned members of 17 REASONS, LLC, owning of record the number of shares entitled to vote as set forth, hereby consent to the following company actions.

The purpose of this consent is to expel member David Canaan from 17 REASONS, LLC. The standard by which a member can be expelled from 17 REASONS, LLC is set forth in the operating agreement of the LLC:

A Member may be expelled from the Company upon a vote of two-thirds majority in interest of the Company Membership. Such expelled Member shall have the rights of a transferee under this Agreement and the remaining Members shall be entitled to purchase the expelled Member's Membership Interest in accordance with this Agreement.

Three of the four members have agreed that Mr. Canaan should be expelled from the LLC. As such, three-fourths of the LLC membership meets the requirements of expulsion set forth in the governing documents.

The governing documents do not require that the voting members set forth any cause or reason to expel a member. Nevertheless, the undersigned members wish to expel Mr. Canaan for the following reasons:

*Mr. Canaan has not met his employment responsibilities with the LLC; he has preferred to devote his time to other businesses.

*Mr. Canaan failed to make a required capital contribution.

This written consent is effective as of the date set forth below.

_____

John Farnsworth

_____

Lisa Knowles

_____

David Stapleton

LLC Form 9: Notice to Member of Expulsion from LLC

17 REASONS, LLC
1010 Mission Street
San Francisco, CA 94107
September 30, 2007

David Canaan
48 Sanchez Street
Austin, TX 7875

Dear Mr. Canaan,

This is an important notice that concerns your ownership and membership of 17 Reasons, LLC. As you know, the operating agreement that governs 17 Reasons, LLC contains a provision allowing for a two-thirds majority of the owners of 17 Reasons to expel a member. The section reads:

A Member may be expelled from the Company upon a vote of two-thirds majority in interest of the Company Membership. Such expelled Member shall have the rights of a transferee under this Agreement and the remaining Members shall be entitled to purchase the expelled Member's Membership Interest in accordance with this Agreement.

On September 29, 2007, three of the four members of 17 Reasons voted, by written consent, to expel you from 17 Reasons.

Within the next 30 days, we will order an appraisal to value your interest in 17 Reasons so that you may be compensated for your terminated interest. We wish you the best in the future.

_____
John Farnsworth

_____
Lisa Knowles

_____
David Stapleton

LLC Form 10: Resolution Authorizing Manager to Transfer Property

RESOLUTION BY WRITTEN CONSENT OF THE MEMBERS OF 17 REASONS, LLC

The undersigned, who constitute the entire membership of 17 Reasons, LLC, a Michigan LLC (the "LLC"), acting pursuant to the operating agreement of the LLC, and pursuant to the Laws of the State of Michigan, hereby adopt and approve the recitals and resolutions set forth below, which shall have the same force and effect as if adopted and approved at a duly held meeting.

RESOLVED, that the Manager for the LLC, Michael Heskett, a member in good standing of the bar of the State of Michigan, is hereby authorized to transfer all of the following property and is furthermore authorized to execute all instruments and documents to effect such transfer, such as deeds, stock powers, etc.:

*The LLC's interest in shares of stock of Initech Corporation.

*The LLC's interest in a parcel of real property known as 123 14th Street in Dearborn, Michigan.

Witness our signatures to be effective the 5th day of February, 2008.

_____
John Farnsworth

_____
Lisa Knowles

_____
David Stapleton

LLC Form 11: Resolution Authorizing a One-Time Mandatory Capital Contribution from LLC Members

RESOLUTION OF THE MEMBERS OF 17 REASONS, LLC REQUIRING A ONE-TIME MANDATORY CAPITAL CONTRIBUTION FROM LLC MEMBERSHIP

The undersigned, who constitute the entire membership of 17 Reasons, LLC, a Michigan LLC (the "LLC"), acting pursuant to the operating agreement of the LLC, and pursuant to the Laws of the State of Michigan, hereby adopt and approve the recitals and resolutions set forth below, which shall have the same force and effect as if adopted and approved at a duly held meeting.

WHEREAS, the operating agreement of the LLC states the following, concerning the members' obligations to make capital contributions:

4.2 Additional Capital Contributions. The Members shall have no obligation to make any additional Capital Contributions to the Company. The Members may make additional Capital Contributions to the Company as the Members unanimously determine are necessary, appropriate, or desirable.

RESOLVED, that after careful deliberation, the members have unanimously determined and resolved hereby that it is in the interest of the LLC and its members that the members make a one-time mandatory capital contribution to the LLC as follows:

*Each member shall pay a capital contribution based upon his or her percentage ownership in the LLC.

*As such, each 1% of LLC ownership shall obligate a member to a $100 capital contribution.

RESOLVED, therefore, that each member (owning equal shares of 33.33% each) shall make capital contribution of $3,333.00 to the LLC.

RESOLVED, that the articles of organization are not amended or modified in any way by these resolutions.

_____

John Farnsworth

_____

Lisa Knowles

_____

David Stapleton

LLC Form 12: Notice of Year-End Distribution

December 31, 2007

To: John Farnsworth
993b Hayes Street
San Francisco, CA 92110

This notice concerns your (25%) membership interest in 17 Reasons, LLC. As you know, it is the policy of 17 Reasons, LLC to distribute year-end profits to members in proportion to their membership interests.

As such, your membership interest entitles you to a pro-rata share of the year-end distribution of profits. A check for your distribution is included.

_____

Lisa Knowles
LLC Manager

LLC Form 13: Resolution of Members Converting
Member-Managed LLC into Manager-Managed LLC

RESOLUTION OF THE MEMBERS OF 17 REASONS, LLC CONVERTING MEMBER-MANAGED LLC INTO MANAGER-MANAGED LLC AND ADOPTING CHANGES TO LLC OPERATING AGREEMENT

The undersigned, who constitute the entire membership of 17 Reasons, LLC, a Michigan LLC (the "LLC"), acting pursuant to the operating agreement of the LLC, and pursuant to the laws of the State of Michigan, hereby adopt and approve the recitals and resolutions set forth below, which shall have the same force and effect as if adopted and approved at a duly held meeting.

RESOLVED, that the LLC is hereby converted from a member-managed LLC into a manager-managed LLC.

RESOLVED, that the following paragraph is hereby stricken from the operating agreement of the LLC:

7.1 Management by Members. The Company shall be managed by its Members, who shall have full and exclusive right, power, and authority to manage the affairs of the Company and to bind the Company to contracts and obligations, to make all decisions with respect thereto, and to do or cause to be done any and all acts or things deemed by the Members to be necessary, appropriate, or desirable to carry out or further the business of the Company.

RESOLVED, that the following paragraph is hereby inserted into the operating agreement of the LLC:

7.1 Management by Manager(s). The Members shall elect and appoint Manager(s) who shall have the full and exclusive right, power, and authority to manage the affairs of the Company and to bind the Company, to make all decisions with respect thereto, and to do or cause to be done any and all acts or things deemed by the Members to be necessary, appropriate or desirable to carry out or further the business of the Company. All decisions and actions of the Manager(s) shall be made by majority vote of the Manager(s) as provided in Section 12.3. No annual meeting shall be required to reappoint Manager(s). Such Person(s) shall serve in such office(s) at the pleasure of the Members and until his, her, or their successors are duly elected and appointed by the Members. Until further action of the Members as provided herein, the Person(s) whose names appear on Table B below are the Manager(s) of the Company.

Table B: Manager(s)

Name of Managers	Address of Managers

_____

John Farnsworth

_____

Lisa Knowles

_____

David Stapleton

Glossary

Acquisition: The purchase of one business entity by anoFther, through the purchase of either its shares or its assets.

Administrative Dissolution: The involuntary dissolution of a corporation or an LLC by the secretary of state or equivalent department, due to the failure of the business entity to meet statutory requirements, such as periodic filing and tax reporting.

Advisory Board: A body that advises the board of directors or managers of a corporation or LLC but does not have authority to vote on company matters.

Agent for Service of Process: The person or entity

authorized to receive legal papers on behalf of a corporation or an LLC.

Alter Ego Liability: The doctrine that attaches liability to corporate shareholders or LLC members in cases of commingling of assets and failure to observe corporate formalities.

Amendment of Articles of Organization: The procedure by which one or more changes are made to an LLC's articles of organization.

Annual Meeting of Directors: A legally mandated meeting held each year to elect officers of a corporation and to address other corporate matters, usually following immediately after an annual meeting of shareholders.

Annual Meeting of Managers: A meeting of the managers of a manager-managed LLC. Annual meetings of managers are generally not mandated by state law, but represent sound LLC governance.

Annual Meeting of Members: A meeting of the owners (members) of an LLC. Annual meetings of members are generally not mandated by state law, but represent sound LLC governance.

Annual Meeting of Shareholders: A legally mandated meeting held each year to elect directors for the corporation and to address other corporate matters.

Apportionment: The allocation of income earned from activities in a particular state or assets present in a particular state to determine the tax due in that state.

Arm's-Length Relationship: A term used to describe the condition of a business transaction, indicating that the parties to the transaction are independent and have equal bargaining strength, in order to avoid any appearance of favoritism or a conflict of interest.

Articles of Formation: See *Articles of Organization*.

Articles of Incorporation: The document that gives birth to a corporation. Articles cover foundational matters, such as the name of the corporation, the shares it is authorized to issue, its corporate purpose, and its agent for service of process. Articles of incorporation are to corporations what articles of organization are to LLCs. Sometimes known as certificate of incorporation or corporate charter.

Articles of Organization: The document that gives birth to an LLC. Articles of organization cover foundational matters, such as the name of the LLC, its business purpose, and its agent for service of process. Articles of organization are to LLCs what articles of incorporation are to corporations. Sometimes known as articles of formation or certificate of formation.

Authorized Capital: The total number of a corporation's authorized shares multiplied by the par value of a share. For example, 1,000,000 authorized shares of stock with a one cent par value constitute an authorized capital of $10,000.

Authorized Shares: The number of shares of stock that a corporation has the authority to issue. The authorized shares of a class of stock are stated in a corporation's articles of incorporation.

Basis: The measuring rod by which gain or loss is determined when an asset is sold. Basis is an important tax concept.

Blue Sky Laws: The securities laws of individual states, collectively. These laws seek to protect people from investing in sham companies—companies that offer nothing more than "blue sky."

Board of Directors: The directors of a corporation, collectively. The directors of a corporation are its governing board. Elected by shareholders, they vote on major corporate matters, such as issuing shares of stock, electing officers, and approving mergers and acquisitions.

Bond: An interest-bearing instrument issued by a corporation or other entity that serves as evidence of a debt or obligation.

Business Judgment Rule: The rule that shields directors of corporations and managers and officers of LLCs from liability for mismanagement of the entities that they serve.

Bylaws: The internal operating rules of a corporation, usually set out in a five- to 20-page document. Bylaws govern such matters as holding meetings, voting, quorums, elections, and the powers of directors and officers.

C Corporation: Any corporation that has not elected S corporation status.

Capital Contribution: The total amount of cash, other property, services rendered, promissory notes, and/or other obligations contributed to a company for the owners' interest in that company.

Certificate, Stock: A legal document that certifies ownership of a specified number of stock shares in a corporation. Also known as certificate of stock or share certificate.

Certificate of Authority: A document issued by the secretary of state or equivalent department that authorizes a foreign corporation to operate in a state other than its state of incorporation.

Certificate of Good Standing: A document issued by the secretary of state or equivalent department certifying that a corporation is validly existing and in compliance with all periodic and taxation requirements.

Certificate of Incorporation: See *Articles of Incorporation*.

Charter, Corporate: See *Articles of Incorporation*.

Charter Document: The form by which a corporation or a limited liability company is created—articles of incorporation for the former and articles of organization for the latter.

Close Corporation: A corporation owned by a small number of individuals. Corporations must elect to be close corporations by inserting a statement in their articles of incorporation. State laws typically permit close corporations to be operated more informally than other corporations.

Closely Held Corporation: A public corporation whose shares are held by a small number of shareholders who are typically not willing to sell, so ownership of the corporation remains in the hands of a few. The definition is fluid and subjective: there are no specific limits of the "small number."

Common Stock: A corporation's primary class of stock. Common stockholders typically have voting rights.

Consent Resolution: Any resolution in writing, signed by all of the directors or shareholders, that authorizes an action.

Control and Domination: A term used by courts to characterize the influence the influence that owners exercise over their business entities that makes them vulnerable to a piercing of their corporate or LLC veil.

Conversion Rights: Rights allowing the holder of shares of stock or other financial instruments to convert to other shares of stock.

Convertible Instrument: Any financial instrument such as bonds or notes that can be converted into shares of stock. Shares of stock may also be convertible into shares of another class.

Corporate Charter: See *Articles of Incorporation*.

Corporate Secretary: A corporate officer, elected by the directors, usually charged with record-keeping responsibilities.

Corporate Veil: The legal separation between a corporate entity and its officers and directors that provides immunity from personal liability for damages caused by the corporation under their control. See also *Pierce the Corporate Veil*.

Corporation: A legal structure that allows individuals to organize a business as a separate legal entity.

Cumulative Voting: A system of voting shares of stock used in some states. Cumulative voting gives minority shareholders additional voting power by allowing them to combine their votes for a single director.

DBA: See *Doing Business As*.

Deadlock: The circumstance that arises when either the board of directors or shareholders or a corporation or the managers or owners of an LLC are evenly split on a vote and cannot take action. Deadlock can lead to judicial resolution of the underlying dispute.

Debt Financing: A method of financing in which the company receives a loan and gives its promise to repay the loan. See also *Equity Financing*.

Derivative Suit: A civil lawsuit filed by shareholders on behalf of a corporation or owners on behalf of an LLC asserting rights of the corporation or LLC when the corporation or LLC is refusing to act in a manner to protect the corporation's or LLC's rights.

Dilution: The effect of reducing an existing shareholder's or owner's interest in a corporation, LLC, or partnership when new shares are issued.

Director: A member of the governing board of a corporation. Elected by shareholders, the directors vote on major corporate matters, such as issuing shares of stock, electing officers, and approving mergers and acquisitions.

Dissolution: The process of shutting down a corporation, an LLC, or a partnership, settling its affairs, and ending its life. Dissolution can be administrative, judicial, or voluntary.

Distribution: A transfer of profits or property by a business entity to its owners.

Dividend: A share of profits issued to the holders of shares in a corporation. Dividends may be paid in shares of stock or other property, such as shares in a subsidiary or parent company.

Dividend Priority: Special rights enjoyed by holders of a secondary class of stock that entitle them to receive dividends before other shareholders.

Doing Business As (DBA): Operating under a name other than its legal name. Some states require a corporation operating under any names other than its legal name to file DBA or fictitious business name registration forms for the protection of consumers conducting business with the corporation.

Domestic Corporation or Limited Liability Company: In general, a corporation or an LLC whose articles of incorporation or organization are filed in the state in which it operates and maintains its principal office.

Equity: Ownership interest in a company. Also Equity Interest.

Equity Financing: A method of financing in which a company issues shares of its stock and receives money in return. See also *Debt Financing*.

Equity Interest: Ownership interest in a company.

Fictitious Business Name: Any name under which a company operates that differs from its legal name. Some states require DBA (doing business as) or fictitious business name filings to be made for the protection of consumers conducting business with the entity.

Fiduciary: One who holds or administers property for another and is held to a high standard of trust and responsibility with respect to that property.

Fiduciary Relationship: A special relationship in which one party, the fiduciary, owes heightened duties of good faith and responsibility to the other party with respect to the property and rights of the other party.

Foreign Corporation: In general, a corporation that operates in one state but whose articles of incorporation are filed in another state. The state in which an out-of-state entity operates refers to it as foreign. The term also refers to corporations chartered in other nations.

Foreign Limited Liability Company: In general, an LLC that operates in one state but whose articles of organization are filed in another state. The state in which an out-of-state entity operates refers to it as foreign. The term also refers to LLCs chartered in other nations.

Franchise Tax: A tax levied in consideration for the privilege of either incorporating or qualifying to do business in a state. A franchise tax may be based upon income, assets, outstanding shares, or a combination.

Friends and Family Offering: A period in which parties who are connected in some way to the owner(s) of a new enterprise are invited to invest in that enterprise. Such an offering must adhere to state and federal laws. Also known as a friends and family round or a seed round

Fully Reporting Company: A public company that is subject to the Securities and Exchange Commission's periodic reporting requirements.

Go Public: The process of becoming a public, fully reporting company, either by filing a registration statement with the SEC or by merging with a public company.

Good Standing: The state a corporation enjoys when it is in full compliance with the law.

Illiquidity Discount: A discount in the value of an interest in a business because of legal restrictions on the resale of that interest.

Incorporator: The person or entity that organizes a corporation and files its articles of incorporation. The incorporator can take corporate action before directors and officers are appointed.

Indemnification: A legal concept by which a person, either through contractual agreement or pursuant to principles of equity, is legally bound to reimburse another person in case of loss arising from an act.

Initial Director: One of the first directors of a corporation, named in the articles of incorporation filed with the secretary of state.

Initial Public Offering (IPO): The first time that a corporation offers to sell its shares to people outside the company. See also *Go Public*.

Instrumentality Rule: Principle by which a court disregards the legal separation between a subsidiary corporation and the parent corporation when it views the subsidiary as organized and controlled by the parent to such an extent that the subsidiary is only an instrument of the parent and the court then holds the parent corporation responsible for the obligations of its subsidiary. The instrumentality rule now seems to apply beyond parent/subsidiary situations.

Inter Vivos: Between living persons, generally used in reference to transactions, trusts, or gifts.

Involuntary Dissolution: The forced dissolution of a corporation or a limited liability company by a judicial or administrative action.

Judicial Dissolution: The forced dissolution of a corporation or a limited liability company by a court at the request of a state attorney general, an owner, or a creditor.

Liability: Legal responsibility for an act or an omission. When two or more people are responsible, their liability can be joint—as a group—or several—individually.

Liability Shield: The protection from liabilities, debts, and lawsuits enjoyed by the owners of a well-operated LLC or corporation that maintains its good standing. The owners of such an LLC or corporation are said to be "shielded from liability."

Limited Liability Company (LLC): A flexible business organization that offers the advantages of liability protection and the simplicity of a partnership.

Limited Partnership: A business organization that allows limited partners to enjoy limited personal liability while general partners have unlimited personal liability.

Liquidation: The conversion of assets into cash; in law, the process by which a company (or part thereof) is brought to an end and its assets are distributed.

Liquidation Preference: The priority inherent in certain classes of stock (usually preferred stock) that entitles holders of that stock to be paid first in the event that the corporation's assets are liquidated.

Liquidity: The ease with which an asset can be converted into cash.

Manager: A person who is granted the authority to manage and operate an LLC.

Manager-Managed LLC: An LLC that is managed by managers appointed by the members (owners) of the LLC.

Member: An owner of a limited liability company.

Member-Managed LLC: An LLC that is managed by its members (owners) and not by appointed managers.

Membership Ledger: A ledger indicating the owners of an LLC and their proportion of ownership. A corporation's ledger is called a share ledger.

Merger: The combination of one or more corporations, LLCs, or other business entities into a single business entity.

Minority Shareholder: Any shareholder owning less than 50% of the stock in a corporation.

Minutes: The official instant written record of a meeting.

No-Par Shares: Shares for which there is no designated par value.

Nonprofit Corporation: A business organization that serves some public purpose and therefore enjoys special treatment under the law. Nonprofit corporations, contrary to their name, can make a profit, but cannot be designed primarily to be profitable. Distributions upon liquidation typically must be made to another nonprofit.

Offering Circular: A formal written offer to sell securities that presents the facts about a business enterprise that a prospective investor needs to make an informed decision about investing in that enterprise. The offering circular contains information about the business of the company, financial facts, a description of the security offered, risk factors of the investment, uses of the proceeds, organization of the company, officers and directors, any pending litigation, and other relevant information. The information in an offering circular should be presented clearly and concisely in a way that enables potential investors to understand it.

Officer: A manager of a corporation, such as the president, chief executive office (CEO), chief financial officer (CFO), and secretary. The officers are appointed by the board of directors.

Operating Agreement: The agreement that governs the internal structure and operation of an LLC and governs the relationship between its members and managers. Usually set out in a 5- to 20-page document, the operating agreement governs such matters as holding meetings, voting, quorums, elections, and the powers of directors and officers.

Organizer: The person or entity that organizes a limited liability company and files its articles of organization.

Outside Director: An independent member of the board of directors who is not a shareholder or regular employee of a corporation.

Ownership Ledger: See *Membership Ledger*.

Par Value: The issued price of a security that bears no relation to the market price.

Parent Corporation: A corporation that either owns outright or controls a subsidiary.

Partnership: A business organization formed when two or more persons or entities come together to operate a business for profit. Liability is not limited in a general partnership; a limited partnership provides limited liability for the limited partners but not for the general partners.

Partnership Agreement: The written document that governs the internal structure and operation of a partnership and governs the relationship among its partners.

Pass-Through Taxation: Treatment of a business entity by a taxing agency that allows profits to pass through the entity without being subject to taxation until they are distributed among the owners, who each then pay personal income tax on their share of those profits. Partnerships, LLCs, and S corporations.

Percentage Ownership: An individual's ownership in an LLC, partnership, or corporation, expressed as a percentage of the total ownership.

Pierce the Corporate Veil: The doctrine that attaches liability to corporate shareholders in cases of commingling of assets and failure to observe corporate formalities.

Preemptive Rights: Rights enjoyed by shareholders to purchase additional shares of stock in the same proportion as their current holdings.

Preferred Stock: A separate and/or secondary class of stock issued by some corporations. Preferred stock typically has limited or no voting rights, but its holders are paid dividends or receive repayment priority in the event that the corporation is liquidated.

Professional Corporation: A corporation whose members are all licensed professionals, such as doctors, lawyers, accountants, and architects.

Professional LLC: An LLC organized to offer services that normally require a license, such as the practice of medicine or law.

Prospectus: A legal document that businesses use to provide all material information about the securities they are offering for sale to potential investors.

Proxy: An authorization by a shareholder giving another person the right to vote the owner's shares. Proxy also refers to the document granting such authority.

Qualification: The process in which a foreign corporation registers in a state of operation other than its state of incorporation.

Quorum: The minimum percentage of owners, managers, or directors who must be present at a meeting in order for any vote to be legally effective.

Record Date: The date, set by a company, used to determine when an individual must own shares or units in a company in order to receive certain benefits from a company, such as dividend rights and voting rights. The record date is important to shareholders in publicly traded companies because shares are constantly changing hands.

Redemption: A repurchase of shares from shareholders by a corporation.

Redemption Rights: The right enjoyed by a corporation to repurchase certain shares of stock.

Registered Agent: The person or entity authorized to receive legal papers on behalf of a corporation.

Registered Office: The official address of a corporation, typically the same as that of the registered agent. See also *Resident Agent*.

Representative Management: The form of management of a business entity in which the owners elect managers, directors, and officers to operate and manage the business entity.

Resident Agent: The person or entity authorized to receive legal papers on behalf of a corporation or LLC. See also *Registered Agent*.

Resolution: A formal decision by the corporation that has been adopted by either the shareholders or the board of directors.

S Corporation: A corporation that elects to be treated as a partnership for taxation purposes by filing with the IRS. Also known as a subchapter S corporation.

Secretary (Corporate Secretary): A corporate officer, elected by the directors, usually charged with record-keeping responsibilities.

Secretary of State: A state official charged with responsibility for the filing of legal documents, including corporation papers. In some states and the District of Columbia, this responsibility falls upon another department, such as Hawaii's Department of Commerce and Consumer Affairs or Arizona's Corporation Commission.

Securities: The broad term that refers to shares of stock, bonds, and some debt instruments.

Securities and Exchange Commission: A federal agency created pursuant to the Securities Act of 1933 and the Securities Exchange Act of 1934, whose mission is "to protect investors, maintain fair, orderly, and efficient markets, and facilitate capital formation."

Service Mark: Any symbol, word, or combination thereof used to represent or identify a service.

Share Ledger: A ledger indicating the owners of a corporation and their proportion of ownership, as well as transfers of such ownership. Also known as a share transfer ledger. An LLC's ledger is called a membership ledger.

Shareholder: An owner of a corporation; one who holds stock in a corporation.

Shareholders' Agreement: An agreement among shareholders of a corporation for any of various purposes, such as a commitment to vote particular persons as directors and allowing other shareholders to have a right of first refusal to purchase the shares of departing shareholders. Also known as a shareholder agreement.

Shelf Corporation: A fully formed corporation without operations, assets, or liabilities that remains in inventory (on a shelf), waiting for a buyer. The advantages of a shelf corporation are that it can be operating within hours and it uses its original formation date.

Shell Corporation or LLC: A company that is formed legally (incorporated or organized) but that has no significant assets or business operations.

Simple Majority: With respect to shareholder and director voting, more than 50%.

Sole Proprietorship: Simply, a business owned and managed by one person. Sole proprietorships do not enjoy liability protection.

Sole Proprietorship: Simply, a business owned and managed by one person. Sole proprietorships do not enjoy liability protection.

Special Allocation: A device whereby the profits of an LLC or a corporation are divided in proportions not equal to the ownership percentages of the entity.

Special Meeting of Directors: A meeting of directors called for a specific purpose, not an annual meeting.

Special Meeting of Managers: A meeting of LLC managers that is not mandated as a periodic meeting in the LLC's governing documents; special meetings are often called for a specific purpose.

Special Meeting of Members: A meeting of LLC members that is not mandated as a periodic meeting in the LLC's governing documents; special meetings are often called for a specific purpose.

Special Meeting of Shareholders: A meeting of shareholders called for a specific purpose, not an annual meeting.

Statute of Limitations: A law setting the maximum period during which one can be charged with breaking a law or during which one may file a lawsuit. Periods vary in length by state.

Stockholder: An owner of a corporation; one who holds at least one share of stock in a corporation.

Subchapter S Corporation: See *S Corporation*.

Subscribe: To contract to purchase the shares of a corporation or LLC.

Subscriber: A person who contracts to purchase the shares of a corporation or LLC.

Subscription Agreement: A contract to purchase the shares of a corporation or LLC.

Subsidiary: A corporation or LLC that is either owned outright or controlled by a parent corporation or LLC.

Supermajority: With respect to shareholder and director voting in a corporation or member or manager voting in an LLC, any required percentage higher than 50%.

Tort: Any action or failure to act (when there is a duty to act) that causes damage to another. Examples of tort actions include personal injuries, fraud, misrepresentation, negligence, battery, assault, trespass, and invasion of privacy. A tort can be intentional or result from negligence.

Trademark: Any symbol, word, or combination thereof used to represent or identify a product or a service. See also *Service Mark*.

ULLCA: The Uniform Limited Liability Company Act. The ULLCA is a set of LLC statutes drafted by the National Conference of Commissioners on Uniform State Laws and adopted by a few states.

Undercapitalization: The condition that exists when a company does not have enough cash to carry on its business and pay its creditors.

Voluntary Dissolution: The intentional dissolution of a business entity by its own management and owners.

Voting Right: The right granted through a share of stock for the shareholder to vote at corporation meetings.

Warrant: An instrument that grants its holder the option or right to purchase shares of stock at a future date at a specific price.

Winding Up: The process of paying creditors and distributing assets that occurs before the dissolution of a business entity.

Written Consent: A document executed by either the shareholders or the directors of a corporation to take action on a specific matter in lieu of voting on the matter in a formal meeting.

Index